COUNTDOWN

A colour-coded guide to the
calorie and carbohydrate content of
manufactured foods

British Diabetic Association

10 Queen Anne Street, London W1M 0BD
Telephone (01) 323 1531

First published September 1982
Second Edition (with revisions) June 1984
Third Edition (totally revised) December 1985
Fourth Edition (totally revised) December 1986
Fifth Edition (completely updated and revised) April 1988
Sixth Edition (totally revised) April 1989

Published by:
THE BRITISH DIABETIC ASSOCIATION
ISBN 0 9503537 4 4
Designed, Typeset and Printed by:
PRESSBOX LIMITED
London
01-524 5807

WHY USE COUNTDOWN?

- It is the only book of its kind currently in the UK;

- It lists over 1000 foods from over 250 manufacturing companies;

- It categorises a food according to the fat, fibre and sugar content — a valuable aid to the health conscious in planning a modern diet;

- It provides calorie and carbohydrate values of many foods per serving so you know exactly what's on your plate;

- It is produced professionally and meticulously using accurate nutritional analyses;

. . . and most importantly it enables you to make an informed choice of everyday foods.

This book was originally designed to help people with diabetes fit manufactured foods into their diet. However, it is now recognised that the so-called "diabetic diet" is not a special diet, it is in fact a health diet, and recommended for the whole population. So Countdown is valuable for anyone who wishes to eat more healthily.

PLANNING A HEALTHY DIET

Countless books will remind us that we should eat more fibre, less fat and less sugar. Why?

Fibre

Fibre is found in wholemeal bread, granary bread, wholegrain cereals, lentils, beans, fruits and vegetables. Certain types of fibre (such as that from oats, lentils and fruit) can cause a slower rise in blood sugar when compared to low fibre foods. This is particularly important for people with diabetes.

Fibre foods being bulky also tend to be more filling. A high fibre diet is often low in fat and therefore calories. So, including these foods can help you keep to a calorie controlled diet. Remember that it is important to increase your fluid intake when you eat more fibre. Constipation is often associated with a low fibre diet.

Fat

Eating too many fatty foods almost invariably leads to a high calorie intake. Weight for weight, fat has twice the calories of carbohydrate and protein. High fat diets are usually associated with high blood cholesterol. The British Government's Committee on Medical Aspects of Food (COMA) recommended in 1984 that we should reduce our consumption of high fat foods, particularly those containing saturated fat. Eating too much saturated fat (eg. meat and dairy products) may increase the risk of developing coronary heart disease, and as people with diabetes are at a higher risk, restriction of fat is especially important.

Sugar

Sugary foods often tend to be high in fat too, for example cakes, chocolates, sweet pastries.

Sugar can cause tooth decay, particulary if sweet foods are eaten at intervals throughout the day. People with diabetes are advised to limit their sugar intake. Any sugary food eaten should ideally be taken as part of a meal rather than on its own as an inbetween meal snack. This is because the other foods in the meal (especially those high in fibre) can lead to a relatively slower rise in blood sugar.

Azmina Govindji BSc SRD
Chief Dietitian
Head of Diet Information Service
British Diabetic Association
10 Queen Anne Street
London W1M 0BD
Telephone (01) 323 1531

PRACTICAL POINTS

All the figures quoted are in terms of grams of carbohydrate and calories. On a diabetic diet sheet, 10 grams is often referred to as one exchange/one portion/one line. For slimming purposes, the calorie column will be most useful. For general health, green section foods should be eaten more often that foods from the other sections.

The BDA is continuously in close touch with the manufacturers represented in this book. Any amendments are closely monitored and will be published in the BDA bi-monthly magazine 'Balance' and in the annual update of Countdown. A few figures were not available at the time this edition was printed — these foods have been designated an 'n/a' symbol. All data is believed to be correct at the time of going to press.

If you have any queries about Countdown please contact Azmina Govindji, Chief Dietitian or Joy Payne, Countdown Co-ordinator at the BDA.

THE BRITISH DIABETIC ASSOCIATION (BDA)

The BDA has provided an information and education service to people with diabetes and their families for over 50 years. Specific aspects on individual treatment are left to the expertise of local medical and dietetic professionals. All BDA members receive the bi-monthly magazine BALANCE. This provides news of progress in medical care and research, advice on diet, nutritious recipes and practical hints on day to day problems. The Association depends entirely on voluntary support.

Subscription rates:

- **Life Membership:** A single payment of £105.00 or seven years covenent of £15.00 per year.

- **Annual Membership:** £5.00 per year.

- **Reduced Rate Membership:** (Pensioner/DHSS Benefit Recipient/ Student on Government Grant) £1.00 per year.

ACKNOWLEDGEMENTS

The BDA would like to thank the food manufacturers for their continued help and cooperation in the production of this booklet. We are also indebted to Jill Metcalfe for originating this book.

MEMBERSHIP

To become a member fill in the application form below and send it with your subscription (see page V) to:

British Diabetic Association
10 Queen Anne Street
London W1M OBD

Please enrol me as a member of the British Diabetic Association for which I enclose the sum of:

(Use Block Letters Please)

Surname . . . .

First Name . . . .

Address . . . .

. . . .

Date of Birth . . . .

Occupation . . . .

Date . . . .

Signature . . . .

(This information will be treated as strictly confidential.)

British Diabetic Association — A Company Limited by Guarantee.
Registered Office — 10 Queen Anne Street, London W1M OBD.
Registered in England. Registration No. 339181.

INFORMATION FOR DIETITIANS
Quantitative Criteria

	Sugar	Dietary Fibre	Fat	Notes
GREEN	<15%	>5%	<15%	If dietary fibre exceeds 5%, foods with an added sugar content of up to 20% will be placed in the green section.
AMBER	<20%	<5%	can be >15%	Foods with up to 25% added sugars and more than 5% fibre will be classified as AMBER.
RED	>20%	<5%	can be high in fat	

INDEX

Think of your diet instructions as a set of traffic lights directing your diet:

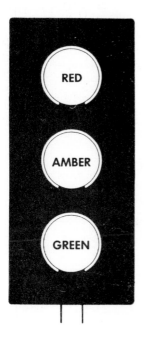

GO SLOW
Stop and think.
Try to save these foods
for special occasions.

GO EASY
Foods from this section
should ideally not make
up a large part of the diet.

GO
Eat these foods regularly.

WHITE SECTION — A selection of alcoholic drinks.
TO BE USED WITH CARE

Please note that the page numbers given refer to the page number for that particular colour coded section.

G = Green Section
A = Amber Section
R = Red Section
W = ALCOHOL

	G	A	R
Fortts		4	5
Fox's	9	4	5
Holly Mill	9	4-5	5
Huntley and Palmer		5	5
Iceland			5
Itona			5
Jacobs		5	5-6
J L Bragg		5	
KP			6
Littlewoods	9	5	6
Lyons			6
MacDonalds			6
Mackies	9		
Marks and Spencer	9	5	6-7
McVitie		5	7
Morrisons			7
Nabisco	9	5	7
Nairns	10		
Newform Foods	9		
Paterson-Bronte	9	5-6	7
Paterson's Scottish Shortbread		6	
Peek Freans		6	7-8
Prewetts	9		
Quaker			8
Renshaw			8
RM Scott	10	6	
Safeway	10	6	8-9
Sainsbury	10	6	9
Simmers	10		
Slymbrand	10	6	
Tesco	10	6-7	9-10
Waitrose	10	7	11
Walkers Shortbread	10	7	11
Walls Ice Cream Wafers		7	

Crackers

	G	A	R
Bahlsen Biscuits		8	
Burton's	11		
Co-Op		8	
Crawford		8	
Jacobs	11	8	

	G	A
Kallo Foods		8
Marks and Spencer	11	8
McDougalls	11	8
McVitie	11	
Morrisons		8
Nabisco	11	8
Parkstone Bakeries		8
Peek Freans		8
Rakusen Foods	11	8-9
Safeway	11	9
Sainsbury	11	9
Tesco		9
Waitrose	11	9

Crispbreads

	G	A
Allinson	12	
Boots "Shapers"	12	
Crawford	12	
Lyons	12	10
Marks and Spencer		10
Morrisons		10
Newform Foods	12	
Primula	12	
Ryvita	12	
Sainsbury	12	
Slymbrand	12	10

BREAD, BREAD PRODUCTS AND PIZZA BASES

	G	A
Uncut Bread – Standards		11
Allinson	13	11
Bejam		11
Boots	13	
Buitoni		11
Co-Op	13	11
Crusty Gold		11
Granny Smith		11
Granose	13	
Hovis	13-14	11
Marks and Spencer	14	12

	G	A	R
Master Chef		12	
McDougalls		12	
McVitie's Frozen Foods		12	
Mighty White		12	
Mothers Pride	14	12-13	
Mr Harvey's Stuffing	14		
Nimble		13	
Paxo		13	
Pitta's	14		
Pitta Bread - Standards		13	
Sainsbury	14-15	13	
Sunblest	15	13-14	
Tesco	15	14	
Vitbe	15		
Waitrose		14	
Whole Earth	15		
Windmill Bakery	15-16		

Pizza Bases

	G	A	R
Safeway	17		

CAKES, CAKE MIXES AND TEA BREADS

Cakes

	G	A	R
Bahlsen Cakes			12
Bejam		15	
Birds Eye		15	12
Cadbury			12
Chambourcy			12
Eden Vale			12
Iceland		15	
Littlewoods		15	12
Lyons		15	12-13
Marks and Spencer		15	13-14
McVitie's Cakes			14
McVitie's Frozen Foods			14
Mr Kipling		15	14-15
Ross			15
Safeway		16	15
Sainsbury		16	15
St Ivel			16

	G	A	R
Sunblest			16
Tesco		16	16
Tiffany			16
Vitbe			16
Waitrose			16
Walkers Shortbread		16	16
Youngs			16

Cake Ingredients

	G	A	R
Cake Ingredients - Standards			17
Homepride			17
Pearce Duff			17
Renshaw			17

Cake Mixes

	G	A	R
Granny Smith		17	18
Green's Cake Mixes		17	18-19
Lyons Tetley			19
McDougalls		17	
Royal			19
Tesco		17	19
Viota		17	20
Whitworths		18	20

Tea Breads

	G	A	R
Allinson	18		
Boots	18		
Granose		19	
Hovis	18		
Imperial Bakeries	18	19	
Littlewoods	18		
Marks and Spencer	18	19	
Mothers Pride		19	
Sainsbury	18	19	
Sunblest		19	
Sunmalt		19	
Tesco	18	19-20	
Vitbe	18		
Waitrose		20	
Windmill Bakery	18		

	G	A	R
Cereals			
Allinson	19	21	
Argyll Stores (Presto)	19		
Beechams		21	
Bejam	19		
Bird's		21	
Boots "Second Nature"	19	21	
Cheshire Whole Foods	19		
Co-Op	19	21	
Family Choice	19		
Force		21	
Granose	19-20		
Holland & Barrett	20		
Holly Mill	20		
Jordans	20		
Kellogg	20	21	21
Laws	20		
Lyons Tetley	20		
Mapleton's		21	
Nabisco	20		
Pearce Duff	21		
Presto	21		
Prewetts	21		
Quaker	21	21	21
Ryvita	21		
Safeway	21	22	
Sainsbury	21	22	21
Sunwheel Foods	22		
Superdrug	22		
Tesco	22	22	
Waitrose	22		
Weetabix	22		21
Whitworths	22		
Whole Earth	22		
William Low	22		
Yorkshire Co-Op	22		

COOKING AIDS, MIXES AND SAUCES

	G	A
Baxters		23
Bisto		23
Bovril		23
Buitoni		23
Buxted		23
Campbells		23
Colman Foods		23-24
Crosse and Blackwell		24-25
Fray Bentos		25
Granny Smith		25
Green's		25
Homepride		25
HP Foods		26
J A Sharwood		26
Knorr		26
Lea and Perrins		26
Marks and Spencer		27
McCormick Foods		27
Oxo		27
Paxo		27
Quaker		27
Quorn		27
Safeway		27-28
Sainsbury		28
Schwartz		28
Shippams		28
Tesco		29
Viota		29
Waitrose		29
Whitworths		29
Whole Earth		29

DAIRY PRODUCTS & DAIRY SUBSTITUTES

Cheese

	G	A
Cheese – Standards	23-24	30
Applewood		30
Dairy Crest	23	30
Eden Vale	23	

	G	A
Heinz Weight Watchers	24	
Kraft		30
Prewett's	24	
Primula	24	
Rowntree-Mackintosh (Sunpat)	24	
Sainsbury	24	
Senoble	24	
Somerset Soft Cheese	24	
St Ivel	24	
Yoplait		31

Cream

	G	A
Creams – Standards		32
Plamil		32
Van Den Berghs		32

Milks & Milk Drinks

	G	A
Milks – Standards	25	33
Dairy Crest		33
Eden Vale		33
Express		33
Marks and Spencer		33
Milram	25	
Raines Dairy Foods		33
St Ivel	25	
Waitrose		33

Milk Substitutes

	G	A
Cadbury		34
Carnation		34
Granose	26	34
Haldane Foods	26	
Itona		34
Plamil	26	34
Provamel	26	34
Safeway	26	34

Low Fat Spreads & Pastes

	G	A
Low Fat Spreads – Standards	27	
Cauldron Foods	27	
Co-Op	27	

	G	A	R
Shippams	27		
Sutherland	27-28		
Tesco	28		

Sweetened Dairy Products

	G	A	R
Carnation			22
Farley Health Products			22
Fussell's			22
Kellogg			22
Nesquik			22
Nestle			22
Rayner & Co			22

Yogurt

	G	A	R
Yogurt - Standards	29	35	
Argyll Stores (Presto)	29		
Boots	29		
Chambourcy		35	
Cool Country		35	
Dairy Crest		35	
Dunsters Farm		35	
Eden Vale		35-36	
Express (Milkman)		36	
Fage		36	
Littlewoods		36	
Loseley		36	
Marks and Spencer	29	36-37	
Milram		37	
Morrisons		37	
Raines Dairy Foods		37	
Safeway	29	37-38	
Sainsbury	29	38	
Ski	29		
Sojal	29		
Spelga		38	
Stapleton Farm	29	38	
St Ivel	30	38	
Sudmilch	30	39	
Tesco		39	
Waistline	30		

	G	A	R
Waitrose	30	39	
Yoplait	30	39-40	

DESSERTS

	G	A	R
Jellies – Standards			23
Ambrosia		41	23
Batchelors			23
Bejam			23
Birds	31	41	23-24
Birds Eye			24
Brown and Polson			24
Casanova Ice Cream	31		
Chambourcy			24
Chivers			25
Co-Op			25
Eden Vale			25
Findus			25
Granose		41	
Greens			25
Golden Wonder			26
Heinz			26
Heinz Weight Watchers		41	
HP Foods			26
Itona		41	26
Libby			26
Littlewoods			26
Lyons Maid		41	26
Marks and Spencer		41	26-27
McDougalls			27
McVitie's Frozen Foods			27
Milram		41	
Modern Health Products		42	
Nestle			27
Pearce Duff			27
Provamel		42	
Robertsons			27
Ross			27
Rowntree Mackintosh			27-28
Royal			28
Safeway			28

	G	A	R
Sainsbury			28-29
Sojal		42	
St Ivel	31		29
Tesco			29
Tiffany			29
Vitari		42	
Waitrose			29
Walls			29
Whitworths			30
Youngs			30

DRESSINGS, PICKLES, SAUCES

Dressings

	G	A	R
Dressings – Standards	32	43	
Heinz	32	43	
Safeway	32		
Sainbury	32		
Waitrose	32		
Whole Earth		43	

Pickles

	G	A	R
Pickles – Standards		44	
Boots	33		
Down to Earth Wholefoods		44	
Whole Earth		44	

Sauces

	G	A	R
Sauces – Standards		45	
Boots	34		
Heinz		45	
Hellmann's	34		
Pearce Duff		45	
Sainsbury	34		
Waitrose	34		
Whole Earth		45	

DRINKS

Cordials & Squashes

	G	A	R
Squashes – Standards	39		32
Beechams			32-33

	G	A	R
Boots			33
Britvic			33
Corona			33
Masonline			33
PLJ	39		
Quosh	39		33
Robinsons	39		
Schweppes			34
Somportex			34
Svali	39		

Fizzy Drinks

	G	A	R
Fizzy Drinks – Standards	35		35
Boots	35		
Britvic			35
Britvic Slimsta	35		
Cariba			35
Coca Cola	36		35
Corona			35
Dexters	36		
Hunts	36		
Idris			36
Kenwood Cascade			36
Littlewoods			36
Marks and Spencer	36		36
One-Cal	36		
Pepsi	36		36
Rowntree Mackintosh			36
Safeway	34		
Schweppes			36-37
Schweppes Slimline	36-37		
Silver Spring	37		
Soda Stream	37		37
Tango	37		37
Top Deck	37		38

Fruit Drinks

	G	A	R
Fruit Juices – Standards		46	
Adams Foods		46	
Birds			39

	G	A	R
Boots		46	
Britvic		46-47	39
Campbells		47	
Coca Cola		47	39
Del Monte		47	
Food Brokers		47	
Green Gate Foods		47	
Heinz			39
HP Bulmer		47	39
Hunts		47	39
Kellogg			39
Libby		47	39-40
Marks and Spencer		48	
Safeway		48	
Schweppes		48	40
Shloer		48	
Showerings		49	
St Ivel		49	
Stute Foods		49	
The Taunton Cider Company		49	
Walls		49	
Whole Earth		49	

Hot Beverages

	G	A	R
Hot Beverages – Standards			41
Boots	38		
Cadbury			41
Carnation		50	41
Caro			41
George Payne			41
Horlicks			41
Knorr	38		
London Herb & Spice Co	38		
Ridpath Pek		50	

FISH

Canned Fish

	G	A	R
Canned Fish – Standards	40-41		

Frozen Fish

	G	A	R
Bejam	42		

G

Birds Eye	42
Co-Op	43
Findus	43
Littlewoods	43
Marks and Spencer	43
McCain	43
Olaf Foods	43
Ross	43
Safeway	43-44
Sainsbury	44
Tesco	44
Waitrose	44
Young's Seafoods	44

Prepared Fish Dishes

Bejam	45
Birds Eye	45
Co-Op	45
Findus	45-46
Gorcy of France	46
Iceland	46
Marks and Spencer	46-47
Mr Chang's Ready Meals	47
Olaf Foods	47
Ross	47
Safeway	47
Sainsbury	47
Tesco	47
Waitrose	48
W A Turner	48
Young's Seafoods	48

FRUITS & PIE FILLINGS

Tinned

Tinned	
Co-Op	49
Del Monte Foods	49
John West	49-50
Libby	50
Safeway	51

	G	A	R
Sainsbury	51		
Tesco	51-52		
Waitrose	52		
T.W. Beach	52		

Fruit-in-Syrup

Fruit-in-Syrup – Standards			42

Fruit Pie Fillings

Armour			43
Batchelors			43
Bird's			43
Chivers			43
Co-Op			43
Greens			43
Morton			43-44
Pickerings			44
Royal			44
Sainsbury			44
Tesco			44

ICE CREAM AND LOLLIES

Ice Cream

Ice Cream – Standards			45
Bejam			45
Birds Eye			45
Co-Op			45
Lyons Maid			45-46
Pearce Duff			46
Pendletons			46
Ross			47
Safeway			47
Sainsbury			47
Tesco			47
Waitrose			47
Walls			47-48

Ice Lollies

Bejam			48
Lyons Maid			48
Pearce Duff			48

	A	R
Pendletons		48
Safeway		48
Walls		49

INSTANT MEALS AND QUICK SNACKS

	A	R
Batchelors	51	
Boots	51	
Crosse & Blackwell	51	
Golden Wonder	51-52	
KP	52	
Tesco	52	

JAMS, PASTES AND SPREADS

	A	R
Peanut Butter - Standards	53	
Boots	53	
Country Basket	53	
Ethos (No-Sugar Added)	53	
Granose	53	
Hedgehog Foods	53	
Heinz	53-54	
Heinz Weight Watchers	54	
Ledbury Preserves	54	
Lifecycle	54	
Nature's Store	54	
Robertson Today's Recipe	54	
Safeway	54	
Saffron Whole Foods	54	
Sunwheel Foods	54	
Thursday Cottage	54	
Waitrose	55	
Welsh Lady	55	
Whole Earth	55	

MEAT, MEAT PRODUCTS

Canned

	A	R
Canned - Standards	53	56
Armour	53	
Baxters	53	
Campbells	53	

	G	A
Co-Op	53	
Crosse & Blackwell	53-54	
Fray Bentos	54	
Goblin	54	
Gold Dish	54	
Iceland	54	
Marks and Spencer	54-55	
Robert Wilson	55	
Sainsbury	55	
Shippams	55-56	
Tesco	56	
Waitrose	56	

Chilled/Frozen

	G	A
Bejam	57	
Bernard Matthews	57-58	
Birds Eye	58	
Bowyers	58	56
Brains		56
Buxted	58-59	
Co-Op	59	56
Crosse & Blackwell		56
Dalepak	59	56
Findus	59	
Iceland	59	
Marks and Spencer	59-60	
Mattesson Walls	60	57
McCain	60	
Millers		57
Plumtree Farms	60	
Robirch	60	57
Ross	60	57
Safeway	61	57
Sainsbury	61	
Slaters Foods	61	
Tesco	61	57
Tiffany	61-62	
Waitrose	62	
W A Turner		57

Prepared Meat/Poultry Dishes

Bejam	63
Birds Eye	63
Brains	63
Buxted	63
Campbells	63
Chesswood	63
Co-Op	64
Crosse & Blackwell	64
Dorset	64
Findus	64
Freshbake Foods	64
Goblin	64
Healthline Foods	64
Iceland	64-65
Katie's Kitchen	65
Littlewoods	65
Lockwoods Foods	65
Marks and Spencer	65-66
Mr Chang's Ready Meals	66
Plumrose	66
Robert Wilson	66-67
Ross	67
Safeway	67
Sainsbury	67
Shippams	67
Shiva	67-68
Tesco	68
Tyne Brand	68
Waitrose	68-69
W A Turner	69

PANCAKES

Savoury

Bejam	58
Birds Eye	58
Findus	58
Gorcy of France	58
Marks and Spencer	58
Mr. Chang's	58

	A	R
Ross	58	
Safeway	58	
Sainsbury	59	
Shippams	59	
Waitrose	59	

Sweet

	A	R
Marks and Spencer	60	
Mothers Pride		31
Sainsbury	60	31
Sunblest Teatime	60	31
Tesco	60	

PASTA

	A	R
Batchelors	61	
Co-Op	61	
Crosse and Blackwell	61	
Heinz	61	
Iceland	61-62	
Royal Norfolk	62	
Safeway	62	
Sainsbury	62	
Tesco	62	
Waitrose	62	

Pasta Prepared Dishes

	A	R
Birds Eye	63	
Buitoni	63	
Eden Vale	63	
Findus	63	
Heinz	63	
Katie's Kitchen	63-64	
Lockwoods	64	
Marks and Spencer	64	
McVitie's Frozen Foods	64	
Mr. Chang's Ready Meals	64	
Safeway	64	
Spaghetti House	65	
Tesco	65	
Waitrose	65-66	

PASTRY, PASTRY GOODS

Pastry	A	R
Bejam	67	
Dorset Foods	67	
Granny Smith	67	
Greenrose Frozen Foods	67	
Jus-Rol	67	
McDougalls	67	
Palethorpes	67-68	
Safeway	68	
Sainsbury	68	
Saxby's	68	
Tesco	68	
Waitrose	68	
Whitworths	68	

Pastry Goods	A	R
Adams Pork Products	69	
Bejam	69	
Birds Eye	69	
Bowyers	69-70	
Buxted	71	
Co-Op	71	
Dorset Foods	71-72	50
Findus	72	50
Fray Bentos	72	
Freshbake Foods	72	50
Goblin	72-73	
Gorcy of France	73	
Greenrose Frozen Foods	73	
Holland & Barrett	73	
Iceland	73-74	
Jus-Rol	74	50
Kraft	74	
Littlewoods	74-75	50
Lockwoods	75	
Lyons		50
Marks and Spencer	75-76	50
McVities Frozen Foods		51
Millers	76	
Mr Kipling		51

	A	R
Olaf Foods	76	
Peter's Savoury Products	76	
Pork Farms	76	
Robirch	77	
Ross	77	51
Safeway	77-78	51
Sainsbury	78	51
Saxby's	78-79	
Tesco	79-80	51
Tiffany	80	
Tyne Brand	80-81	
Waitrose	81	
Walter Holland	81-82	
W A Turner	82	

PATÉS

	A	R
Bowyers	83	
Culrose	83	
Granose	83	
John West	83	
Marks and Spencer	83	
Mattesson Walls	83	
Plumrose	83-84	
Princes	84	
Robirch	84	
Sutherland	84	

PIZZAS & PIZZA BASES

	A	R
Bejam	85	
Birds Eye	85	
Buitoni	85	
Co-Op	85	
Findus	85	
Granny Smith	85	
Haldane Foods – Hera	85	
Iceland	86	
Marietta Frozen Foods	86	
Marks and Spencer	86	
McCain Pizzas	86-87	
McVitie's Frozen Foods	87	

	A	R
Ross	87	
Safeway	87	
Sainsbury	87	
Tesco	87-88	
Tiffany	88	
Waitrose	88	

POTATO PRODUCTS

	A	R
Chips – Standards	89	
Batchelors	89	
Bejam	89	
Birds Eye	89	
Cadbury	89	
Co-Op	89	
Eden Vale	89	
Findus	90	
Freshbake Foods	90	
Goblin	90	
Heinz	90	
Jus-Rol	90	
Katie's Kitchen	90	
Littlewoods	90	
Lockwoods	90	
Marks and Spencer	90	
McCain	90-91	
Ross	91	
Safeway	91	
Sainsbury	91	
Tesco	91	
Waitrose	91	
Whitworths	91	
Yeoman	92	

PRESERVES AND SPREADS

	A	R
Preserves –Standards		52
Cadbury		52
Ledbury Preserves		52

READY MEALS

Prepared Fish Dishes

	A	R
Bejam	93	

	G	A
Birds Eye		100
Iceland		100
Kellogg		100
Lockwoods		100
Marks and Spencer		101
Mr. Chang's Ready Meals		101
Safeway		101
Tesco		101
Whitworths		101
Whole Earth		101

SALADS AND VEGETABLES

Salads

Coleslaw – Standards	70	
Argyll Stores (Presto)	70	
Eden Vale	70-71	
Heinz	71	
Holland & Barrett	71	
Itona	71	
Littlewoods	71	
Lockwoods	71	
Marks and Spencer	71	
Safeway	71-72	
Sainsbury	72	
St Ivel	72	
Tesco	72	

Vegetables — Frozen

Vegetables – Standards	73	
Bejam	73	
Birds Eye	73	
Findus	73	
Marks and Spencer	73	
Ross	74	
Safeway	74	
Sainsbury	74	
Tesco	74	

Vegetables — Tinned

Vegetables – Standards	75-76	

	G	A
Batchelors	76	
Buitoni	76	
Crosse & Blackwell	76	
Heinz Weight Watchers	76-77	
Marks and Spencer	77	
Safeway	77	
Shippams	77	
Waitrose	77	
Whole Earth	77	

SAUSAGES, SAUSAGE PRODUCTS

	G	A
Sausages – Standards		102
Sausage Products – Standards		102-103
Bejam		103
Bernard Matthews		103
Bowyers		103
Buxted		103
Co-Op		103
Findus		103
Fresh Bake Foods		103
Iceland		103
Marks and Spencer		103
Mattesson Walls		104
Millers		104
Plumrose		104
Robirch		104
Ross		104
Sainsbury		104
Saxby's		104
Tesco		104

SNACKS, NUTS & SWEETS
LOW SUGAR

	G	A
Allinson	78	
Bahlsen Biscuits		105
Bejam		105
BN Biscuits & Foods		105
Booker Health	78	105
Burton's		105
Callard & Bowser		105

SOUPS

	A	R
Batchelors	115-116	
Baxters	116	
Campbells	116-118	
Co-Op	118	
Crosse & Blackwell	118-119	
Heinz	119-120	
Knorr	120	
Littlewoods	120	
Marks and Spencer	121	
Mr Chang	121	
Safeway	121	
Sainsbury	121-122	
Tesco	122	
Waitrose	122-123	

SWEETS

	A	R
Standards		53
Allinson		53
Barker & Dobson		53
Bassett		53
Beechams		53
Boots		53-54
Cadbury		54-55
Callard and Bowser		55
Clarnico		55
Dextrosol		55
Ferrero		56
Fox's		56
Granose		56
Halls		56
Horlicks		56
Itona		56
Kalibu		56
Littlewoods		56
Lofthouse of Fleetwood		57
Marks and Spencer		57
Mars		57-58
Nestle		58
Pascall		59
Renshaw		59

	G	R
Rowntree Mackintosh		59-60
Safeway		60
Sainsbury		60-61
Sharps		61
Terry		61
The Wrigley Company		61
Trebor		61-62

VEGETARIAN PREPARED FOODS

	G
Boots	81
Care Foods	81
Cauldron Foods	81
Direct Foods	81
Granose	81-82
Haldane Foods	82
Holly Mill	83
Itona	83
Morinaga	83
Prewett's	83
Sunwheel Foods	83
The Realeat Company	83

Prepared Dishes

	G
Bejam	84
Be-Well Nutritional Products	84
Birds Eye	84
Boots	84
Brooke Bond	84
Direct Foods	84
Emile Tissot Foods	84
Granose	84-85
Haldane Foods	85
Hofels Pure Foods	85
Holland & Barrett	85
Itona	85-86
Katie's Kitchen	86
Marks and Spencer	86
Prewett's	86
Sainsbury	86
Tesco	86

G

The Realeat Company	86
Vegetarian Feasts	87
Waitrose	87
Whole Earth	87

Notes

Notes

Notes

Notes

Notes

Notes

GREEN SECTION

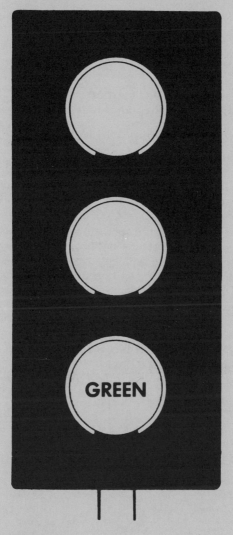

GO
Eat these foods regularly.

GREEN SECTION FOODS

Why are these called the 'best choice foods'? Is it because they're healthy foods? But what is a 'healthy food'?

All foods are made up of a combination of nutrients such as protein, carbohydrate, fat, vitamins, minerals and water. As outlined in the introduction, it is wise to try to reduce out intake of fat and sugar while having more fibre containing foods.

The majority of the foods listed in this section are a significant source of fibre, and are low in added sugar and fat. Fibre can help to slow down the rise in blood sugar after meals. So if a food contains a lot of fibre as well as a small amount of sugar, the effect of that sugar on blood sugar levels is not so great. The more fibre a food contains the more effective it is in minimising swings in blood sugar and this can help the control of diabetes.

The low fat, high fibre, low sugar foods in this section can also help you keep to a calorie controlled diet.

GREEN
EAT THESE FOODS REGULARLY

Baby Foods

Parents should consult their doctor or dietitian before including commercially prepared baby products into the diets of their diabetic children.

COW AND GATE
STAGE 1 (STRAINED/BABYMEALS)
Introductory Size—

Main Courses — 80g jars	Carbohydrate in grams	Calories
Beef Dinner	6	55
Chicken Dinner	5	50
Vegetable and Rice Casserole	8	50

Desserts — 80g jars		
Peach Melba	11	45

No Added Sugar Desserts — 80g jars		
Fruit Delight Dessert	13	50

Breakfasts — 110g jars		
Creamed Porridge	14	75
Fruit and Cereal Breakfast	17	65
Muesli Breakfast	14	70

Main Courses — 110g jars		
Beef and Bone Broth	7	70
Beef Dinner	8	80
Cheese and Tomato Savoury	7	65
Chicken Dinner	7	70
Chicken Risotto	8	80
Fish in Cheese Sauce	7	50
Lamb Dinner	7	70
Spaghetti Bolognaise	9	70
Vegetable and Rice Casserole	11	70

Desserts — 110g jars		
Cherry Treat Dessert	15	60
Chocolate Pudding	22	100
Creme Caramel	12	65
Peach Melba	15	60
Strawberry Fool with VitC	17	75

No Added Sugar Yogurt Desserts — 110g jars		
Apple Dessert	17	65
Apple and Banana Dessert	16	60
Apple and Orange Dessert	17	70
Fruit Delight Dessert	18	70
Mixed Fruit	14	65
Pear	15	70

3

COW AND GATE — Continued

Yogurt Desserts — 110g jars	Carbohydrate in grams	Calories
Apple and Blackcurrant	16	70
Banana	16	70
Cherry	15	70
Peach Melba	16	70
Raspberry	16	70
Strawberry	16	70

STAGE 2 (JUNIOR) BABYMEALS

Breakfasts — 150g jars		
Bacon, Egg & Tomato Breakfast	7	80
Creamed Porridge	19	105
Fruit and Cereal Breakfast	23	90
Muesli Breakfast	20	95

Main Courses — 150g jars		
Beef Dinner	10	105
Beef and Kidney Dinner	9	95
Cheese and Tomato Savoury	9	90
Chicken Dinner	9	95
Chicken Risotto	10	105
Fish in Cheese Sauce	9	70
Lamb Dinner	10	100
Lamb and Noodle Casserole	9	105
Spaghetti Bolognaise	12	95
Vegetable Casserole with Pasta	14	100

Desserts — 150g jars		
Cherry Treat Dessert	20	80
Chocolate Pudding	30	140
Creme Caramel	16	90
Peach Melba	21	85
Strawberry Fool	23	105

No Added Sugar Dessert — 150g jars		
Apple Dessert	24	90
Apple and Banana Dessert	22	85
Apple and Orange Dessert	24	90
Fruit Delight Dessert	24	95
Pineapple Dessert	20	75

COW & GATE

Liga Rusks all flavours (1)	6	30
Pure Concentrated Juice with Vitamin C all flavours, 10ml	6	25
Pure Juice with Vitamin C all flavours, 125ml bottle	13	50

FARLEY HEALTH PRODUCTS

Breakfast Timers —		
Fruit & Yogurt 2 level tablespoons (10g weight)	7	45

FARLEY HEALTH PRODUCTS — Cont

	Carbohydrate in grams	Calories
Muesli		
2 level tablespoons (10g weight)............	7	45
Oat & Apple		
2 level tablespoons (10g weight)............	7	45
Original Recipe		
2 rounded tablespoons (10g weight)	7	40
Farex Fingers (1)	7	40
Farex Weaning Food		
1 level teaspoon*............................	1	4
Farley's Breakfast Cereal		
1 level teaspoon*............................	1	4
Farley's Low Sugar Rusks (1).................	13	70
Farley's Granulated Rusk		
1 level teaspoon*............................	1	5
Farley's Original Rusks (1)	14	67
Farley's Rusks with Wholemeal (1)..........	12	67
Oster Rusks (1)	6	35

HEINZ
FOODS FOR BABIES AGED 3-9 MONTHS
Breakfast & Savoury Varieties
— 4.52oz/128g cans

Beef and Carrot Casserole	10	90
Beef and Oxtail Dinner........................	11	90
Bone & Beef Broth with Veg	11	80
Braised Lamb Dinner...........................	13	95
Braised Steak and Kidney	12	90
Chicken Casserole with Vegetables	12	85
Country Lamb with Carrot....................	11	100
Egg and Bacon Breakfast	9	95
Golden Chicken Dinner........................	11	80
Turkey Dinner	12	70

FOODS FOR BABIES AGED 3-9 MONTHS
Breakfast & Savoury Varieties
— 4.52oz/128g jars

Beef Broth with Vegetables	11	85
Chicken Broth Supper	10	75
Country Chicken Dinner.......................	11	75
Steak and Kidney Dinner......................	13	100

FOODS FOR BABIES AGED 3-9 MONTHS
Dessert Varieties — 4.52oz/128g cans

Apples with VitC...............................	22	85
Apricot Custard	17	80
Banana Dessert with VitC	16	65
Chocolate Pudding............................	20	105
Cream Caramel Dessert	17	115
Creamed Rice Pudding	19	125
Egg Custard with Rice.........................	16	105
Fruit Salad......................................	17	70
Pear Dessert....................................	18	75

* 1 level 5ml spoon of powder

HEINZ — Continued
FOODS FOR BABIES AGED 3-15 MONTHS

Dessert Varieties — 4.52oz/128g jars	Carbohydrate in grams	Calories
Apple Yogurt Dessert	22	100
Apricot Yogurt Dessert	23	100
Baby Muesli	16	85
Banana Yogurt Dessert	22	105
Chocolate Dessert	17	115
Egg Custard with Rice	18	120
Orange Dessert with VitC	24	95
Orange Yogurt Dessert	22	100
Pear Yogurt Dessert	21	100
Pineapple Dessert with VitC	20	75
Strawberry Yogurt	20	90

FOODS FOR BABIES AGED 3-15 MONTHS

Pure Fruits — 4.52oz/128g cans/jars		
Apple and Apricot	16	65
Apple and Banana	18	70
Apple and Orange	15	60
Apple and Pear	15	60
Just Apple	15	60
Mixed Fruit	18	70

FOODS FOR BABIES AGED 3-15 MONTHS

Vegetable Meals — 4.52oz/128g cans		
Golden Vegetables	16	90
Spring Vegetables	15	90

FOODS FOR BABIES AGED 7-15 MONTHS
Breakfast & Savoury Varieties

— 4.52oz/128g cans		
Beef and Bone Hotpot	15	90
Cheese, Bacon and Egg Supper	7	85
Chicken and Ham Dinner	14	85
Chicken Supreme Dinner	15	100
Country Lamb and Liver Dinner	12	90
Egg and Bacon Breakfast	9	90
Farmhouse Pork Dinner	11	100
Lamb Casserole with Vegetables	13	100
Liver and Bacon Dinner	12	85
Spaghetti Hoops and Sausages Supper	15	95
Steak and Kidney Dinner	12	85
Steak Hotpot	11	75

FOODS FOR BABIES AGED 7-15 MONTHS

Dessert Varieties — 4.52oz/128g cans		
Apple Dessert	14	80
Apricot Dessert with Rice	19	90
Banana Rice and Rosehip Dessert	20	80
Chocolate Pudding with Tapioca	21	95
Creamed Rice Pudding	19	125
Egg Custard with Tapioca	20	120
Fruit Dessert with Tapioca	23	85

HEINZ — Continued
FOODS FOR BABIES AGED 7-15 MONTHS

Savoury — 170g jars	Carbohydrate in grams	Calories
Beef Broth with Vegetables	19	130
Chicken Broth Supper	15	120
Country Chicken and Ham Dinner	15	115
Steak and Kidney Lunch	18	115

MILUPA
All figures are per **30g** of dried product as per instructions on packet for infants.

INFANT FOODS BREAKFAST CEREALS

7 Cereal Breakfast	20	130
Oat Breakfast Cereal with Apple............	20	130
Sunshine Orange Breakfast	22	130
Wheat Breakfast Honey	21	130

INFANT FOODS DINNER-TIME DESSERTS

Autumn Fruit	22	130
Caribbean Fruit	20	130
Chocolate and Hazelnut	20	135
Rice Dessert	23	130
Semolina and Honey	22	130

INFANT FOODS DINNER-TIME SAVOURIES

Autumn Vegetable Hotpot....................	20	125
Mixed Vegetable	20	130
Spring Vegetable Dinner	20	130
Summer Salad Variety	20	130
Winter Vegetable Casserole	20	130

INFANT FOODS FRUITS

Apple and Rosehip............................	23	130
Mixed Fruit	22	130
Pear and Orange	22	130

INFANT AND JUNIOR DRINKS

per 50ml prepared drink....................	3	10

INFANT FOODS YOGURTS

Banana and Apple Delight	22	125
Soft Fruit Surprise	22	125
Summer Fruit Cocktail........................	22	125

JUNIOR FOODS

Beef and Vegetable Hotpot	20	130
Beef Stew.......................................	20	130
Braised Steak and Tomato Dinner	20	125
Chicken and Vegetable Casserole..........	20	130
Muesli Breakfast	25	125

PLAIN CEREALS

Pure Rice Cereal	25	105

MILUPA — Continued

RUSKS

	Carbohydrate in grams	Calories
Granulated Rusks	20	130
Granulated Rusk with Mixed Fruit	20	130
Fruit Rusk (1)	10	50
Muesli Rusk (1)	9	50

ROBINSON'S BABY FOODS
All figures are for dried weight of product.

Desserts — Small size pack — per **3** dessertspoons/10g

Apple and Banana with VitC	9	40
Apple Dessert with VitC	9	40
Banana Yogurt Dessert	9	40
Egg Custard	8	40

Desserts — Standard Size Pack
— per **3** dessertspoons/10g

Banana and Pineapple Treat with VitC	9	40
Chocolate Pudding	9	40
Creamed Rice Pudding	8	40
Strawberry Surprise	9	40
Summer Fruit Salad with VitC	9	40

Infant/Junior Cereals — per **3** dessertspoons/10g

Apple and Blackberry	8	40
Baby Rice	8	40
Granulated Rusk	8	40
Mixed Cereal	7	40
Muesli	7	40
Orange and Banana	8	40
Porridge Oats	7	40

Infant Meals — per **3** dessertspoons/10g

Beef Casserole with Vegetables	6	40
Beef Dinner with Vegetables	6	40
Cauliflower Cheese	6	40
Chicken Casserole with Vegetables	6	40
Chicken Dinner with Vegetables	6	40
Country Vegetable Casserole	7	40
Egg and Cheese Savoury	6	40
Farmhouse Bone and Vegetable Broth	7	40
Lamb Dinner with Vegetables	6	40
Mixed Vegetable Dinner	7	40

Junior Meals — per **2** tablespoons/15g

Beef Dinner	10	60
Chicken Casserole	10	60
Chicken Dinner	10	60
Lamb Hotpot	10	60
Steak and Kidney Casserole	9	60
Tomato, Cheese and Egg Noodle	10	65
Vegetable Hotpot	10	60

8

Biscuits, Crackers, Crispbreads

HIGH FIBRE
BISCUITS

	Carbohydrate in grams	Calories
ALLINSON		
Bran Oatcake 1 from a pack of 7............	7	50
DOVES FARM		
Wholemeal Gingernuts (1)....................	5	32
FOX'S		
Wholemeal Bran (1)...........................	7	59
HOLLY MILL		
Fibretime Biscuits(1)...........................	8	85
LITTLEWOODS		
Wholemeal Bran Biscuits (1)..................	8	62
MACKIES		
Oatcakes (1)...................................	8	60
MARKS AND SPENCER		
Wholemeal Bran Biscuits (1)..................	9	65
NABISCO		
Wholewheat Teabreak (1)....................	6	38
NEWFORM FOODS - COUNTRY BASKET		
Hazelnut (1)....................................	4	35
Muesli Fruit (1).................................	4	40
Oatmeal (1)	3	35
Six Grain (1)	4	35
Wholewheat Bran (1).........................	4	35
Yoghurt (1)....................................	5	40
PATERSON - BRONTE		
Bran Oatcakes (1)	8	55
Farmhouse Oatcakes (1)......................	14	96
PREWETT'S		
'No Added Sugar' Biscuits —		
Apple and Bran (1)	7	80
Carob Chip (1)............................	8	83
Raisin and Coconut (1)...................	7	81
Rich Fig (1)	8	79
Sesame and Sunflower (1)	7	83
Stem Ginger (1)	8	78

	Carbohydrate in grams	Calories
RM SCOTT		
Husky Bran Biscuits (1)	6	39
SAFEWAY		
Wholemeal Bran Biscuits (1)	8	62
SAINSBURY		
Wholemeal Bran Biscuits (1)	8	71
Wholemeal Shortbread Fingers (1)	8	74
SIMMERS		
Oatcakes (1).....................................	8	60
SLYMBRAND		
Digestives (1)	5	37
TESCO		
Wholemeal Shortbread Fingers (1)	11	80
WAIRNS		
Oatcakes (1).....................................	8	60
WAITROSE		
Wholemeal Shortbread Fingers (1)	12	100
WALKERS SHORTBREAD		
Oatcakes –		
Bran (1).....................................	8	64
Fine/Highland (1)	8	60
Wholemeal Shortbread (1)	11	95

CRACKERS

	Carbohydrate in grams	Calories
BURTON'S		
Golden Harvest Crackers (1)	5	27
JACOBS		
Farmhouse Crackers (1)	5	39
MARKS AND SPENCER		
Wheaten Crackers (1)	3	30
McDOUGALLS		
Hovis Cracottes (1)	5	27
Wholemeal Cracottes (1)	4	20
McVITIE		
Kracka Wheat (1)	4	38
Toasted Wheat Crisp (1)	2	22
NABISCO		
Wholemeal Cheese & Onion Sandwich (1)	5	47
RAKUSEN FOODS		
Hilo Crackers (1)	3	15
Wheaten Matzos (1)	4	18
SAFEWAY		
Wheat Cracker (1)	5	38
SAINSBURY		
Wheat Crackers (1)	5	37
WAITROSE		
Wheat Crackers (1)	5	38

CRISPBREADS

	Carbohydrate in grams	Calories
ALLINSON		
Salt Free Wholemeal Crispbread (1)	3	15
Wholemeal Crispbread (1)....................	3	15
BOOTS "SHAPERS"		
Whole Rye Crispbread (1)	3	15
CRAWFORD		
Ry King Brown Crispbread (1)................	5	33
Ry King Cheese Snack (1).....................	15	155
Ry King Fibre Plus (1)........................	5	28
Ry King Golden Crispbread (1)	6	34
LYONS		
Whole Rye Krispen (1)........................	3	16
Wholewheat with Bran Krispen (1)...........	3	16
NEWFORM FOODS - COUNTRY BASKET		
Wholewheat Crisp-Bread (1)	5	30
PRIMULA		
Extra Thin Crispbread (1)	4	19
Rye-Bran Extra Thin (1).......................	2	13
Rye-Bran Thick (1)............................	5	22
Rye Crispbread (1)............................	5	23
RYVITA		
Ryvita High Fibre (1).........................	4	22
Ryvita Original (1)	5	25
Ryvita Swedish Style Brown (1)	5	25
SAINSBURY		
Wholemeal Krispwheat (1)....................	4	18
SLYMBRAND		
Rye Slymbred (1).............................	2	17
Sesame Slymbred (1)	2	19
Slymbred (1).................................	2	17
Wholemeal Slymbred (1)......................	2	17

Bread, Bread Products and Pizza Bases

HIGH FIBRE

BREAD AND BREAD PRODUCTS

	Carbohydrate in grams	Calories
ALLINSON		
Bran Bread Mix		
20oz/566g packet	440	2000
100% Stoneground Wholemeal Baps (1) ...	25	155
100% Stoneground Wholemeal Bread		
large loaf, medium sliced (1 slice)	12	70
large loaf, thick sliced (1 slice)	16	85
large uncut loaf (whole loaf)	365	1680
small loaf (1 slice)	10	55
100% Stoneground Wholemeal Cob		
small loaf (whole loaf)	175	850
100% Wholemeal (Rollerground)		
large loaf (1 slice)	13	70
small loaf (1 slice)	11	55
Wholemeal Snack Rolls (1)....................	18	105
Wholewheat Bread Mix		
20oz/566g packet	390	1875
BOOTS		
Country Grains Loaf		
large loaf (whole loaf)	345	1730
large loaf (1 slice)	15	75
Country Grains Roll (1)	37	195
Wholemeal Loaf		
large loaf (1 slice)	15	80
small loaf (whole loaf)	170	860
Wholemeal Rolls (1)	25	130
CO-OP		
Wholemeal Bread		
large loaf (1 slice)	15	75
small loaf (1 slice)	12	60
GRANOSE		
Wholemeal Toasties (1) approx	7	45
HOVIS		
Country Grain Wholemeal Bread		
large loaf (1 slice)..........................	16	85
Malted Wheatgrain Brown Bread		
large loaf (1 slice)	20	95
Stoneground Baps (1)	21	125
Stoneground Wholemeal Bread		
large loaf (1 slice)	14	72
small loaf (1 slice)	11	60

13

HOVIS — Continued

	Carbohydrate in grams	Calories
Traditional Wheatgerm Bread		
small loaf (1 slice)	12	60
Wholewheat and Bran Baps (1)..............	20	115

MARKS AND SPENCER

Brown Big Country Rolls (1)...................	22	115
Hi-Bran Bread		
large loaf, medium sliced (1 slice)..........	14	70
large loaf, thick sliced (1 slice).............	17	80
small loaf, medium sliced (1 slice)	11	55
Mini Hovis Loaves (1)...........................	18	95
Mixed Grain Loaf		
large loaf (whole loaf)......................	375	1840
small loaf (whole loaf)	190	920
Multi-Grain Bread		
(1 slice).....................................	11	60
Multi-Grain Roll (1)	25	140
Soft Brown Rolls (1)	20	125
Vitbe Wheatgerm Bread		
large loaf (1 slice)...........................	14	75
small loaf (1 slice)	11	60
Wholewheat (Allinson label)		
large loaf (1 slice)...........................	15	70
small loaf (1 slice)	12	55

MOTHERS PRIDE

Brown Morning Rolls (1).......................	21	110

MR HARVEY'S STUFFING

Chestnut		
85g packet	60	270
Parsley and Thyme		
85g packet	55	265
Sage and Onion		
85g packet	55	265

PITTA'S

Wholemeal		
— most brands (1)	40	180
Mini Wholemeal Pittas 35g (1)..............	19	90

SAINSBURY

Bran Rolls		
(1 from pack of 6)............................	28	150
Brown Floury Batch Baps (1)..................	21	120
Granary Wholemeal		
large loaf (1 slice)...........................	15	80
small loaf (1 slice)	12	65
Granary Wholemeal Baps (1).................	25	150
Stoneground Wholemeal Baps (1)...........	20	125
Stoneground Mini-loaves (1)..................	25	120

	Carbohydrate in grams	Calories
Stoneground Wholemeal		
large loaf (1 slice)	12	60
Wholemeal Baps sliced (1)	28	140
Wholemeal		
large loaf (1 slice)	12	65
Wholemeal Hoagies (1)	45	220
Wholemeal Rolls		
all shapes (1)	21	105
SUNBLEST		
Long Loaf Brown		
large loaf (1 slice)	14	75
TESCO		
Bran Bap (1)	25	135
Bran Loaf		
large loaf (1 slice)	15	75
small loaf (1 slice)	12	60
Brown Bread		
large loaf, medium sliced (1 slice)	15	75
Brown Morning Rolls (1)	24	125
Brown Snack Rolls (1)	14	70
Stoneground Wholemeal Baps (1)	22	120
Wholemeal Loaf		
large loaf (1 slice)	15	75
small loaf (1 slice)	12	60
VITBE		
Hi-Bran Brown Bread		
large loaf, medium sliced (1 slice)	12	75
large loaf, thick sliced (1 slice)	15	100
small loaf (1 slice)	8	55
Hi-Bran Rolls (1)	17	115
Wheatgerm Bread		
large loaf (1 slice)	13	75
small loaf (1 slice)	10	60
WHOLE EARTH		
Whole Earth Bread		
400g loaf (whole loaf)	165	835
WINDMILL BAKERY		
Country Brown		
large loaf (1 slice)	16	75
Granary		
small loaf (1 slice)	12	58
Hi-Fibre Wholemeal Bread		
large loaf (1 slice)	13	70
White High Fibre		
large loaf (1 slice)	15	75
Wholemeal Baps (1)	23	130

WINDMILL BAKERY - Continued

	Carbohydrate in grams	Calories
Wholemeal		
large loaf, medium sliced (1 slice)	14	80
large loaf, thick sliced (1 slice)	16	85
small loaf (1 slice)	11	55
Wholemeal Scotch Rolls (1)	20	110

PIZZA BASES

SAFEWAY
Wholemeal Pizza Base

	Carbohydrate in grams	Calories
1 from pack of 2	120	515
1 from pack of 4	60	260

Cakes and Teabreads

HIGH FIBRE TEABREADS

	Carbohydrate in grams	Calories
ALLINSON		
Wholemeal Malt Loaf........................	120	610
Wholemeal Hot X Buns (1)	34	210
BOOTS		
Fruited Wholemeal Scones (1)...............	28	200
HOVIS		
Wholewheat and Bran Muffins (1)...........	24	135
IMPERIAL BAKERIES		
Soreen Bran Malt Loaf.......................	130	580
LITTLEWOODS		
Fruit Malt Loaf	145	645
MARKS AND SPENCER		
Raisin and Bran Muffins (1)	30	140
SAINSBURY		
Mini Wholemeal Spiced Fruit Buns (1).......	18	85
Wholemeal and Raisin Muffins (1)...........	30	140
Wholemeal Fruit Scones (1)..................	30	180
Wholemeal Muffins (1)	30	155
Wholemeal Spiced Fruit Buns (1).............	30	175
TESCO		
Wholemeal Muffin 65g approx..............	25	135
Wholemeal Muffin 75g	30	155
Wholemeal Spiced Bun (1)	31	185
VITBE		
Hi-Bran Fruit & Honey Malt Loaf		
whole loaf....................................	110	590
WINDMILL BAKERY		
Wholemeal Spiced Fruit Buns (1).............	26	155

Cereals

HIGH FIBRE

Porridge oats contain 20g carbohydrate and 100 calories per 1oz serving of the uncooked oats. This figure is the same for traditional and quick cooking brands.

	Carbohydrate in grams	Calories
ALLINSON		
Bran Muesli 1oz	16	95
Bran Plus 1oz	9	65
Breakfast Muesli 1oz	19	100
Broad Bran 1oz	5	45
Brunch Muesli Pot Snack 95g packet	65	330
ARGYLL STORES (PRESTO)		
Bran Cereal 1oz	12	70
Branflakes 1oz	20	90
Dutch Wholewheat Crispbakes (1)	6	35
Muesli-Bran 1oz	16	85
Wheat Bisks (1)	11	60
Wheatflakes 1oz	19	95
BEJAM		
Fruit and Nut Muesli 1oz	20	95
High Fibre Bran Muesli 1oz	16	80
BOOTS "SECOND NATURE"		
Branflakes with Sultanas & Apples 1oz	19	85
Deluxe Muesli 1oz	17	95
Muesli Cereal 1oz	21	105
No Added Sugar Muesli 1oz	18	105
Unprocessed Bran 1oz	7	60
CHESHIRE WHOLE FOODS		
Fruit and Fibre Muesli 1oz	18	85
High Fibre Muesli 1oz	17	100
Muesli 1oz	18	100
CO-OP		
Bran Flakes 1oz	24	105
Wholewheat Cereal Biscuits(1)	11	50
Wholewheat Flakes 1oz	23	105
Wholewheat Muesli 1oz	17	95
FAMILY CHOICE		
Bran Breakfast Cereal 1oz	14	80
Sultana Bran 1oz	23	90
GRANOSE		
Bircher Muesli 1oz	20	110

	Carbohydrate in grams	Calories
GRANOSE – Continued		
Crunchy Nut Cereal 1oz	17	140
'8' Fruit Muesli 1oz	18	115
Soya Bran 1oz	10	30
Wholegrain Fruit Muesli 1oz	21	115
HOLLAND AND BARRETT		
High Fibre Fruit & Nut Muesli 1oz	17	100
HOLLY MILL		
Apple and Banana Bran Brek 1oz	17	125
Bran Brek 1oz	16	125
Fruit & Nut Porridge 1oz	19	100
Muesli Base 1oz	21	100
Muesli Sugar Free 1oz	18	100
JORDANS		
Country Muesli with Fruit & Wholenuts 1oz	16	100
Natural Country Bran 1oz	8	50
Original Crunchy		
Natural 1oz	15	115
Tropical 1oz	15	110
with Bran and Apple 1oz	16	115
with Honey Almonds and Raisins 1oz	15	110
Special Receipe Muesli 1oz	15	95
KELLOGG		
All Bran 1oz	13	70
Bran Buds 1oz	16	80
Bran Flakes 1oz	19	90
Nutrigrain		
Brown Rice with Raisins 1oz	23	100
Rye and Oats 1oz	20	105
Rye and Oats with Raisins 1oz	21	95
Raisin Splits 1oz	20	100
Sultana Bran 1oz	19	85
Summer Orchard 1oz	17	90
LAWS		
Muesli 1oz	17	100
LYONS TETLEY		
Coco Brek 1oz	21	110
Golden Brek 1oz	22	115
Ready Brek Original 1oz	21	110
NABISCO		
Cubs 1oz	21	100
Harvest Home Bran Flakes 1oz	20	105
Raisin Fruit Wheats 1oz	19	90
Shredded Wheat (1)	16	80
Shreddies 1oz	21	95
Team 1oz	18	85

	Carbohydrate in grams	Calories
PEARCE DUFF		
Muesli de Luxe 1oz	18	105
PRESTO		
Fruit and Nut Muesli 1oz	17	100
PREWETT'S		
Bran Muesli 1oz	16	95
Fruit and Nut Muesli 1oz	18	95
Muesli Deluxe 1oz	17	110
Natural Wheat Bran 1oz	5	45
Tropical Museli 1oz	17	100
Whole Wheat Flakes 1oz	20	95
QUAKER		
Harvest Crunch 1oz	18	125
Harvest Crunch Bran and Apple 1oz	17	120
Instant Hot Bran 1oz (uncooked)	16	95
Oat Krunchies with Added Bran 1oz	20	110
Puffed Wheat 1oz	20	95
Warm Start 1oz (uncooked)	19	105
RYVITA		
Bran Breakfast Cereal 1oz	14	80
Cracked Wheat Flakes 1oz	20	100
Hi-Bran Crispy Rice 1oz	20	100
High Fibre Cornflakes 1oz	23	105
Morning Bran 1oz	14	80
SAFEWAY		
Crunchy Oat Cereal 1oz	18	120
Fibre Bran 1oz	12	70
Fruit and Nut Muesli 1oz	17	95
Hot Oat Cereal 1oz	19	110
Swiss Style Cereal 1oz	18	95
Wholewheat Biscuits (1)	12	55
Wholewheat Flakes 1oz	19	90
SAINSBURY		
Branflakes 1oz	20	95
Crunchy Oat Cereal with Apple & Bran 1oz	17	110
Instant Oat Cereal 1oz	19	105
Mini Wheats 1oz	22	100
Muesli 1oz	19	110
Natural High Fibre Wheat Bran Cereal 1oz	12	70
Oat and Bran Flakes 1oz	18	105
Puffed Wheat 1oz	20	95
Sultana Bran 1oz	20	90
Toasted Bran 1oz	17	85
Wheatflakes 1oz	24	105
Wholewheat Bisk (1)	13	60

	Carbohydrate in grams	Calories
SUNWHEEL FOODS		
Barley Kernals 1oz	20	100
De Luxe Muesli 1oz	20	105
Fruit and Nut Muesli 1oz	16	100
SUPERDRUG		
Bran Breakfast Cereal 1oz	14	80
TESCO		
Bran Flakes with Sultanas 1oz	20	90
Bran Muesli 1oz	14	100
Porridge Oats with Bran 1oz	16	100
Rye & Raisin Cereal 1oz	20	90
Swiss Style Breakfast 1oz	19	100
Unsweetened Swiss Style Muesli 1oz	18	95
Wholewheat Cereal 1oz	14	70
Wholewheat Flakes 1oz	22	95
Wholewheat Fruit and Nut Muesli 1oz	16	105
WAITROSE		
Bran Flakes 1oz	20	100
Bran Muesli 1oz	20	105
Fruit and Fibre Muesli 1oz	19	85
Fruit and Nut Muesli 1oz	16	100
Muesli Cereal 1oz	19	110
Wheat Flakes 1oz	22	95
WEETABIX		
Alpen 1oz	19	105
Alpen with Tropical Fruit 1oz	19	110
Bran Fare 1oz	10	65
Farmhouse Bran with Apple & Apricot 1oz	19	95
Toasted Farmhouse Bran 1oz	17	85
Weetabix (1)	12	60
Weetaflake 1oz	19	95
Weetaflake 'n' Raisin 1oz	21	100
WHITWORTHS		
Breakfast Booster 1oz	13	80
WHOLE EARTH		
Almond Crunch Cereal 1oz	17	120
WILLIAM LOW		
Luxury Muesli 1oz	18	105
YORKSHIRE CO-OP		
Muesli 1oz	19	100

Dairy Products and Dairy Substitutes

LOW FAT
CHEESE

There is very little variation in the carbohydrate and calorie values for Natural Cottage Cheese from one manufacturer to another. Below are carbohydrate and calorie values which are a useful guide for the majority of the popular brands:

	Carbohydrate in grams	Calories
Natural Cottage Cheese		
4oz/113g pot	2	100-120
8oz/227g pot	3	200-230
Cottage Cheese with Chives		
4oz/113g pot	2	120
Cottage Cheese with Date and Walnut		
8oz/227g pot	23	270
Cottage Cheese with Onion and Cheddar		
4oz/113g pot	2	140
Cottage Cheese with Peanuts and Sweetcorn		
4oz/113g pot	3	150
Cottage Cheese with Pineapple		
4oz/113g pot	5-8	100-110
Cottage Cheese with Pineapple and Peanuts and Curry Dressing		
4oz/113g pot	7	150
Cottage Cheese with Salmon and Cucumber		
4oz/113g pot	3	130
Diet Cottage Cheese 1oz....................	1	25
Diet Cottage Cheese with Chives/Onions 1oz	1	25
Diet Cottage Cheese with Pineapple 1oz...	2-3	25

DAIRY CREST
Tendale Cheddar Cheese 1oz	neg	70
Tendale Cheshire Cheese 1oz...............	neg	70

EDEN VALE
Cottage Cheese with Apricot & Apple		
8oz/227g pot	12	210
Crunchy Cottage Cheese		
8oz/227g pot	5	260
Seafood Cottage Cheese		
6oz/170g pot	3	160

	Carbohydrate in grams	Calories
HEINZ WEIGHT WATCHERS		
Reduced Fat Processed Cheese Slices (1) ...	neg	40
PREWETT'S		
Reduced Fat Vegetarian Cheese 1oz	neg	75
PRIMULA		
Low Fat Dairy Spreads		
all flavours 150g pack	6	270
ROWNTREE MACKINTOSH (SUN-PAT)		
Low-Line Low Fat Spread		
all flavours 150g pack	15	265
SAINSBURY		
Low Fat Dutch Cheese 1oz	neg	70
Virtually Fat Free Fromage Frais 1oz........	<1	15
SENOBLE		
Low Fat Cheese with Apricot		
200g pot.....................................	24	265
Low Fat Cheese with Strawberry		
200g pot.....................................	24	265
SOMERSET SOFT CHEESE		
Low Fat 1oz	<1	40
ST IVEL		
Shape low fat soft cheese, 1oz...............	neg	40
Shape Cheese, 1oz	neg	80
MOST BRANDS		
Curd Cheese 1oz	neg	40
Quark Plain		
Low Fat Soft Cheese 1oz...................	1	35
Medium Fat Soft Cheese 1oz..............	1	45
Skimmed Milk Cheese 1oz.................	1	25
Quark Savoury 1oz...........................	1	40

MILKS

	Carbohydrate in grams	Calories
Standard skimmed 1pt......................	28	190
Standard semi-skimmed 1pt................	28	260

MILRAM
Buttermilk with Fruits – 500ml pot

all varieties	55-60	280-300

ST IVEL

Shape Low Fat Milk, 1pt	31	255

MILK SUBSTITUTES

	Carbohydrate in grams	Calories
GRANOSE		
Soya Milk – Sugar Free		
500ml carton	7	210
1 litre carton	14	420
HALDANE FOODS		
Hera Sojal Soya Milk		
1 litre carton	25	440
PLAMIL		
Soya milk (Sugar Free Blue Label)		
14ml mini pot	neg	15
420ml can	neg	370
500ml tetrapak	neg	440
PROVAMEL		
Soya Milk – no sugar, no salt		
500ml carton	3	190
SAFEWAY		
Unsweetened Soya Milk		
500ml carton	3	180

LOW FAT SPREADS & PASTES

There is very little variation in the carbohydrate and calorie values of spreads labelled "low fat" spread.

	Carbohydrate in grams	Calories
"Low Fat Spread" 1oz	neg	110

Useful brands: "Delight", "Outline", "Slimmers Gold", "St Ivel Gold", "Weight Watchers".

CAULDRON FOODS
Vegetable Paté

100g pack	2	190

CO-OP
Pastes — 75g pot

Chicken and Ham	<4	160
Salmon and Shrimp	<4	125

SHIPPAMS
Pastes & Spreads — 35g jar

Anchovy/Bloater/Crab	1	65
Beef	1	75
Chicken and Ham	neg	75
Chicken	neg	80
Ham	2	60
Ham and Beef	neg	70
Liver and Bacon	1	70
Salmon and Shrimp	neg	60
Sardine and Tomato	1	65

Pastes & Spreads — 75g jar

Anchovy/Bloater	2	130
Beef	2	155
Chicken and Ham	1	165
Chicken	1	165
Crab	2	140
Ham and Beef	1	150
Liver and Bacon	2	145
Pilchard & Tomato	2	130
Salmon and Shrimp	1	130
Sardine and Tomato	2	140

Sandwichmakers — 95g cans
Savoury Recipe Base with

Beef & Onion	10	125
Chicken & Stuffing	7	135
Ham & Bacon	9	130

SUTHERLAND
Crab Spread

35g pot	2	55
53g pot	3	80

SUTHERLAND - Continued	Carbohydrate in grams	Calories
Meat Spreads - all varieties		
35g pot	<2	65
53g pot	<3	100
Potted & Minced - 78g pot		
Beef	neg	160
Chicken & Ham in Jelly	neg	110
Salmon with Butter	neg	125
Sardine and Tomato Spread		
35g pot	neg	60
53g pot	<2	90
Tasty Pastes - 100g pot		
Meat varieties	<5	210
Salmon	7	130
TESCO		
Pastes — 75g pots		
Beef	3	155
Chicken & Ham	1	150
Salmon & Shrimp	1	85
Sardine & Tomato	3	135

YOGURTS

There is very little variation in the carbohydrate and calorie values for Natural Low Fat Yogurt from one manufacturer to another. We therefore give below carbohydrate and calorie values which will be a useful guide for all the popular brands:

	Carbohydrate in grams	Calories
Natural Low Fat Yogurt		
4.2fl.oz/120g pot............................	8-10	65-80
5.3fl.oz/150g pot............................	10-12	80-100
Natural Set Yogurt (low fat)		
125g pot.....................................	6	45
142g pot.....................................	9	65
150g pot.....................................	10	75
Very Low Fat Pasteurised		
Natural Yogurt 125g pot	6	50
ARGYLL STORES (PRESTO)		
Diet Yogurt – 125g pot		
all flavours.................................	9	60
BOOTS		
Shapers Yogurt – 150g pot		
all flavours.................................	14	90
MARKS AND SPENCER		
"Lite" Yogurt – 150g pot		
all flavours.................................	9	60
SAFEWAY		
Trimrite Yoghurt – 125g pot		
all flavours.................................	10	60
SAINSBURY		
Diet Yogurt – 125g pot		
all flavours.................................	9	55
SKI		
Diet Yogurts – 125g pot		
all flavours.................................	7	50
SO JAL		
Dairy Free Yoga – 125g pot		
Natural.....................................	6	60
Raspberry	7	65
Strawberry	7	65
STAPLETON FARM		
Sugar-Free Live Yogurts – 142g pot		
4 flavours..................................	10	65

	Carbohydrate in grams	Calories

ST IVEL
Shape Multigrain Yogurt – 125g pot
all flavours... **10** **65**
Shape Yogurts – 125g pot
all flavours... **8** **55**

SUDMILCH
Country Love Yogurt
150g pot... **6** **100**

WAISTLINE
Low Fat Yogurts – 125g pot
all flavours... **12** **65**

WAITROSE
Diet Yogurt
(1 from pack of 6) 125g pot.................... **8** **55**

YOPLAIT
Diet Yogurt – 125g pot........................... **9** **60**

30

Desserts

	Carbohydrate in grams	Calories
BIRD'S		
Sugar Free Jelly Crystals - all flavours		
1 sachet approx.	5	50
per serving approx.	neg	10
CASANOVA ICE CREAM		
Trimanova Vanilla Ice Dessert		
1 scoop (50g weight)	3	45
ST IVEL		
Fromage Frais Desserts - 80g pot		
Apricot	4	50
Orange	5	50
Raspberry	6	55
Strawberry	6	55

Dressings, Pickles, Sauces

LOW SUGAR
DRESSINGS

	Carbohydrate in grams	Calories
Basic Oil & Vinegar type dressings reduced calorie		
1 tablespoon................................	neg	25
HEINZ		
Reduced Calorie Dressing for Salads		
1 tablespoon	<3	25
SAFEWAY		
Low Calorie Vinaigrette Dressing		
1 tablespoon	neg	5
SAINSBURY		
Reduced Calorie Vinegar & Oil Dressing		
1 tablespoon................................	<2	25
WAITROSE		
Low Calorie Vinaigrette Dressing		
1 tablespoon	neg	5

PICKLES

BOOTS
Shapers Reduced Calorie -
Sweet Pickle

	Carbohydrate in grams	Calories
1 level tablespoon	<3	10

SAUCES

	Carbohydrate in grams	Calories
BOOTS		
Shapers Reduced Calorie – Mayonnaise		
1 level tablespoon	<3	60
HELLMANN'S		
Reduced Calorie Mayonnaise		
1 level tablespoon	1	45
SAINSBURY		
Reduced Calorie French Mayonnaise		
1 level tablespoon	2	40
WAITROSE		
Low Sugar Tomato Ketchup		
1 tablespoon	2	7

Drinks - Low Sugar

FIZZY DRINKS

There is very little variation in the carbohydrate and calorie values of fizzy drinks labelled "low calorie". Below is an approximate guide to cover all popular brands.

	Carbohydrate in grams	Calories
American Ginger Ale		
250ml bottle	neg	10
330ml can	neg	15
Bitter Lemon		
250ml bottle	2	10
330ml can	3	15
Cola		
250ml bottle	2	10
330ml can	3	15
Dry Ginger		
250ml bottle	2	10
330ml can	3	15
Indian Tonic Water		
250ml bottle	2	10
330ml can	3	15
Lemonade		
250ml bottle	2	10
330ml can	3	15
Orange		
250ml bottle	2	10
330ml can	3	10

Useful Brands: **Boots, Diet Corona, Mandora, Safeway, Sainsbury, Tesco, Waitrose, Weight Watchers.**

BOOTS "SHAPERS"
Low Calorie Shandy Flavour

330ml can	neg	12

BRITVIC SLIMSTA
Apple Crush		
170ml bottle	2	7
Blackcurrant Crush		
170ml bottle	1	5
250ml bottle	2	7
Orange Crush		
170ml bottle	2	8
250ml bottle	3	12
Pineapple Crush		
170ml bottle	2	8
Shandy		
270ml can	4	16

COCA COLA
(Sweetened with NutraSweet)
Diet Coke

	Carbohydrate in grams	Calories
330ml can	neg	1

DEXTERS
Low Calorie Isotonic Drink

25cl can	neg	<5

HUNTS
Diet Bitter Orange Drink

170ml bottle	<1	5
Diet Drinks – 600ml bottle		
Sparkling American Ginger Ale............	neg	8
Sparkling Bitter Lemon	<1	3
Sparkling Indian Tonic Water..............	neg	3
Bitter Sweet Sparkling Lemon & Lime		
250ml can	2	11
Bitter Sweet Sparkling Orange		
250ml can	3	12

MARKS AND SPENCER
Citro Pineapple/Grapefruit Drink

320ml can	3	13
Low Calorie Cola		
320ml can	3	3
Low Calorie Orange Crush		
250ml can	2	10

ONE-CAL
1-Cal Drinks, whole range

330ml can	neg	1

PEPSI
(Sweetened with NutraSweet)
Diet Pepsi Cola

330ml can	neg	1

SCHWEPPES SLIMLINE
(Sweetened with NutraSweet)
American Ginger Ale

113ml bottle	neg	neg
180ml bottle	neg	neg
250ml bottle	neg	1
500ml bottle	neg	2
Bitter Lemon		
113ml bottle	neg	2
180ml bottle	neg	3
250ml bottle	1	5
500ml bottle	2	9
Cariba		
330ml can	3	15

SCHWEPPES SLIMLINE — Continued

	Carbohydrate in grams	Calories
Lemonade		
180ml bottle	neg	neg
250ml bottle	neg	1
330ml can	neg	1
Lemonade and Beer Shandy		
330ml can	1	21
Sparkling Limon Crush		
330ml can	2	10
Sparkling Orange Crush		
330ml can	2	10
Tonic Water		
113ml bottle	neg	neg
180ml bottle	neg	1
250ml bottle	neg	1
SILVER SPRING		
(Sweetened with NutraSweet)		
Diet Rola Cola		
1 litre bottle	neg	10
Diet Spring-Up Lemonade		
1 litre bottle	neg	10
SODA STREAM		
One Cal* all flavours		
25ml	neg	<1
TANGO		
Diet Drinks - 330ml can		
Sparkling Orange	2	10
Sparkling Orange & Pineapple	2	8
TOP DECK		
Diet Low Calorie Lemonade with Beer		
330ml can	5	35

HOT BEVERAGES

	Carbohydrate in grams	Calories
BOOTS		
Beefy Beverage		
1 level teaspoon	neg	10
KNORR		
Hot Light Drinks – all flavours		
1 serving	4	20
LONDON HERB & SPICE CO.		
Natural Break		
1 sachet	neg	<10

SQUASHES - LOW CALORIE

There is very little variation in the carbohydrate and calorie content of squashes or dilutable drinks labelled "Diabetic" or "Low Calorie". The table below is an accurate guide. Values are given for undiluted quantities of the squashes.

	Carbohydrate in grams	Calories
Apple and Blackberry 1fl oz/25ml	neg	2
Blackcurrant 1fl oz/25ml.................	neg	neg
Grapefruit 1fl oz/25ml.................	neg	2
Lemon 1fl oz/25ml.................	neg	<5
Lemon and Lime 1fl oz/25ml.................	neg	<5
Lemon Barley 1fl oz/25ml	neg	3
Lime 1fl oz/25ml.................	neg	<5
Orange 1fl oz/25ml.................	neg	<5
Orange and Grapefruit 1fl oz/25ml	neg	<2
Orange and Pineapple 1fl oz/25ml..........	neg	<5
Tropical Fruit 1fl oz/25ml	neg	3

Useful brands: **Boots Diabetic, Boots Shapers, Braid Soft Drinks, Co-op, Edwin Cheshire, Low Sugar Quosh, Magpie Soft Drinks, Peels Pure Squashes, Renpro (Diabetic), Rimark Soft Drinks, Robinson's, Roses, Safeway, Sionon, Strathmore Springs, Sunpure, Tesco, Weight Watchers.**

PLJ
Lemon Juice, Less Sharp
1fl oz/25ml .... <1   7
Original
1fl oz/25ml .... <1   7

QUOSH
Low Calorie Orange Drink
250ml tetra brik............................... 2   13

ROBINSONS
Special R - No Added Sugar
 Apple & Blackcurrant 1fl oz/25ml .... neg   neg
 Orange 1fl oz/25ml .... neg   neg

SVALI
Lemon Drink, Ready to drink
 250ml pack 3   13

Fish

CANNED FISH

There is only a small variation in the carbohydrate and calorie content of the various brands of Fish in Brine/Oil/Sauce. The table below is sufficiently accurate for everyday use and does take into account the small variation from brand to brand.

Useful brands: **Armour, John West, Plumrose, Princes, Safeway, Sainsbury, Shippams, Tesco, Waitrose.**

	Carbohydrate in grams	Calories
Crab		
198g tin	neg	125
Crabmeat in Brine		
170g tin	neg	140
Herring Fillets in Savoury Sauce		
200g tin	8	235
Herring Fillets in Tomato Sauce		
200g tin	8	275
Kipper Fillets		
200g tin	neg	455
Kipper Fillets in Oil		
198g tin	neg	590
Mackerel Fillets in Oil		
125g tin	neg	400
Mackerel Steaks in Natural Juices		
200g tin	neg	500
Mackerel Fillets in Tomato Sauce		
125g tin	neg	215
425g tin	8	860
Mackerel Steaks in Tomato Sauce		
200g tin	2	405
Pilchards in Tomato Sauce		
156g tin	neg	200
215g tin	2	300
425g tin	4	590
Pink Salmon		
99g tin	neg	155
213g tin	neg	330
426g tin	neg	660
Prawns in Brine		
100g tin	neg	90
200g tin	neg	175
Red Salmon		
99g tin	neg	210
213g tin	neg	450
426g tin	neg	660
Sardines in Tomato Sauce		
120g tin	neg	220
Sardines in Vegetable Oil		
120g tin	neg	235

	Carbohydrate in grams	Calories
Shrimps		
113g tin...........................	**neg**	**70**
184g tin...........................	**neg**	**110**
Sild in Oil		
110g tin...........................	**neg**	**250**
Sild in Tomato Sauce		
110g tin...........................	**1**	**190**
Tuna in Brine		
100g tin...........................	**neg**	**110**
200g tin...........................	**neg**	**220**
Tuna in Oil		
100g tin...........................	**neg**	**200**
200g tin...........................	**neg**	**395**
Tuna in Lemon Jelly		
185g tin...........................	**neg**	**125**

FROZEN FISH

There is very little variation from one manufacturer to another for all white breaded filleted fish, i.e. cod, haddock, plaice, whiting, 1oz before cooking is approximately 3 - 5g carbohydrate and 30 - 40 calories.

BEJAM

	Carbohydrate in grams	Calories
Boil in the Bag Kipper Fillets with Butter 200g pack	neg	380
Cod Bites when baked (1)	3	35
Cod Fish Cakes (1)	12	120
Cod Fish Fingers when grilled (1)	5	45
Cod Steaks in Crispy Batter when deep fried (1)	13	250
Haddock Steaks in Crispy Batter when deep fried (1)	12	220
Oven Cod oven baked (1)	22	300

BIRDS EYE

	Carbohydrate in grams	Calories
Big Value Fish Cakes when grilled (1)	9	85
Captain's Fishburgers when baked/grilled (1)	8	100
Cod Fillet Fish Fingers when grilled (1)	5	50
Cod Steaks in Wholemeal Crumb when baked/grilled (1)	13	195
Cod Steaks in Crisp Crunch Crumb when baked/grilled (1)	13	185
Crispy Cod Steaks when shallow fried (1)	12	190
Crispy Haddock Steaks when shallow fried (1)	12	180
Fish Cakes in Wholemeal Crumbs		
Cod when grilled (1)	10	90
Salmon when grilled (1)	8	90
Fish Fingers in Crispy Batter when fried (1)	5	65
Haddock Steaks in Crisp Crunch Crumb when grilled (1)	13	185
Oven Crispy Cod Steaks when baked/grilled (1)	12	215
Oven Crispy Haddock Steaks when baked/grilled (1)	12	215
Plaice Steaks in Crisp Crunch Crumb (1)	15	200
Value Fish Fingers when grilled (1)	4	45

	Carbohydrate in grams	Calories

CO-OP
	Carbohydrate in grams	Calories
Cod Fish Fingers (1)	5	55
Cod Steaks in Butter		
1 from pack of 4	4	100
Fish Cakes (1)	10	65

FINDUS
Batter Crisp Cod Portions (1)	20	265
Battered Cod/Haddock Steaks		
Batter Crisp (1)	20	255
Cod Fish Cakes (1)	10	60
Crumb Crisp Cod/Haddock Portions (1)	17	265
Crumb Crisp Haddock Fish Fingers (1)	5	65
Haddock Portion Batter Crisp (1)	20	270
Wholemeal Crumb Crisp Cod		
Fish Fingers (1)	5	55

LITTLEWOODS
Battered Cod		
50g (1)	9	115
100g (1)	18	235
Cod Fish Fingers (1)	5	55
Value Fish Fingers (1)	5	50

MARKS AND SPENCER
Battercrisp Cod Portions		
1 from pack of 2	12	245
Battercrisp Haddock Portions		
1 from pack of 2	12	185
Breaded Lemon Sole Fillets 1oz	4	35
Cod Fish Fingers (1)	4	50

McCAIN
Fillet Fish Fingers (1)	4	45
Fish Cakes (1)	10	80

OLAF FOODS
Surfers (1)	15	190

ROSS
Battered Fishcakes (1)	8	100
Cod Fish Fingers (1)	5	60
Crispy Cod (1)	14	180
Crispy Haddock (1)	14	180
Fish Cakes (1)	11	60
Jumbo Battered Cod Fingers (1)	11	140
Oven Cod (1)	14	210

SAFEWAY
Cod in Batter		
200g pack	20	400
Fish Cakes (1)	10	60

	Carbohydrate in grams	Calories
SAFEWAY — Continued		
Fish Fingers Cod (1)..............................	5	50
Haddock in Batter		
200g pack...................................	20	400
SAINSBURY		
Cod Fillet Fish Fingers (1)	5	65
Cod Steaks in Natural Crispy Crumb (1)....	11	195
Fish Cakes (1)	10	90
TESCO		
Cod Steaks in Batter (1).......................	15	200
Fish Cakes (1)	9	55
Fish Fingers (1)	5	50
WAITROSE		
Minced Cod Fish Fingers (1)	5	55
YOUNG'S SEAFOODS		
CHILLED PRODUCTS		
Smoked Haddock Croquettes 1oz..........	5	55
Whole Scampi Tails in Breadcrumbs 1oz ...	5	60

PREPARED FISH DISHES

	Carbohydrate in grams	Calories
BEJAM		
Boil-in-Bag Fish – 1 packet		
Cod in Butter Sauce	4	140
Cod in Cheese Sauce........................	5	170
Cod in Mushroom Sauce..................	4	180
Cod in Parsley Sauce	4	140
Cod and Prawn Pasta		
10oz/283g pack	25	275
Cod and Prawn Pie		
1 from pack of 2	30	410
Cod Crumble		
1 from pack of 2	40	485
Smoked Haddock Lasagne		
10oz/284g pack	45	400
Stuffed Plaice with Prawn & Mushrooms		
when baked (1)	20	410
BIRDS EYE		
Captains Pie		
10oz/283g tray..............................	28	335
Cod in Butter Sauce		
1 packet	8	155
Cod in Cheese Sauce		
1 packet	8	175
Cod in Mushroom Sauce		
1 packet	8	160
Cod in Parsley Sauce		
1 packet	10	150
Cod in Seafood Sauce		
1 packet	7	165
Cod Mornay		
1 packet	25	420
Fisherman's Choice		
1 packet	30	320
Haddock Platter		
340g pack....................................	25	345
Salmon & Broccoli Mornay		
1 packet.......................................	15	310
CO-OP		
Cod Steaks in Butter Sauce		
170g pack....................................	5	155
300g pack....................................	9	270
Cod in Parsley Sauce		
170g pack....................................	7	125
FINDUS		
Cod Steak in Butter Sauce		
170g pack....................................	7	190

FINDUS — Continued

	Carbohydrate in grams	Calories
Cod Steak in Cheese Sauce		
170g pack	4	170
Cod Steak in Parsley Sauce		
170g pack	7	170
Cod Steak in Seafood Sauce		
170g pack	9	140
Lean Cuisine Range - 1 packet		
Fillet of Cod Florentine	15	220
Fillet of Cod with Broccoli	15	265

GORCY OF FRANCE

Marie Seafood Coquilles (1)	5	120

ICELAND

Cod in Butter Sauce		
per sachet	5	130
Cod in Parsley Sauce		
per sachet	5	130
Cod in Parsley Sauce with Vegetables		
per pack	12	170

MARKS AND SPENCER

Cod and Prawn Pie		
1 from pack of 2	20	300
Cod and Ratatouille Gratin		
(Serves 2) 454g pack	15	570
Cod Floretine		
(Serves 1) 340g pack	10	310
Cod in Butter Sauce		
184g pack	5	175
Cod in Parsley Sauce		
184g pack	2	150
Crowns of Plaice		
(Serves 2) 400g pack	10	460
Fisherman's Pie		
8oz/227g pack	20	310
16oz/454g pack	35	620
Haddock & Courgette Bake		
(Serves 1) 283g pack	15	260
Haddock Mornay		
(Serves 2) 400g pack	10	445
Mariners Bake		
454g pack	45	485
Ocean Pie		
8oz/227g pack	20	245
16oz/454g pack	35	485
Salmon a la Creme		
(Serves 2) 454g pack	45	605

	Carbohydrate in grams	Calories
Traditional Fish Pie		
(Serves 2) 454g pack	50	510

MR CHANG'S READY MEALS
Prawn Curry
6oz/170g pack............................... | 10 | 90

6oz/170g pack...............................	10	90

OLAF FOODS
Bellarena Salmon & Broccoli au Gratin
227g pack..................... | 15 | 300

Bellarena Salmon & Mushroom Pasta
227g pack..................... | 25 | 260

Bellarena Salmon Crumble
227g pack..................... | 30 | 430

227g pack.....................	15	300
227g pack.....................	25	260
227g pack.....................	30	430

ROSS
Fish in Sauce -150g pack

Cod Steaks in Butter Sauce................	5	140
Cod Steaks in Parsley Sauce..............	3	130
Cod Steaks in Sweetcorn Sauce...........	6	130

Special Recipe Meals -per serving

Cod Crumble.............................	35	595
Cod Mornay..............................	25	385
Haddock and Prawn Crumble.............	35	550
Ocean Pie	30	320

SAFEWAY
Cod in Butter Sauce

5.29oz/150g pack	5	135
300g pack	9	270

Cod in Parsley Sauce

5.29oz/150g pack	3	120
300g pack................................	6	240

SAINSBURY
Cod and Broccoli Pie (frozen)
350g pack.................... | 20 | 365

Cod and Prawn Pie with Grapes (frozen)
300g pack.................... | 30 | 445

Cod and Vegetable Pasta
300g pack.................... | 25 | 275

Mariners Pie (frozen)
227g pack.................... | 24 | 225

350g pack....................	20	365
300g pack....................	30	445
300g pack....................	25	275
227g pack....................	24	225

TESCO
Cod in Butter Sauce
170g pack.................... | 7 | 165

Cod in Parsley Sauce
170g pack.................... | 8 | 150

170g pack....................	7	165
170g pack....................	8	150

	Carbohydrate in grams	Calories
WAITROSE		
Cod/Broccoli Mornay		
16oz/454g pack	25	465
Prawn Curry		
250g pack....................................	25	500
W A TURNER		
Traditionally British Cod in Parsley Sauce		
16oz/454g pack	40	480
YOUNG'S SEAFOOD		
CHILLED PRODUCTS		
Filled Plaice with Butter Sauce 1oz	5	45
Filled Plaice with Mornay Sauce 1oz	5	45
Haddock Dippers 1oz........................	4	55
Lemon Sole Goujons 1oz	5	65
Sea Scallops in Breadcrumbs 1oz............	4	50
Seafood Sticks 1oz	3	25

Fruits

TINNED

	Carbohydrate in grams	Calories
CO-OP		
Apricot Halves in natural juice		
411g can	35	150
Fruit Cocktail in natural juice		
411g can	55	215
Grapefruit Segments in natural juice		
411g can	30	125
Mandarin Oranges in natural juice		
298g can	25	95
Peach Slices in natural juice		
411g can	35	155
Pear Halves in natural juice		
411g can	40	155
Pineapple Chunks in natural juice		
420g can	50	200
Pineapple Slices in natural juice		
420g can	50	200
Raspberries in natural juice		
220g can	15	65
Strawberries in natural juice		
213g can	20	70
DEL MONTE FOODS		
Fruit Cocktail in natural juice		
415g can	50	195
Peach Slices in natural juice		
415g can	50	190
Pear Halves in natural juice		
415g can	50	200
Pineapple Chunks in natural juice		
220g can	35	140
415g can	65	260
Pineapple Slices in natural juice		
220g can	35	140
415g can	65	260
830g can	130	520
JOHN WEST		
Apple Slices		
383g can	30	120
Apricots in fruit juice		
285g can	35	135
Blackberries in fruit juice		
300g can	20	75
Black Cherries in natural juice		
285g can	40	115
Blackcurrants in fruit juice		
300g can	25	100

JOHN WEST — Continued

	Carbohydrate in grams	Calories
Fruit Cocktail in fruit juice		
285g can	35	145
Fruit Salad in fruit juice		
285g can	25	95
Grapefruit Segments in natural juice		
285g can	30	95
540g can	60	180
Guava Halves in fruit juice		
285g can	25	100
Kiwi Fruit in natural juice		
310g can	30	130
Loganberries in fruit juice		
285g can	20	85
Loquats in natural juice		
300g can	25	100
Mandarin Oranges in natural juice		
298g can	20	90
Peach Slices in fruit juice		
285g can	30	130
Pear Quarters in fruit juice		
285g can	30	125
Pineapple Cubes in natural juice		
340g can	35	170
455g can	45	225
Pineapple Rings in natural juice		
425g can	65	255
440g can	70	265
Prunes in fruit juice		
300g can	50	190
Raspberries in fruit juice		
300g can	15	70
Strawberries in fruit juice		
300g can	20	75

LIBBY

	Carbohydrate in grams	Calories
Natural Chunky Mixed Fruit		
415g can	55	220
Natural Peach Halves		
411g can	50	195
Natural Peach Slices		
411g can	50	200
Natural Pear Halves		
411g can	50	200
Pineapple Slices in natural syrup		
425g can	60	230

	Carbohydrate in grams	Calories
SAFEWAY		
Crushed Pineapple in natural juice		
425g can	55	215
Grapefruit in natural juice		
540g can	55	215
Mandarins in fruit juice		
298g can	30	135
Peach Slices in natural juice		
411g can	50	180
Pear Halves in natural juice		
411g can	55	205
Pineapple Pieces in natural juice		
425g can	55	215
822g can	105	410
Pineapple Rings in natural juice		
227g can	30	115
425g can	55	215
822g can	105	410
Prunes in natural juice		
220g can	65	260
437g can	135	510
SAINSBURY		
Apricot Halves in fruit juice		
411g can	35	125
Blackcurrants in fruit juice		
213g can	20	85
Flavourseal Grapefruit Segments in natural juice		
400g can	40	160
Peach Slices in fruit juice		
411g can	35	145
Pear Halves in fruit juice		
411g can	40	145
Pineapple Pieces in natural juice		
227g can	35	150
Prunes in fruit juice		
425g can	110	450
Raspberries in fruit juice		
400g can	25	120
Satsuma Oranges in fruit juice		
298g can	30	120
Unsweetened Blackberries in fruit juice		
213g can	20	75
TESCO		
Fruit Cocktail in juice		
410g can	55	210
Grapefruit Segments in juice		
538g can	50	195
Peach Halves in juice		
411g can	45	180
Peach Slices in juice		
411g can	45	180

TESCO - Continued	Carbohydrate in grams	Calories
Pear Halves		
410g can	55	225
Pear Slices in juice		
411g can	50	195
Pineapple Slices in juice		
810g can	105	420
WAITROSE		
Apricots in juice		
425g can	40	165
Fruit Cocktail in juice		
205g can	30	100
411g can	60	200
Grapefruit in juice		
539g can	50	195
Mandarins in juice		
295g can	25	110
Pears in juice		
205g can	25	105
411g can	50	200
Pineapple Pieces in juice		
425g can	60	250
Pineapple Slices in juice		
227g can	35	130
425g can	60	250
Raspberries in juice		
400g can	35	130
Sliced Peaches in juice		
205g can	20	75
411g can	40	145
TW BEACH		
Orange Marmalade Mix		
822g tin	40	80

Meats, Poultry, Prepared Meat Dishes

CANNED

There is very little variation in the carbohydrate and calorie values for certain canned/chilled meats from one manufacturer to another. Below is a useful guide per ounce for all the popular brands:

	Carbohydrate in grams	Calories
Beef 1oz..	neg	40
Corned Beef 1oz	neg	60-70
Ham (Honey Roast, Maryland, Premier)		
1oz	neg	30-35
Pressed Pork Tongue 1oz	neg	50
Silverside 1oz	neg	50
Turkey and Ham Loaf 1oz	neg	40

ARMOUR
Corned Beef Loaf

11oz/312g tin	20	645

BAXTERS
Scottish Haggis

411g tin......................................	85	715
Scotch Mince		
432g tin......................................	30	430

CAMPBELLS
Quick Snack – 425g tins

Chicken & Pasta Supreme	40	565
Vegetable Casserole........................	50	300
Tinned Meats — 15oz/425g tins		
Meatballs in Curry Sauce	40	510
Meatballs in Gravy	30	375
Meatballs in Onion Gravy	35	380
Meatballs in Tomato Sauce...............	45	435
Minced Beef and Vegetable..............	35	425

CO-OP
Minced Beef and Onion in Gravy

218g tin......................................	15	350
425g tin......................................	30	680
Stewed Steak in Gravy		
15oz/425g tin	4	595

CROSSE AND BLACKWELL
Ham and Beef Roll

5oz/142g tin.................................	20	320
8oz/227g tin.................................	32	515

CROSSE AND BLACKWELL – Continued

	Carbohydrate in grams	Calories
Ham and Chicken Roll		
5oz/142g tin...............................	15	300
8oz/227g tin...............................	20	485

FRAY BENTOS

	Carbohydrate in grams	Calories
Chicken and Mushroom Pie Filling		
15oz/425g tin	20	455
Minced Steak and Onion Pie Filling		
15oz/425g tin	20	840
Savoury Minced Beef with Onions & Gravy		
213g tin.......................................	10	360
425g tin.......................................	20	715
Steak and Kidney Pie Filling		
15oz/425g tin	12	630
20oz/568g tin	15	835
Steak and Mushroom Pie Filling		
15oz/425g tin	15	615
20oz/568g tin	20	815
Steak and Onion Pie Filling		
15oz/425g tin	20	670
Vegetable and Steak Pie Filling		
15oz/425g tin	25	620
20oz/568g tin	35	825

GOBLIN

	Carbohydrate in grams	Calories
Hamburgers with Onions and Gravy		
440g tin.......................................	30	620
Minced Beef and Onion		
5oz/142g tin...............................	10	285
15oz/425g tin	30	850
Pie Fillings		
15oz/425g tin	20	555

GOLD DISH

	Carbohydrate in grams	Calories
Chicken Breast		
7oz/200g tin.................................	neg	190

ICELAND

	Carbohydrate in grams	Calories
Minced Beef with Vegetables		
(Serves 1) 10oz/283g pack..................	15	235
Quick Cook Casserole – 454g pack		
Beef...	25	630
Lamb	30	495

MARKS AND SPENCER

	Carbohydrate in grams	Calories
Chicken in Rich Cream Sauce		
418g tin.......................................	10	555
Chunky Chicken in Savoury White Sauce		
205g tin.......................................	10	310
418g tin.......................................	20	630
Chunky Curried Beef		
439g tin.......................................	20	435

54

	Carbohydrate in grams	Calories
Chunky Steak in Rich Gravy		
212g tin	5	215
439g tin	10	440
Mild Curried Chicken		
425g tin	17	480
Minced Beef in Rich Gravy		
212g tin	5	320
439g tin	10	660
ROBERT WILSON		
Chunky Steak with Gravy		
7oz/198g tin	2	310
15oz/425g tin	4	635
Cottage Pie Filling		
15oz/425g tin	40	415
Curried Beef		
15oz/425g tin	25	460
Hamburgers with Onions and Gravy		
15oz/425g tin	30	565
Meat Balls in Brown Sauce		
7oz/198g tin	8	200
15oz/425g tin	20	420
Meat Balls in Curry Sauce		
15oz/425g tin	30	435
Meat Balls in Onion Sauce		
15oz/425g tin	20	415
Meat Balls in Tomato Sauce		
15oz/425g tin	25	435
Minced Beef and Onions		
7oz/198g tin	10	265
15oz/425g tin	20	715
Minced Beef and Onion Pie Filling		
7oz/198g tin	12	250
15oz/425g tin	25	535
Minced Beef in Gravy		
7oz/198g tin	5	320
15oz/425g tin	15	710
Pie Fillings — 15oz/425g tins		
Steak	20	360
Steak and Kidney	16	380
Steak and Onion	22	365
SAINSBURY		
Chicken in White Sauce		
206g tin	8	310
Beef Curry		
15oz/425g tin	25	450
SHIPPAMS		
Beef Taco Filling		
205g tin	12	365

SHIPPAMS — Continued

	Carbohydrate in grams	Calories
Chunky Chicken in Barbecue Sauce'		
7.23oz/206g tin	13	270
Chunky Chicken in Curry Sauce		
7.23oz/206g tin	8	265
14.7oz/418g tin	17	540
Chunky Chicken in Mushroom Sauce		
7.23oz/206g tin	9	350
14.7oz/418g tin	18	700
Chunky Chicken in White Sauce		
4.87oz/138g tin	7	210
7.23oz/206g tin	10	315
14.7oz/418g tin	20	640

TESCO

Economy Minced Beef and Onion Pie Filling		
425g tin	30	500
Minced Beef and Onions in Gravy		
15oz/425g tin	25	630

WAITROSE

Spicy Meatballs		
350g tin	30	525

CHILLED/FROZEN

In the majority of cases figures for beefburgers, steaklets, etc are given before cooking. The carbohydrate content will not change whichever cooking method you choose, i.e. baking, bar-be-cue, frying, grilling, microwaving etc. However, the choice of cooking method does affect the calorie content. If you GRILL some fat will drip away – in some cases between 50-150 calories can be saved. If you fry or cook on a solid surface less fat will be lost and smaller savings in calories made. If you microwave, place the item on absorbable kitchen paper and remove immediately when cooked.

	Carbohydrate in grams	Calories
BEJAM		
Beef Loaf		
20oz/568g pack	50	1775
100% Beef Burgers		
when grilled (1)............................	neg	100
80% Beef Burgers		
when grilled (1)............................	3	95
Beefburger with Onion		
when grilled (1)............................	4	125
Golden Bake – 1 when oven baked		
Chicken Bites (1)...........................	3	35
Chicken Breast Steaks (1)..................	15	255
Chicken Drumsticks 1oz portion............	6	65
Chicken Fingers (1)	2	45
Chicken Nibbles (1)	9	120
Chicken Nuggets (1)	3	40
Chicken Portions 1oz.......................	4	60
Turkey Steaks (1)	12	165
Grillsteaks – 1 when grilled		
Chinese-Style Pork Rib-Steaks (1)..........	4	205
Lamb Grills (1)..............................	neg	230
Pork Rib-Steaks (1)	9	230
Steak Grills (1)..............................	2	205
Low Fat Beefburgers		
when grilled (1)............................	4	95
Low Fat Thick Pork Sausages		
when grilled (1)............................	4	95
Quarter-Pound Beef Burger		
when grilled (1)............................	2	210
Turkey Bites		
when oven baked (1).......................	3	45
BERNARD MATTHEWS		
Crispy-Crumb Turkey Steaks		
(uncooked) (1).............................	12	170
Gammon-Style Turkey Steaks		
(uncooked) (1).............................	neg	105

BERNARD MATTHEWS — Continued	Carbohydrate in grams	Calories
Low Fat Sausages		
(uncooked) (1)......................................	7	105
Turkey Breast Roast		
567g approx	neg	900
Turkey Leg Roast		
567g approx	neg	1020
Turkey Steaks (uncooked) (1)..................	neg	180
BIRDS EYE		
100% Beefburgers		
when grilled (1)................................	neg	120
Cheesies		
when grilled (1)................................	7	75
Chicken Grills in Natural Wheat Crumb		
when grilled/baked (1).......................	9	195
Economy Burgers		
when grilled (1)................................	4	90
Grillsteaks		
Beef (when grilled)...........................	1	175
Lamb (when grilled)	1	190
Low Fat Beef Burgers		
when grilled (1)................................	2	85
MenuMaster – Traditional Meals		
Braised Kidneys in Gravy		
1 packet....................................	6	200
Gravy and Lean Roast Beef		
4oz/113g tray	3	95
Liver with Onion and Gravy		
1 packet....................................	6	190
Roast Chicken Joint & Gravy		
1 packet....................................	6	300
Original Beefburgers		
when grilled (1)................................	2	120
Prizesteak		
when grilled (1)................................	neg	215
Quarter Pounders		
when grilled (1)................................	4	235
Value Chicken Grills		
when grilled/baked (1).......................	13	190
BOWYERS		
Low Fat Sausages –		
Chilled (1).....................................	6	125
Frozen (1).....................................	6	105
BUXTED		
Chicken Crunchies		
when oven baked (1)........................	2	35
Chicken Topovers		
Cheese when baked (1)......................	14	190

BUXTED — Continued	Carbohydrate in grams	Calories
Tomato when baked (1)...............	15	170
Cooked Chicken Quarters (1)	neg	360
Crispy Turkey Fries		
10oz/284g pack when deep fried	50	780
Southern Fried Chicken Drumsticks		
1 when baked approx........................	8	145
Southern Fried Chicken Nibbles		
16oz/454g pack when baked..............	50	1000
Turkey Meat Loaf		
1lb/454g pack when baked................	45	915
CO-OP		
Beefburgers with Onions (1)...................	4	200
Beefy Grills (1)	2	260
DALEPAK		
BBQ Pork Rib Steak		
1 x 3.5oz	6	285
Beef Dale Steak (frozen)		
1 x 4oz	neg	295
Beef Quick Steak (frozen)		
1 x 3oz	4	250
Beef Steaklet (frozen)		
1 x 3oz	5	290
Chicken Dale Steak (frozen)		
1 x 2.75oz....................................	neg	185
Lamb Dale Steak (frozen)		
1 x 4oz	neg	295
Lamb Quick Steak		
1 x 3oz	2	265
Turkey Steaklet		
1 x 3oz	4	220
FINDUS		
Beef Grill Steak (1)	neg	200
Roast Beef in Gravy		
100g (serves 1)................................	2	105
ICELAND		
Low Fat Beefburgers		
when grilled (1)................................	3	105
Low Fat Grillsteaks		
when grilled (1)................................	neg	185
Low Fat Sausages –		
Cocktail (1)....................................	2	25
Pork (1)	8	190
Thick Pork & Beef (1).......................	14	210
Thin Pork & Beef (1)........................	7	110
MARKS AND SPENCER		
Bacon Burgers (1).............................	16	395

MARKS AND SPENCER – Continued	Carbohydrate in grams	Calories
Beef Burgers Fresh (1)	2	120
Beef Burgers Frozen (1)	2	150
Beef Loaf		
20oz/568g	25	1475
Low Fat Pork Sausages (1)	5	105
Pork Kebabs (1) approximately	neg	200
Quarter Pounder (1)	neg	280
Turkey Breast with Chestnut Stuffing		
1 packet	5	235
Turkey Kebabs		
(1) approximately	7	125
Vegetable Cutlets (1)	25	85

MATTESSONS WALLS
'Original' Pork Sausages (1)	5	120
Pre-Packed Meats – 4oz/113g pack		
Lunch Tongue	2	295

McCAIN
Tenderchoice Chicken –		
Chunks (1)	2	35
Fingers (1)	5	70
Steaklets	12	160

PLUMTREE FARMS
Low Fat Sausages (1)	10	135

ROBIRCH
Haslet 1oz	5	75
Low Fat Pork & Beef Sausages (1)	7	115
Pork & Tongue Tub 1oz	neg	50
Pre-Packed Meats – 4oz packs		
Stuffed Pork Loaf	18	270

ROSS
American Hamburgers		
1 x 4oz	neg	380
Barbecue Ribs (1)	6	255
Beefburgers Economy (1)	3	140
Beefburgers 100% 1.75oz (1)	neg	170
Beefwich (1)	neg	115
Breaded Veal Cutlets (1)	14	320
Cheese and Onion Fries (1)	24	130
Chinese Ribs (1)	8	260
Grillsteaks (1)	neg	290
Jumbo Quarter Pounders (1)	4	315
Jumbogrills (1)	15	260
Kebabs		
Lamb (1)	2	255
Pork (1)	2	160
Quickgrills (1)	5	285

SAFEWAY

	Carbohydrate in grams	Calories
Beefburgers		
1 x 2oz	neg	170
1 x 4oz (Quarter Pounder)	3	340
Beef Loaf		
680g pack	50	1930
Breaded Beef Grill (1)	12	340
Breaded Pork Grill (1)	12	360
Economy Burgers (1)	4	145
Pork Loaf		
680g pack	40	1990
Prime Steak Burger (1)	neg	275
Quick Cook Beefburger (1)	5	320
Ranch Style Beefburger		
1 x 2oz	2	150
1 x 4oz	5	295
Ranch Style Porkburger (1)	5	290

SAINSBURY

	Carbohydrate in grams	Calories
Low Fat Beef Burgers		
when grilled (1)	1	75
Low Fat Sausages		
when grilled (1)	5	100

SLATERS FOODS

	Carbohydrate in grams	Calories
Economy Burgers with Onion		
before cooking (1)	4	150
Quarterpounders		
before cooking (1)	2	315
Steak Canadien Beef Sandwich Slices		
before cooking (1)	neg	100
Steakettes		
before cooking (1)	6	255

TESCO

	Carbohydrate in grams	Calories
Beefburgers with/without Onion (1)	neg	120

TIFFANY

	Carbohydrate in grams	Calories
Beefburgers		
50g	2	135
56g	2	150
Clubsteaks		
85g	3	230
Corned Beef Hash		
92g	17	230
Economyburgers		
50g	2	130
Gammon and Pork Steaklets		
113g	2	295
Lamb King Sized Savouries		
100g	12	210

TIFFANY - Continued

	Carbohydrate in grams	Calories
Savouries - **Beef Lamb**		
66g	14	160
Sizzles -		
Beef, Chicken, Cheese & Onion, Cheese & Tomato		
56g	11	130
Steakburgers		
113g	4	305
Turkey Savouries		
66g	11	140
Veal Cordon Blue		
142g	21	335
Veal King Sized Savouries		
100g	14	190
WAITROSE		
Beefburgers		
frozen (1)	2	160
Pork Sausages - 60% Pork (1)	4	80

PREPARED MEAT/POULTRY DISHES

	Carbohydrate in grams	Calories
BEJAM		
Chili Con Carne		
9oz/255g pack..............................	40	350
BIRDS EYE		
MenuMaster – Traditional Meals		
Beef Stew and Dumpling		
1 packet....................................	32	320
Chicken and Mushroom Casserole		
1 packet....................................	7	160
Minced Beef with Veg in Gravy		
1 packet....................................	10	150
Shepherds Pie		
1 packet....................................	22	270
BRAINS		
Cottage Pie		
12oz/340g pack	30	320
Family Shepherd's Pie		
16oz/454g pack	40	400
BUXTED		
Chicken Cordon Bleu		
1 from pack when baked....................	20	335
Chicken in Curry Sauce		
1lb/454g pack when baked.................	30	440
Chicken Supreme		
1lb/454g pack when baked.................	30	425
Chicken Sweet 'n' Sour		
1lb/454g pack when baked.................	35	430
Chicken Kiev		
1 from pack when baked....................	17	360
CAMPBELLS		
Beef Stew		
15oz/425g tin	35	300
Chicken Stew		
15oz/425g tin	30	285
Steak and Kidney Stew		
15oz/425g tin	25	275
Quick Snack — 425g tins		
Beef Curry	40	425
Chicken Curry	40	480
Chili Con Carne	45	600
CHESSWOOD		
Curry with Beef and Mushrooms		
15oz/425g tin	40	380
Curry with Chicken and Mushrooms		
15oz/425g tin	45	350

CO-OP

	Carbohydrate in grams	Calories
Irish Stew		
15oz/425g tin	35	385
Shepherds Pie		
8oz/227g pack	30	265

CROSSE AND BLACKWELL

Faggots 'n' Peas		
15oz/425g tin	55	555

DORSET

Cottage Pie		
6oz/170g pack	15	155

FINDUS

Beef Teriyaki		
283g pack	45	360
Broccoli with Chicken Gratin		
241g pack	25	405
Cumberland Pie		
10.2oz/289g pack	35	465
Lean Cuisine Range – 1 packet		
Beef Provencale	15	270
Moussaka		
283g pack	15	575

FRESHBAKE FOODS

Shepherds Pie (Frozen)		
1 from pack of 4	20	205

GOBLIN

Beef Casserole		
15oz/425g tin	35	425
24oz/680g tin	60	680
Irish Stew		
15oz/425g tin	35	425
Ready Dinner		
15oz/425g tin	35	425
24oz/680g tin	60	680

HEALTHLINE FOODS

Healthy Cuisine — 300g pack		
Chicken Tuscany	20	200
Chilli Con Carne	25	230
Elizabethan Spiced Beef	20	155
Lamb a la Grecque	25	185
Liver Mexicaine	25	190
Turkey Napoleon	20	160

ICELAND

Chicken in Asparagus & Mushrooms		
per pack	30	385

	Carbohydrate in grams	Calories
Gammon Steak Platter		
340g pack	20	345
Moussaka		
284g pack	30	930
KATIE'S KITCHEN		
Bolognese & Courgette Bake		
435g pack	40	610
Coronation Chicken		
340g pack	40	640
Moussaka		
450g pack	40	530
LITTLEWOODS		
Cottage Pie		
283g pack	20	265
LOCKWOODS FOODS		
Beef Casserole		
330g pack	20	300
Chicken Casserole		
330g pack	20	330
Lamb Casserole		
330g pack	20	300
MARKS AND SPENCER		
Barbecue Pork Spare Ribs		
13oz/369g pack	30	880
Beef Stew and Dumplings		
(Serves 2) 1lb/454g pack	65	670
Calorie Counted Meals – 1 packet		
Beef and Spinach Layer	15	245
Braised Beef and Vegetables	25	255
Chicken Pizzaiola	20	190
Chicken Casserole		
(Serves 2) 625g pack	40	660
Chicken Curry		
18oz/510g pack	15	810
Chicken Italienne		
(Serves 2) 454g pack	5	790
Chicken Kiev		
(Serves 2) 312g pack	30	820
Chicken Supreme		
(Serves 2) 397g pack	12	560
Chicken Tandoori		
1 pack approximately	7	870

	Carbohydrate in grams	Calories
Chilli Con Carne		
(Serves 1) 250g pack	25	350
(Serves 2) 454g pack	40	635
Chilli Con Carne		
425g tin...............................	40	470
Cottage Pie		
large	50	535
Duckling a la Orange		
19oz/540g pack	30	1010
Fresh Potato Cottage Pies		
Family...............................	70	995
Individual	25	260
Large...............................	50	555
Liver and Bacon		
(Serves 2) 482g pack	35	665
Moussaka		
(Serves 1) 250g pack	25	330
(Serves 2) 510g pack	45	675
Roast Chicken Leg Meal		
397g pack...............................	35	480
Shepherds Pie		
Individual	40	455
Steak and Vegetable Fresh Potato Pie		
330g pack...............................	30	310

MR CHANG'S READY MEALS

Beef Chop Suey		
6oz/170g pack...............................	8	110
Beef Curry		
6oz/170g pack...............................	13	115
Chicken Curry		
6oz/170g pack...............................	13	130
Chicken and Mushroom		
6oz/170g pack...............................	14	145
Pineapple & Chicken		
6oz/170g pack...............................	20	210
Spare Ribs in BBQ Sauce		
8oz/227g pack...............................	10	300
Sweet and Sour Chicken		
6oz/170g pack...............................	19	140

PLUMROSE

Bacon Grill		
170g tin...............................	12	480
300g tin...............................	21	850

ROBERT WILSON

Beef Casserole		
15oz/425g tin	25	450
Chicken Casserole		
15oz/425g tin	25	380

	Carbohydrate in grams	Calories
Chilli Con Carne		
15oz/425g tin	50	480
Irish Stew		
15oz/425g tin	25	340
Lancashire Hot Pot		
15oz/425g tin	25	400
ROSS		
Shepherd's Pie		
8oz/277g pack..............................	30	260
16oz/454g pack	60	525
Stir-Fry Meals - 340g pack		
Chicken Provencale	25	240
Chinese Chicken............................	25	275
Indian Chicken	30	310
SAFEWAY		
Bar-B-Que Style Pork Ribs		
350g pack...................................	15	720
Chilli Con Carne (Fresh)		
454g pack...................................	15	520
Hot Pot (Frozen)		
454g pack...................................	40	485
Moussaka (Fresh)		
454g pack...................................	35	820
Shepherd's Pie (Frozen)		
8oz/277g tray..............................	25	280
16oz/454g tray.............................	50	560
Stir Fry - 340g pack		
Chinese Style Chicken	25	220
Indian Style Chicken	45	315
SAINSBURY		
Beef Curry		
425g tin....................................	25	450
Chicken Curry		
418g tin....................................	25	520
Chilli Con Carne		
425g tin....................................	45	450
SHIPPAMS		
Chili Con Carne		
425g tin....................................	40	565
SHIVA		
Beef Curry		
10oz/284g pack	15	400
Chilli Con Carne		
300g pack...................................	45	450
Chicken Curry		
10oz/284g pack	15	400

SHIVA — Continued

	Carbohydrate in grams	Calories
Lamb Curry		
10oz/284g pack	15	400

TESCO

	Carbohydrate in grams	Calories
Beef Hot Pot		
(Serves 2) 514g pack	30	510
Chicken Curry (without Rice)		
425g tin...	30	420
Chilli Con Carne		
(Serves 2) 454g pack	50	555
Cottage Pie – chilled		
large	45	830
small	19	345
Economy Irish Stew		
553g tin...	30	400
Leek and Ham Bake		
(Serves 2) 426g pack	35	460
Shepherds Pie – frozen		
8oz/227g pack...............................	30	300
16oz/454g pack	55	600

TYNE BRAND

	Carbohydrate in grams	Calories
Savoury Mince Vegetables & Beef		
Ready Meal Farmhouse Style		
411g tin	45	415
Savoury Mince Vegetable and Beef		
Ready Meal Mild Curry		
411g tin	35	385

WAITROSE

	Carbohydrate in grams	Calories
Beef Vindaloo		
283g pack......................................	10	515
Chicken with Almonds		
16oz/454g pack	15	820
Chicken Korma Curry		
283g pack......................................	16	690
Chicken Moghlai		
283g pack......................................	10	470
Chicken Tikka Masala		
283g pack......................................	10	460
Chilli Con Carne		
15oz/425g pack	35	495
Cottage Pie		
15oz/425g pack	55	480
Lamb Curry		
250g pack......................................	5	300
Lamb Rogan Josh		
283g pack......................................	25	515
Moussaka (frozen)		
10oz/283g pack	30	485

WAITROSE - Continued

	Carbohydrate in grams	Calories
Moussaka		
424g pack	45	665
850g pack	90	1400
Shepherds Pie		
10oz/283g pack	30	350
567g pack	60	700
Tandoori Chicken Masala		
10oz/283g pack	11	420
W A TURNER		
Traditionally British –		
Beef Stew & Dumpling		
468g pack	45	675
Chicken Casserole		
16oz/454g pack	40	555

Salads & Vegetables

SALADS

There is very little variation in the carbohydrate and calorie content of coleslaw, i.e. "Coleslaw in Vinaigrette", "Coarse Cut Coleslaw", "Diet" or "Low Calorie Coleslaw" from one manufacturer to another. A useful guide is given below.

	Carbohydrate in grams	Calories
Coleslaw		
5oz/142g pot	10-12	180-220
8oz/227g pot	15-20	300-340
Coleslaw in Vinaigrette		
5oz/142g pot	10-12	120-140
8oz/227g pot	15-20	200-220
Diet Coleslaw – Low Calorie		
8oz/227g pot	8-10	120-150
Diet Coleslaw in Vinaigrette		
8oz/227g pot	14-18	70-80

Useful brand names: **Chambourcy, Co-Op, Eden Vale, Littlewoods, Marks & Spencer, Mattessons, Morrisons, Safeway, Sainsbury, St Ivel.**

ARGYLL STORES (PRESTO)

Cheese & Pineapple Salad		
227g pack.....................................	20	425
Curried Vegetable Salad		
227g pack.....................................	40	400
Five Bean Salad		
227g pack.....................................	35	270
Mixed Vegetable Salad		
198g pack.....................................	12	150
Prawn Salad		
170g pack.....................................	12	280

EDEN VALE

Continental Salad		
4oz/113g pot	19	210
Fruity Coleslaw		
8oz/227g pot	22	470
Harvest Salad		
8oz/227g pot	41	335
Mild Vegetable Salad		
4oz/113g pot	15	235
Prawn		
5oz/141g pot	11	220

EDEN VALE – Continued

	Carbohydrate in grams	Calories
Spicy Coleslaw		
4oz/113g pot	14	230
8oz/227g pot	28	460
Vegetable		
8oz/226g pot	31	320
HEINZ		
Vegetable Salad		
7.41oz/210g tin	28	320
HOLLAND & BARRETT		
Coleslaw		
8oz/227g pot	8	310
Mixed Bean		
8oz/227g pot	35	750
ITONA		
Golden Archer Bean Salad		
426g tin	55	300
LITTLEWOODS		
Bean and Potato Salad		
227g pack	45	480
Florida Salad		
227g pack	32	285
Prawn Salad		
142g pack	11	210
Sweetcorn with Red Peppers		
227g pack	33	368
LOCKWOODS FOODS		
Carrot & Raisin Salad		
240g pack	20	170
Vegetable Salad		
240g pack	25	430
MARKS AND SPENCER		
Carrot & Nut Salad		
10oz/283g pack	40	715
Florida Salad		
8oz/227g pot	20	465
Three Bean Salad		
10oz/283g pack	30	420
Waldorf Salad		
6oz/170g pot	7	510
SAFEWAY		
Apple & Sultana Coleslaw		
8oz/227g pack	30	460
Mixed Salad/Beansprout		
7oz/198g pack	5	60

SAFEWAY – Continued	Carbohydrate in grams	Calories
Salad Chinese Leaf & Sweetcorn		
7oz/198g pack	8	50
Salad Walnut & Apple & Raisin		
7oz/198g pack	17	115
Spanish Salad		
8oz/227g pack	15	385
Vegetable Salad		
8oz/227g pack	30	475
SAINSBURY		
Coleslaw with Prawns		
125g pot	7	175
Celery, Apple and Mandarin Salad		
250g pot	20	350
Celery, Peanut and Sultana		
8oz/227g pot	16	400
Three Bean & Celery Salad		
250g pot	30	390
Waldorf Salad		
250g pot	25	375
ST IVEL		
Prawn Salad		
5oz/142g pot	12	220
8oz/227g pot	20	355
TESCO		
Apple Coleslaw		
250g pack	16	395
Celery Nut & Sultana Salad		
250g pack	20	500
Prawn Salad		
150g pack	6	150
Taramasalata Salad		
170g pack	16	740
Three Bean Salad		
250g pack	42	260
Vegetable Salad		
250g pack	25	295

VEGETABLES - FROZEN

Frozen vegetables contain similar amounts of carbohydrate and calories regardless of their brand name.

	Carbohydrate in grams	Calories
Broad Beans 1oz when cooked	2	15
Broccoli 1oz when cooked	1	10
Brussels Sprouts 1oz when cooked	1	10
Carrots 1oz when cooked....................	1	10
Cauliflower 1oz when cooked	neg	5
French Beans whole 1oz when cooked	1	10
Green Beans sliced 1oz when cooked.......	1	10
Mange Tout 1oz when cooked	2	12
Peas 1oz when cooked........................	1	12
Sweet Corn 1oz when cooked................	5	25

BEJAM
Farmhouse Style Mix 1oz	1	10
Mexican Mix 1oz	3	20
Oriental Mix 1oz.............................	2	10
Veg 'n' Rice Mix 1oz	3	15

BIRDS EYE
Broccoli Mornay		
9oz pack	12	280
Casserole Vegetables 1oz	2	10
Cauliflower Peas and Carrots 1oz	1	10
Original Mixed Vegetables 1oz..............	2	15
Peas and Baby Carrots 1oz	1	10
Ratatouille		
10oz pack	20	170
Stir Fry — 12oz/340g packs		
Continental Recipe..........................	30	180
Country Recipe	20	120
Oriental		
10oz/283g pack..........................	30	200

FINDUS
Country Mix 1oz	3	15
Mixed Vegetables 1oz	3	15

MARKS AND SPENCER
Broccoli in Cream Sauce		
16oz/454g pack	25	535
Crispy Mushrooms		
170g pack	20	275
Fresh Vegetable Bake (frozen)		
15oz/425g pack	40	500
Ratatouille (frozen)		
283g pack....................................	8	180

	Carbohydrate in grams	Calories
ROSS		
Casserole Mix 1oz...............................	1	6
Country Mix 1oz.................................	1	9
Farmhouse Mixed Vegetables 1oz	1	9
French Vegetable Mix 1oz....................	neg	7
Onion Ringers 1oz..............................	8	65
Oriental Vegetable Mix 1oz..................	2	11
Special Mix 1oz.................................	2	11
Stewpack Mixed Vegetables 1oz	1	7
Stir Fry Mix1oz.................................	3	14
Stir Fry Sweetcorn 1oz........................	3	20
SAFEWAY		
Fresh Ratatouille Vegetables		
12oz/340g pack	12	60
Mixed Vegetables 1oz	3	15
Stir Fry Mushrooms		
12oz/340g pack	7	80
SAINSBURY		
Crispy Coated Mushrooms		
200g pack.....................................	40	380
TESCO		
Brown Rice with Mixed Vegetables 1oz.....	7	30
Farmhouse Mixed Vegetables 1oz	1	5
Parisienne Mixed Vegetables 1oz	neg	5
Special Mixed Vegetables 1oz...............	3	20

VEGETABLES - TINNED

Tinned vegetables contain similar amounts of carbo-hydrate and calories regardless of their brand name. The following table is a quick guide to the values of various vegetables. (Tin sizes are approximate).

	Carbohydrate in grams	Calories
*Asparagus		
298g	5	45
Baked Beans		
150g	20	110
225g	30	165
450g	60	330
567g	75	415
Baked Beans in Barbecued Sauce		
225g	30	165
Baked Beans with Pork Sausages		
225g	30	280
283g	45	355
425g	70	415
Baked Beans with Hamburgers		
220g	35	275
*Broad Beans		
298g	20	100
*Butter Beans		
213g	20	100
415g	35	200
*Cannelloni Beans		
227g	30	150
445g	55	305
*Carrots		
284g	10	40
Chick Peas		
400g	35	190
Curried Beans		
227g	35	230
Curried Beans with Sultanas		
225g	35	200
*Garden Peas		
284g	15	80
425g	20	125
*Green Beans		
284g	neg	20
*Marrowfat Peas		
284g	25	130
*Mixed Vegetables		
284g	25	100
*Mushrooms		
213g	5	40
Mushrooms Creamed		
213g	15	160

	Carbohydrate in grams	Calories
Mushy Peas		
284g	45	240
425g	65	360
Mushy Peas Chip Shop		
284g	40	215
425g	60	325
Mushy Peas Mint Flavour		
284g	45	355
*New Potatoes		
284g	25	95
539g	45	180
*Processed Peas		
142g	10	65
415g	35	195
*Red Kidney Beans		
213g	25	130
415g	45	250
*Sweet Corn		
340g	45	200
Sweet Corn Creamed		
298g	55	255
*Tomatoes		
400g	10	50

*The Carboydrate and Calorie Values are based on the DRAINED weight

BATCHELORS
Bean Cuisine –14.6oz/415g tin		
Calypso Beans	60	290
Cassoulet Beans	50	270
Chilli Beans	50	270
Pease Pudding		
7.5oz/213g tin	40	220
15oz/425g tin	80	440

BUITONI
Ratatouille		
375g tin	15	150

CROSSE AND BLACKWELL
Healthy Balance Baked Beans		
220g tin	24	140
440g tin	48	280

HEINZ WEIGHT WATCHERS
Bean St Kids		
Beans and Burgerbites		
7.9oz/225g tin	35	270
15.9oz/450g tin	70	535
Beans and Chickbits		
7.9oz/225g tin	35	255

	Carbohydrate in grams	Calories
15.9oz/450g tin............................	70	510
Beans and Minisausages		
7.9oz/225g tin............................	30	295
15.9oz/450g tin............................	65	590
No Added Sugar Baked Beans		
225g tin......................................	19	125
450g tin......................................	38	250
MARKS AND SPENCER		
Ratatouille		
375g tin......................................	15	150
SAFEWAY		
Continental Mixed Vegetables		
410g tin......................................	40	195
Mixed Vegetables		
284g tin......................................	25	105
Ratatouille		
390g tin......................................	15	180
SHIPPAMS		
Jalapeno Bean Dip		
297g tin......................................	40	315
Refried Beans		
453g tin......................................	70	400
WAITROSE		
Baked Beans in Apple Juice		
439g tin......................................	65	340
WHOLE EARTH		
No Sugar Added Baked Beans		
440g tin......................................	58	345

Snacks - High Fibre

	Carbohydrate in grams	Calories
ALLINSON		
Fruit Bars - 35g bars		
Banana..................	19	90
Fruit and Nut	19	115
Muesli	18	110
Wheateats - 25g packet		
Cheese flavour	13	110
Chilli flavour	13	105
Natural.................................	15	105
Onion flavour.................................	14	110
Peanut Butter flavour......................	12	125
Pizza flavour.................................	15	110
BOOKER HEALTH		
Barbaras Cookies		
Tropical Coconut (1)........................	16	230
GRANOSE		
Apricot Date 30g bar (1)	16	85
Blackberry 50g bar (1)...........................	33	190
Cherry 50g bar (1)	33	190
Date 25g bar (1)	19	90
Date and Apricot 25g bar (1)	17	85
Date and Coconut 25g bar (1)	15	105
Date and Fig 25g bar (1)	17	80
Date and Nut 25g bar (1)...................	17	95
Date and Sesame 25g bar (1).................	16	95
Fig and Prune 25g bar (1)......................	17	80
Fig and Raisin 25g bar (1).....................	18	85
Ginger Pear 30g bar (1)........................	17	110
Hazelnut 50g bar (1)	24	240
Lemon 50g bar (1)	32	185
Mixed Fruit 50g bar (1)	27	190
Orange 50g bar (1).............................	35	190
Rose Hip 50g bar (1)	29	190
Strawberry 50g bar (1)	33	190
HOFELS PURE FOODS		
Crispy Soybrits		
15g packet	10	55
HOLLAND AND BARRETT		
Paradise Bounty Mix 1oz	12	120
HOLLY MILL		
Banana Munch Bar (1)	18	145
Fibretime Snack 38g bar (1)	19	150
Fruit and Nut Slice (1)	22	175

HOLLY MILL - Continued

	Carbohydrate in grams	Calories
No Added Sugar Range - 40g bars		
Apple & Cardamom Bar	20	170
Apricot & Almond Bar	19	160
Tangy Citrus Bar (1)	16	145

JORDANS
Original Crunchy Bar with Apple and Bran (1)	16	135

KP
Lower Fat Crisps - 25g packets		
all flavours	12	110

LYME REGIS FOODS
Grizzly Bars - 25g bars		
Apricot & Honey (1)	12	110
Fruit & Honey (1)	12	110
Muesli & Honey (1)	13	115

MARKS AND SPENCER
Lower Fat Crisps - 65g packet		
all flavours	40	320

NATURE'S SNACK
Wholewheat Crisps		
23g packet	12	125
50g packet	25	265

NEILSON FRUIT BARS
Date and Apple (1)	31	155
Date and Apricot (1)	31	155
Date and Banana (1)	30	160
Date and Nut (1)	29	170

NEWFORM FOODS
Country Basket Range Apricot & Date Snack		
35g bar (1)	21	120

PEAK FREANS
Twiglets		
large (1)	1	6
small (2)	1	6
25g packet	15	100

PREWETT'S
Apple and Date Bar (1)	25	110
Banana Bar (1)	23	105
Carob Coated Bars		
Banana (1)	22	130
Date and Fig (1)	21	145

PREWETT'S — Continued	Carbohydrate in grams	Calories
Fruit and Nut (1)	21	150
Muesli Fruit (1)	21	150
Orange and Sultana (1)	21	160
Date and Fig Bar (1)	22	125
Fruit and Bran Bar (1)	24	125
Fruit and Nut Bar (1)	22	135
Muesli Fruit Bar (1)	22	130
Orange and Sultana Bar (1)	23	145

SAFEWAY
Savoury Twigs

50g packet	30	195
100g packet	60	390

SHAWS BISCUITS
Jungle Bars

Apricot and Raisin Bar (1)	20	120
Currant and Apple Bar (1)	18	125

SHEPHERDBOY FRUIT BARS

Apple Fruit & Nut 40g bar (1)	18	140
Banana Fruit & Nut 40g bar (1)	18	165
Bran Fruit & Nut 38g bar (1)	16	125
Carob Fruit & Nut 40g bar (1)	21	165
Coconut/Pineapple Fruit & Nut 38g bar (1).	12	170
Ginger Fruit and Nut 38g bar (1)	15	165
Multi Fruit 38g bar (1)	23	90
Sunflower Fruit & Nut 50g bar (1)	20	205
Tangy Fruit & Nut 38g bar (1)	21	135

SMITHS
Square Crisps (Low Fat) – 25g packet

all flavours	15	125

SOONER FOODS
Sea Shells

1 packet	21	50

SUNWHEEL FOODS
Kalibu No Added Sugar Bars

Raisin Yogurt Coated Snack Bar (1)	16	105

TESCO
Lower Fat Crisps

65g packet	40	315

WAITROSE
Party Twigs

50g packet	30	200
100g packet	60	400

Vegetarian Prepared Foods

CANNED/CHILLED/DRIED

Plain Textured Vegetable Protein (TVP) with no additions except flavourings, spices etc, contains similar amounts of carbohydrate and calories regardless of the brand name.

	Carbohydrate in grams	Calories
TVP (all flavours) 1oz	<5	70-100

Useful brand names: **Boots, Haldane Foods (Hera), Itona.**

BOOTS
Dried Mixes – 200g packs

Vegetable Burger Mix	70	560
Vegetable Sausage Mix	40	940

CARE FOODS

Nutriburger (1)	15	200

CAULDRON FOODS
Plain Tofu

10oz/284 pack	2	330

Smoked Tofu

8oz/227g pack	1	265

Tofu Burgers

Chilli flavour (1)	7	160
Peanut (1)	7	165
Savoury (1)	7	160

DIRECT FOODS
Nut Hawain Croquettes

227g pack	130	855

Protoveg

Natural 1oz dry product	3-4	70
Flavoured 1oz dry product	3-4	70

Protoveg Menu
Burgamix

175g pack	40	680

Jumbo Grills

227g pack	25	580

Minced Soya & Onion Mix

141g pack	50	490

Sizzles

175g pack	40	740

Sosmix

90g pack	25	390

GRANOSE
Bologna/Vegelinks

15oz/425g	50	710

GRANOSE – Continued

	Carbohydrate in grams	Calories
Chinese Tofu		
420g tin	17	255
Dinner Balls		
14oz/400g	32	580
Fricassee		
400g tin	30	520
Frikaletts		
15oz/425g	20	510
Lentil Roast		
200g pack	90	675
Meatless Savoury Cuts		
213g	12	190
15oz/425g	24	375
Nutbrawn		
10oz/284g	35	605
15oz/425g	55	900
Nutloaf		
10oz/284g	14	500
15oz/425g	21	750
Rissolnut		
350g pack	190	1320
Sausalatas		
10oz/284g	20	390
15oz/425g	30	580
Saviand		
10oz/284g	24	565
15oz/425g	35	845
Savoury Pudding		
454g	75	940
Savory Pudding, Country Style		
454g tin	75	760
Soya Pro Beef Flavour		
385g	12	810
Soya Pro Chicken Flavour		
400g tin	12	840
Soyapro Weiners		
385g tin	20	810
Tender Bits		
213g	12	170
425g	25	335
Tofu in Savoury Bean Sauce		
445g tin	45	535

HALDANE FOODS
Hera range –

	Carbohydrate in grams	Calories
Vegetable Soysage		
(Serves 6) 200g pack	90	845
Tofu		
255g pack	6	200

HOLLY MILL

	Carbohydrate in grams	Calories
Singles Range – 60g pack		
English Mix....................	25	160
Hungarian Mix..............................	25	170
Italian Mix	25	160
Mexican Mix.................................	25	160

ITONA

Golden Archer Ready Cook –		
Soya Chunks in Gravy		
284g tin	20	610

MORINAGA

Silken Tofu		
297g pack.....................................	9	160

PREWETT'S

'Just for One' – 110g packs		
Vegetable Curry with		
Brown Rice	65	330
Vegetable Provencale with		
Brown Rice	65	330

SUNWHEEL FOODS

Ever-Fresh Silken Tofu Soybean Curd		
1 serving.....................................	4	80

THE REALEAT COMPANY

VegeBanger Mix		
110g packet†	30	580
VegeBurger — all flavours		
125g packet†	45	540
per beefburger*	11	155
Vegeburgers (1)................................	10	160

† Before preparation.
* When made according to instructions with egg.

83

PREPARED DISHES

	Carbohydrate in grams	Calories
BEJAM		
Cauliflower Cheese		
10oz/284g pack	15	355
BE-WELL NUTRITIONAL PRODUCTS		
Easy Beans Range – 1 serving sachet		
Haricot Bean Goulash	50	265
BIRDS EYE		
Cauliflower Cheese		
10oz/283g pack	25	370
BOOTS		
Country Casserole		
360g pack..................................	50	280
Vegetable Curry		
400g pack..................................	40	300
BROOKE BOND		
Beanfeast Range — 4oz/113g packs		
Beanfeast.....................................	45	320
Beanfeast Bolognaise	45	330
Beanfeast Mexican Chilli....................	55	330
Beanfeast Paella Style.....................	55	350
Beanfeast Soya Mince with Onion........	40	380
Beanfeast Supreme.........................	40	335
DIRECT FOODS		
Protoveg Menu		
Soya Bolognese		
113g pack	50	375
Soya Mince with Vegetables		
113g pack	45	375
EMILE TISSOT FOODS		
Vegetable au Gratin		
342g pack..................................	35	295
Vegetable Biryani		
342g pack..................................	30	220
Vegetable Lasagne		
300g pack..................................	25	280
Wheat Casserole		
300g pack..................................	40	615
GRANOSE		
Bean and Mushroom Stew		
420g tin....................................	60	330
Curry – Chicken Style		
425g tin....................................	40	245

GRANOSE – Continued

	Carbohydrate in grams	Calories
Goulash		
425g tin	40	230
Lentil and Vegetable Casserole		
15oz/425g	50	425
Mexican Bean Stew		
15oz/425g	50	555

HALDANE FOODS
Hera range–

	Carbohydrate in grams	Calories
Vegetable Bolognese		
(Serves 3) 1 sachet from pack of 2	45	335
Vegetable Casserole		
(Serves 3) 1 sachet from pack of 2	45	350
Vegetable Chilli		
(Serves 3) 1 sachet from pack of 2	45	350
Vegetable Curry		
(Serves 3) 1 sachet from pack of 2	50	345
Vegetable Goulash		
(Serves 3) 1 sachet from pack of 2	40	350
Vegetable Stroganov		
(Serves 3) 1 sachet from pack of 2	40	370
Vegetable Supreme		
(Serves 3) 149g pack	75	570

HOFELS PURE FOODS

	Carbohydrate in grams	Calories
Hot Pot		
411g tin	60	460
Savoury Style Curry		
411g tin	60	420
Vegetable Curry Medium Hot		
411g tin	50	320
Vegetable Curry Mild		
411g tin	50	320
Vegetable Curry Vindaloo		
411g tin	50	340

HOLLAND & BARRETT

	Carbohydrate in grams	Calories
Frozen ready meals – 300g pack		
Butter Bean Curry	45	360
Mexican Chilli	35	360
Oriental Savoury Rice	45	390
Veg Burgers – 175g		
Mexican	45	370
Nut	50	480
Tandoori	45	390

ITONA

	Carbohydrate in grams	Calories
Golden Archer Ready Cook Meals –		
Bolognese		
284g tin	10	130
Casserole		
426g tin	45	380

ITONA - Continued

	Carbohydrate in grams	Calories
Chilli		
284g tin	40	200
Curry		
284g tin	20	460

KATIE'S KITCHEN

Cauliflower Cheese		
450g pack	30	550
Vegetable Curry		
450g pack	50	500

MARKS AND SPENCER

Baked Bean Jackets		
1 from pack of 2	30	195
Cabbage and Mushroom Bake		
283g pack	25	300
Cauliflower Cheese		
10oz/283g pack	10	405
16oz/454g pack	15	650
Filled Green Pepper		
250g pack	12	240
Garden Vegetable Pie		
(Serves 1) 250g pack	30	285
Vegetable Chilli		
(Serves 1) 250g pack	35	240
Vegetable Lasagne		
(Serves 1) 250g pack	20	285

PREWETT'S

Vegetable Burger Mix		
125g packet	50	475

SAINSBURY

Cauliflower Cheese		
454g pack	35	520
Vegetable Mornay		
450g pack	30	460

TESCO

Cauliflower Cheese		
(Serves 2) 454g pack	20	590

THE REALEAT COMPANY

Macaroni Florentine		
241g pack	25	310
Pasta Italienne		
241g pack	25	185
Vege Cottage Pie		
241g pack	25	180
Vegelasagne		
258g pack	35	370

VEGETARIAN FEASTS

	Carbohydrate in grams	Calories
Feastburgers – frozen		
Chilli (1)	5	85
Savoury (1)	3	150
Great Grain Burgers (1)	6	90
Oven Ready Meals – 312g pack		
Caribbean Medley	30	315
Shepherdess Pie	30	315
Spicy Bean Casserole	35	190
Spinach and Walnut Lasagne	30	325
Sweet and Sour Almonds	35	240
Tasty Lentil Bake	20	290
Vegetable Chilli	25	300
Vegetable Moussaka	15	245
Wholewheat Macaroni Cheese	30	280

WAITROSE

	Carbohydrate in grams	Calories
Aubergine Gratin		
10oz/284g pack	20	525
Cauliflower Cheese		
14oz/397g pack	15	300
Vegetable Chilli		
255g pack	35	220
Vegetable Curry		
16oz pack	35	420
Vegetable Lasagne		
9oz/225g pack	30	290
18oz/510g pack	65	580
Vegetable Moussaka		
1lb/454g pack	60	660
Vegetable Shepherds Pie		
10oz/284g pack	30	260

WHOLE EARTH

	Carbohydrate in grams	Calories
Vegetarian Chilli		
15.5oz/440g tin	95	420

New Additions

New Additions

New Additions

New Additions

New Additions

New Additions

New Additions

New Additions

New Additions

AMBER SECTION

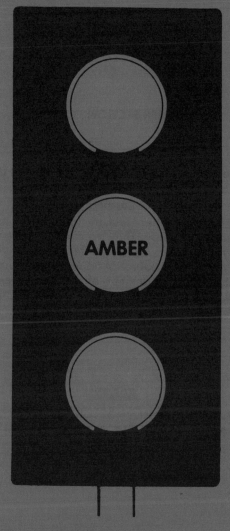

GO EASY
Foods from this section
should ideally not make
up a large part of the diet.

AMBER SECTION FOODS

What does a single amber light on a set of traffic lights signify?

Caution –

Similarly amber section foods are to be treated cautiously. They do contain some fibre but not so much as Green Section foods. They are not a major source of added sugars, but can contain large quantities of fat. Examples are pies, pastries and sausages. It is best to limit our intake of fat containing foods.

AMBER
FOODS WHICH SHOULD IDEALLY NOT MAKE UP A LARGE PART OF THE DIET

Biscuits, Crackers, Crispbreads–Plain

BISCUITS

	Carbohydrate in grams	Calories
ALLINSON		
Scottish Shortbread (1)	8	62
Soft Bake Coconut Cookies (1)	8	115
Wholemeal Tea Biscuits		
Bran (1)	7	53
Fruit and Nut (1)	7	51
Muesli (1)	7	56
ASKEYS ICE CREAM		
Pompadour Wafers (1)	8	40
BAHLSEN BISCUITS		
ABC (1)	2	10
Afrika (1)	2	20
Azora (1)	1	9
Leibniz-Butterkeks (1)	4	22
Rogga (1)	6	30
BEJAM		
Digestive Biscuits (1)	10	64
Rich Tea (1)	6	35
BOOTS		
Healthy Foods –		
Digestive Biscuits (1)	4	32
Fruit Shorties (1)	5	30
Second Nature –		
Sesame Seed Biscuits (1)	10	84
Wheat Biscuits (1)	13	100
BURTON'S		
Bakers Selection		
Coconut Rings (1)	5	39
Digestive		
1 from 200/300g pack	7	51
Fruit and Bran (1)	4	29
Fruit Rings (1)	5	37
Golden Crunch (1)	4	29
Lemon Crisp (1)	4	28
Rich Tea		
1 from 200g pack	5	35
1 from 300g pack	7	44
Shortcake		
1 from 300g pack	6	50
1 from 150g pack	4	28
Royal Edinburgh Shortbread		
Finger — large (1)	12	104
small (1)	7	65

BURTON'S - Continued	Carbohydrate in grams	Calories
Petticoat Tail (1)	7	57
Thistle (1)	12	103
Snapjack (1)	9	72
Wheatmeal Fruit & Nut (1)	6	49

CARR'S
Table Water Biscuits

large (1)	6	33
small (1)	2	15

CO-OP
Cheese Sandwich (1)	5	46
Fruit Shortcake (1)	6	40
Morning Coffee (1)	4	23

CRAWFORD
Balmoral (1)	8	65
Highland Finger (1)	8	63
Marie (1)	5	31
Mini Shorties		
45g packet	35	230
Pennywise		
Finger Nice (1)	4	28
Finger Tea (1)	4	22
Garibaldi (1)	7	36
Malties (1)	6	37
Morning Coffee (1)	4	21
Shortcake (1)	7	53
Shorties (1)	5	37
Petticoat Tail per piece	7	57
Tartan Shortbread (1)	12	97
Thin Arrowroot (1)	5	32

DOVES FARM
Carob Coated Digestives (1)	7	62
Wholemeal Digestives (1)	7	55

FORTTS
Bath Oliver (1)	8	45

FOX'S
Butter Shorties (1)	4	31
Morning Coffee (1)	4	25
Muesli Biscuits (1)	7	56
Petit Burerre (1)	5	31
Royal Dukes (1)	5	33
Sport (1)	5	32
Thick Tea (1)	12	59

HOLLY MILL
Carob Chip Cookie (1)	8	55

	Carbohydrate in grams	Calories
Lemon Crunch Cookie (1)	7	56
Spicy Orange Cookie (1)	8	52

HUNTLEY AND PALMER
Choc Chip N'Nut Cookie (1)	6	46
Digestive (1)	9	63
Raisin Biscuits (1)	8	59
Syrup (Kennett) Biscuits (1)	7	63

JACOBS
Fig Roll (1)	11	54

J L BRAGG
Medicinal Charcoal Biscuits (1)	3	20

LITTLEWOODS
Almond Biscuits (1)	5	44
Butter Biscuits (1)	6	43
Butter Fruit Biscuits (1)	6	42
Fig Rolls (1)	12	58
Lemon Crisp Biscuits (1)	6	40
Rich Tea (1)	7	44
Shortbread Fingers (1)	10	88

MARKS AND SPENCER
All Butter Biscuits (1)	6	46
All Butter Thistle Shortbread (1)	12	104
Almond Biscuits (1)	6	48
Butter Crunch (1)	5	33
Fruit Shortcake (1)	5	35
Oat Crunchies (1)	10	73
Rich Tea Fingers (1)	4	23
Round Rich Tea (1)	7	45
Round Shorties (1)	8	55

McVITIE
Country Cookies		
Cherry & Coconut (1)	10	83
Digestive (1)	11	73
Fruit Shortcake (1)	7	50
Hobnob (1)	10	71
Jaspers (1)	9	67
Lincoln (1)	6	43
Rich Tea (1)	6	34

NABISCO
Hovis Digestive (1)	8	57
Teabreak (1)	7	38

PATERSON – BRONTE
Cherry Fingers (1)	n/a	100

PATERSON-BRONTE - Continued	Carbohydrate in grams	Calories
Coconut Fingers (1)	12	100
Fruit Shrewsbury (1)	11	78
Griddle Oatcake (1)	8	57
Muesli Biscuits (1)	11	79
Rough Oatcake (1)	8	57
Viennese Fingers (1)	12	104

PATERSON'S SCOTTISH SHORTBREAD
Finger Shortbread (1)	9	75
Petticoat Tails (1)	48	375
Tam O'Shanter Assorted Shapes (1)	n/a	30
Shortbread Rounds (1)	n/a	500
Shortie Shortbread (1)	30	250

PEEK FREANS
Currant Crisp (1)	5	30
Digestive small (1)	6	48
Fruit Shortcake (1)	5	36
Lincoln (1)	5	35
Malt Crunch (1)	5	35
Rich Tea (1)	4	26

RM SCOTT
Diabisc Biscuits (1)	5	36

SAFEWAY
Fig Roll (1)	11	54
Fruit Shortcake (1)	6	38
Petticoat Tails 150g (1)	20	150
Rich Tea		
1 from a 200g pack	5	34
1 from a 300g pack	7	44
Shortbread Fingers (1)	12	92
Shortcake (1)	9	68

SAINSBURY
Fruit Digestive Biscuits (1)	7	50
Garibaldi (1)	6	30
Shortcake (1)	9	66

SLYMBRAND
Half Coated Slymbrand Digestive (1)	6	60

TESCO
All Butter Fruit (1)	6	43
Digestive (1)	10	71
Economy Digestive (1)	9	63
Economy Rich Tea (1)	6	36
Economy Shortcake (1)	8	57
Fruit Shortcake (1)	6	37
Garibaldi (1)	8	39

	Carbohydrate in grams	Calories
Malted Milk (1)	6	38
Marie (1)	4	22
Morning Coffee (1)	4	22
Rich Tea (1)	6	36
Rich Tea Finger (1)	4	22
Shortbread Fingers (1)	13	110
Shortcake (1)	7	48
Thistle Shortbread (1)	13	110

WAITROSE
Digestive
1 from a 200g pack	6	43
1 from a 400g pack	10	70
Fruit Shortcake (1)	6	36
Garibaldi (1)	6	29
Nice (1)	7	41
Rich Tea (1)	6	35
Shortbread Fingers (1)	14	110
Shortcake (1)	9	68
Tea Fingers (1)	4	20

WALKERS SHORTBREAD
Tradition Oatcakes (Triangle shape) (1)	8	60
Walkers Pure Butter -		
Almond Shortbread (1)	10	95
Hazelnut Shortbread (1)	10	93
Shortbread Fingers - thick (1)	12	107
Shortbread Fingers - thin (1)	9	80
Shortbread Petticoat Tails		
per segment	8	64
Shortbread Rounds (1)	11	95
Wholemeal Shortbread -		
thick (1)	12	105
thin (1)	9	80

WALLS ICE CREAM WAFERS
Cones
double header (1)	4	18
medium (1)	2	10
large (1)	3	15
sugar (1)	8	50
Wafers (4)	4	20
Wafers - fan (1)	4	22

CRACKERS

	Carbohydrate in grams	Calories
BAHLSEN BISCUITS		
Bits (1)	1	10
Cheese-Crack (1)	1	10
Club-Krack (1)	1	10
Pizzy (1)	2	15
CO-OP		
Cream Crackers (1)	6	35
Crisp Bake Crackers (1)	6	35
CRAWFORD		
Butter Puffs (1)	6	50
Cheddars (1)	2	22
Cream Crackers (1)	9	37
TUC (1)	3	26
JACOBS		
Cornish Wafers (1)	5	43
Cream Crackers (1)	5	33
Rich Water (1)	5	30
Water High Bake Biscuits (1)	6	27
KALLO FOODS		
Rice Cakes all flavours (1)	5	25
MARKS AND SPENCER		
Butter Puffs (1)	6	50
Cheese Sandwich (1)	5	52
McDOUGALLS		
Cheese Cracottes (1)	5	23
Original Cracottes (1)	5	23
MORRISONS		
Cream Crackers (1)	6	33
NABISCO		
Cheese & Onion Sandwich (1)	5	47
Cheese Sandwich (1)	5	48
Cheese Ritz (1)	3	16
Hovis Crackers (1)	4	29
Ritz (1)	3	16
PARKSTONE BAKERIES		
Crackerbread (1)	4	19
PEEK FREANS		
Cheeselets (10)	5	40
RAKUSEN FOODS		
Small Matzos Crackers (1)	4	18

RAKUSEN FOODS – Continued	Carbohydrate in grams	Calories
Superfine Matzos (1)	17	80
Tea Matzos (1)	4	18

SAFEWAY
Cornish Wafer (1)	5	44
Cream Crackers (1)	5	33
Dixie Cracker (1)	3	18
Farmhouse Cracker (1)	5	33
Sesame Cracker (1)	3	20
Small Water Biscuit (1)	3	18
Water High Bake (1)	5	27

SAINSBURY
Cheese Thins (1)	2	20
Cornish Wafers (1)	5	42
Cream Crackers (1)	5	35
High Bake Water (1)	6	30
Sesame Seed Crackers (1)	3	20

TESCO
Cheese Sandwich (1)	4	42
Cheese Thins (1)	2	18
Cream Crackers (1)	8	48
High Baked Water (1)	5	28
Poppy & Sesame Crackers (1)	2	20
Snack Crackers (1)	3	24
Wheat Cracker (1)	5	40

WAITROSE
Cream Crackers (1)	5	35
High Bake (1)	5	25
Savoury Crackers (1)	2	16
Sesame Crackers (1)	3	19
Wheat Crackers (1)	5	38

CRISPBREADS

	Carbohydrate in grams	Calories
LYONS		
Krispen		
Rye (1)	4	17
Standard (1)	4	17
MARKS AND SPENCER		
Rye Light Crispbread (1)	3	17
MORRISONS		
Crispbread (1)	3	17
SLYMBRAND		
Slymbred (1)	3	17
Slymsnaks (1)	5	115
Slymsquares (1)	2	28

Bread, Bread Products

There is very little variation in the figures for UNCUT crusty white bread. A useful guide is given below:

	Carbohydrate in grams	Calories
Bloomer		
large loaf (800g)	390	1830
small loaf (400g)	200	980
Farmhouse		
small loaf (400g)	200	915
Split Tin		
large loaf (800g)	390	1830
ALLINSON		
White Bread Mix		
20oz/568g pack	430	2000
BEJAM		
Burger Buns (1)	24	130
French Half Baguettes (per half)	60	265
French Rolls (1)	30	130
Garlic Bread		
(1 from pack of 2)	80	690
Harvest Bran –		
Bran French Rolls (1)	27	120
BUITONI		
Grissini (1)	3	15
Melba Toast (1)	3	16
CO-OP		
Brown Bread		
large loaf (1 slice)	15	75
Standard White Sliced Bread		
medium sliced (1 slice)	16	75
thick sliced (1 slice)	25	115
thin sliced (1 slice)	13	65
CRUSTY GOLD		
French Stick		
1 approx 300g	140	685
GRANNY SMITH		
White Bread Mix*		
280g pack	190	990
HOVIS		
Traditional Wheatgerm		
large loaf (1 slice)	15	75

* when made up according to instructions

MARKS AND SPENCER	Carbohydrate in grams	Calories
Big Country Rolls		
Sesame (1)	25	135
Big Country White Bread		
(1 slice)	18	90
Breakfast/Morning Rolls (1)	26	130
Croissant Rolls (1)	15	170
Crouton Snacks		
100g pack	50	560
Farmhouse Baps (1)	24	130
Crusty Bread/Sesame Seeded		
whole loaf	215	1000
Old English and Scottish Rolls (1)	24	125
Toasting Loaf		
small loaf (1 slice)	15	80
MASTER CHEF		
Waffles (1)	9	70
Mc DOUGALLS		
Brown Bread Mix		
10oz/283g pack	210	1020
White Bread Mix		
10oz/283g pack	215	1045
McVITIE'S FROZEN FOODS		
Waffles (1)	11	90
MIGHTY WHITE		
Mighty Bite Rolls (1)	40	230
Mighty Muncher Rolls (1)	35	210
Sliced White Bread		
large loaf, medium sliced (1 slice)	16	80
large loaf, thick sliced (1 slice)	21	110
MOTHERS PRIDE		
Bridge Rolls (1)	16	95
Country Pride Danish White		
small loaf (1 slice)	10	50
Croissants (1)	24	220
Crusty Breakfast Rolls (1)	29	145
Crusty Rolls (1)	25	125
Long Rolls (1)	32	185
Scotch Rolls (1)	23	115
Scottish Square Bread		
large loaf (1 slice)	24	120
Soft White Baps (1)	28	140
White Long Loaf		
medium sliced (1 slice)	17	80
thick sliced (1 slice)	20	90
thin sliced (1 slice)	15	65
White Sesame Baps (1)	28	150

MOTHERS PRIDE – Continued

	Carbohydrate in grams	Calories
White Uncut		
Giant Loaf (whole loaf)	625	2820
Long Loaf (whole loaf)	415	1880

NIMBLE

	Carbohydrate in grams	Calories
Family Loaf		
Brown (1 slice)	9	45
White (1 slice)	10	50

PAXO

	Carbohydrate in grams	Calories
Golden Bread Crumbs 1oz	24	315

PITTA BREAD

	Carbohydrate in grams	Calories
Mini Pittas most brands (1)	20	95
Pitta most brands (1)	35-40	160-180

SAINSBURY

	Carbohydrate in grams	Calories
All Butter Croissants (1)	21	200
Baps (1)	28	140
Crusty Breakfast Rolls (1)	27	135
Danish Soft Light White		
medium sliced (1 slice)	12	60
Danish Toaster		
small loaf (1 slice)	12	60
Petit Pain (1)	21	100
Poppy Seed Knots (1)	19	110
White Floury Batch Baps (1)	27	130

SUNBLEST

	Carbohydrate in grams	Calories
Cheese & Mustard Seed Rolls (1)	23	155
Crusty Cob Rolls (1)	28	160
Danish Toaster		
small loaf (1 slice)	9	45
Danish White		
small loaf (1 slice)	7	35
Farmhouse Baps		
(1 from pack of 6 or 12)	24	130
Finger Rolls (1)	16	90
Long Loaf		
medium sliced (1 slice)	15	75
thick sliced (1 slice)	19	90
thin sliced (1 slice)	13	65
Lunch Rolls (1)	24	135
Muesli Toaster Loaf		
1 slice	7	50
Orange Peel Toaster Loaf		
1 slice	8	45
Scottish Morning Rolls		
(1 from pack of 6 or 12)	19	95
Sesame Seeded Burger Rolls (1)	24	135

SUNBLEST – Continued

	Carbohydrate in grams	Calories
Soft Brown Bread Rolls		
(1 from pack of 6 or 12)	20	115
Soft White Bread Rolls		
(1 from pack of 6 or 12)	22	120
White Loaf		
small loaf (1 slice)	12	60

TESCO

	Carbohydrate in grams	Calories
Danish Toaster,		
small loaf (1 slice)	13	65
Natural White Rolls (1)	26	140
Seeded Burger Buns (1)	23	130
White Bread		
large loaf, medium sliced (1 slice)..........	16	75
large loaf, thick sliced (1 slice)..............	20	100
large loaf, thin sliced (1 slice)...............	14	65

WAITROSE

	Carbohydrate in grams	Calories
Cheese Croissants (1).........................	17	220
Garlic Bread 170g............................	70	570
White Bread, large loaf		
thick sliced, 1 slice.........................	20	85
thin sliced, 1 slice...........................	12	55

Cakes, Cake Mixes and Teabreads

CAKES

	Carbohydrate in grams	Calories
BEJAM		
Chocolate Dairy Cream Sponge.............	105	625
Dairy Cream Eclairs (1).......................	6	105
Dairy Cream Sponge	105	625
BIRDS EYE		
Dairy Cream Doughnuts (1)	22	175
Dairy Cream Eclairs (1).......................	10	145
Dairy Cream Sponge	100	780
Strawberry Cream Cake......................	130	870
ICELAND		
Morello Cherry Cream Cake	120	780
Strawberry Cream Cake	105	685
LITTLEWOODS		
Butter Madeira with Cherries/Sultanas 1oz.	17	100
Chocolate Sponge Slice		
188g..	115	685
230g..	140	835
French Jam Sandwich........................	150	930
Oblong Butter Madeira Cake 1oz...........	18	130
Sponge Slice	125	650
LYONS		
Butter Madeira...............................	160	1070
Flan medium..................................	85	455
Trifle Sponges (1)	18	75
MARKS AND SPENCER		
Cherry Cut Cake..............................	170	1155
Chocolate Layer Cake	190	1735
Fresh Cream		
Chocolate Eclairs (1)	12	165
Scones (1)	26	180
Parkin Cut Cake	225	1260
Potato Scones (1)	14	100
Sponge Sandwich Jam Buttercream.........	140	835
MR. KIPLING		
Butter Shorties (1)............................	10	130
Buttercream Walnut Cake....................	170	1370
Chocolate Sponge............................	140	830
Golden Sponge...............................	145	835
Madeira Cake	160	1075
Victoria Sponge..............................	165	735

	Carbohydrate in grams	Calories
SAFEWAY		
All Butter Wholemeal Fruit Cake		
1oz	14	95
14oz	195	1350
All Butter Cherry Cake 402g	210	1270
All Butter Dundee Cake 1oz	17	110
Butter Cherry Genoa 1oz	15	95
Cherry Genoa Cut Cake 340g	210	1080
Dairy Cream Eclair frozen (1)	7	120
Dairy Cream Sponge (frozen)	95	660
Dundee Cake 320g	205	1000
Sultana Cut Cake 320g	205	1160
SAINSBURY		
All Butter Walnut Sandwich 1oz	16	120
Chocolate Decorated Sponge Sandwich	55	390
Madeira Cake 1oz	15	100
Spiced Fruit Cake 1oz	17	105
Sultana and Currant Cake z	18	90
Trifle Sponges (1)	21	90
Wholemeal Carrot & Orange Cake 1oz	11	105
per Cake 360g	140	1325
TESCO		
Dundee Slab Cake 1oz	17	95
Wholemeal Slab Cake 1oz	17	90
WALKERS SHORTBREAD		
Dundee Cake		
(slab) 1oz	15	105
Paradise Cake		
(slab) 1oz	15	100
Rich Fruit Cake		
(slab) 1oz	16	95
Sultana Cake		
(slab) 1oz	16	105

CAKE MIXES

	Carbohydrate in grams	Calories
GRANNY SMITH		
Savoury Crumble Mix*		
8oz/225g packet	140	1015
GREENS CAKE MIXES		
Classic Wholemeal Scone Mix*		
225g packet	140	1070
Fruit Loaf Cake*		
300g packet	230	1320
Wholemeal Fruit & Nut Loaf*		
287g packet	190	1200
Mc DOUGALLS		
Chocolate Sponge*		
8oz/227g packet	170	990
Plain Sponge*		
8oz/227g packet	160	1045
16oz/454g packet	315	2010
Scone Mix*		
8oz/227g packet	165	895
Shortbread Mix*		
6oz/170g packet	130	550
TESCO		
Rock Cakes†		
185g packet	150	635
VIOTA		
Afternoon Tea Cakes*		
219g packet	145	1325
Carnival Cakes*		
198g packet	150	1060
Chocolate Sponge*		
5oz/142g packet	110	1070
Cornish Tea Sponge*		
247g packet (without jam filling)	165	1225
Crumble*		
8oz/227g packet	160	1140
Ginger Cake*		
8oz/227g packet	185	980
Madeira Cake*		
12oz/340g packet	255	1555
Plain Sponge*		
184g packet	135	910
Rock Cakes*		
184g packet	130	1275

†before additions
* when made up according to instructions

VIOTA - Continued	Carbohydrate in grams	Calories
Scones*		
6oz/170g packet............................	135	660
Shortbread*		
6oz/170g packet............................	105	1250
Small Cakes*		
5oz/142g packet (without icing)............	105	670
Walnut Layer Cake*		
233g packet................................	145	1430
WHITWORTHS		
Luxury Sponge Mix*		
8oz/227g packet............................	180	960
Scone Mix*		
8oz/226g packet............................	150	980

*when made according to instructions
†before additions

TEABREADS

	Carbohydrate in grams	Calories
GRANOSE		
Fruit Bread 125g loaf........................	65	390
IMPERIAL BAKERIES		
Soreen Fruity Malt Loaf	140	575
MARKS AND SPENCER		
Bath Buns (1)...................................	28	195
Crumpets (1)...................................	15	70
Sliced Fruit Loaf (1 Slice)	10	50
Spiced Fruit Buns (1)...........................	34	185
Sultana Devon Scones (1)...................	20	125
Tea Cakes (1)	30	155
Teatime Batch.................................	100	500
MOTHERS PRIDE		
Chelsea Buns (1)	32	185
Crumpets (1)...................................	16	75
Currant Buns (1)................................	25	145
Fruited Tea Cake (1)..........................	29	155
Muffins (1)	31	155
Spiced Fruit Buns (1)	18	105
Sultana Scones (1)	28	180
SAINSBURY		
Bath Buns (1)..................................	31	170
Cheese and Chive Muffins (1)	26	155
Crumpets (1)...................................	20	75
Currant Buns (1)................................	26	150
Fruit Scones (1)	36	235
Plain Muffins (1)...............................	32	155
Spiced Fruit Buns (1)	32	175
Teacakes (1)...................................	25	130
SUNBLEST		
Cheese Muffins (1)	29	155
Crumpets (1)...................................	17	80
Currant Buns (1)................................	28	160
Fruit Loaf	155	845
Fruited Teacakes (1)	28	155
Hot X Buns (1).................................	31	185
Standard Muffins (1)..........................	31	160
Sultana Scones (1)	27	160
SUNMALT		
Malt Loaf.....................................	130	630
TESCO		
Fruit Buns (1)	28	140
Hot X Buns (1).................................	30	165

	Carbohydrate in grams	Calories
Muffins (1)	30	160
Sultana Scones (1)	25	160

WAITROSE

Lincoln Plum Bread 400g	180	855
Pikelets (1)	10	50

Cereals

PLAIN

There is very little variation from one brand to another for cornflakes. Below is a useful guide:

	Carbohydrate in grams	Calories
Cornflakes 1oz	24	100

Brand names: **Budgen, Co-Op, Family Choice, Happy Shoppers, Kelloggs, Quinnsworth, Safeway, Sainsbury, Spar, Tesco, VG.**

ALLINSON
Hot Brunch Muesli Pot Snack		
70g pot	42	250
Wheatgerm 1oz	13	100

BEECHAMS
Bemax 1oz	10	85
Crunchy Bemax 1oz	17	90

BIRDS
Grape Nuts 1oz	22	100

BOOTS - "SECOND NATURE"
Stabilised Wheatgerm 1oz	13	100

CO-OP
Swiss Style Cereal 1oz	21	110
Toasted Rice Cereal 1oz	25	100

FORCE
Wheatflakes 1oz	24	110

KELLOGG
Country Store 1oz	20	100
Fruit 'n' Fibre 1oz	21	95
Rice Krispies 1oz	24	100
Toppas 1oz	21	105

MAPLETONS
Bran Crunch 1oz	21	115
Frugrains 1oz	22	95
Fruesli 1oz	19	130
Golden Crunch 1oz	21	125
Sunny Grains 1oz	20	125

QUAKER
Oat Krunchies 1oz	20	110

	Carbohydrate in grams	Calories
SAFEWAY		
Rice Crunchies 1oz............................	24	100
SAINSBURY		
Rice Pops 1oz	23	100
TESCO		
Crisp Puffed Rice 1oz..........................	24	100

Cooking Aids, Mixes, Sauces

	Carbohydrate in grams	Calories
BAXTERS		
Cooking-in-Sauces — 425g tins		
Burgundy Wine	30	250
Medium Curry	60	315
Provencale	40	500
Sweet and Sour	90	400
White Wine	40	420
BISTO		
Bisto		
1 heaped teaspoon approx	4	20
Gravy Granules		
1 heaped teaspoon approx	2	20
BOVRIL		
Ambrosia Dessert White Sauce		
15oz/425g tin	65	415
Vegetable & Chicken Cube (1)	1	12
Vegetable & Meat Cube (1)	1	12
BUITONI		
Sauces — 9.98oz/283g cans		
Bolognese Sauce	25	145
Milanese Sauce	20	135
Napolitan Sauce	15	70
Siciliana	30	210
Tomato Puree		
4.59oz/130g tube	20	95
BUXTED		
Stuffing in Buxted Stuffed Chicken 9oz	70	370
CAMPBELLS		
Prego Sauces — 1 jar		
Bolognese	35	310
Pizza	45	240
Romagna	15	155
Tuscany	20	255
Spaghetti Sauces — 10.6oz/300g tins		
Bolognese	15	270
Siciliana	25	210
Tomato and Mushroom Spaghetti	25	205
COLMAN FOODS		
Cooking Mixes — 1 sachet		
Beef Bourguignon	35	175
Beef Goulash	30	140

	Carbohydrate in grams	Calories
Beef Provencale	30	140
Beef Strogonoff	25	160
Chicken Chasseur	30	125
Chilli con Carne	35	150
Coq au Vin	30	125
Farmhouse Lamb	30	165
Korma Mild Curry	35	145
Liver Casserole	35	175
Madras Medium Curry	35	145
Pork Casserole	30	150

Concentrated Gravy
Gravy Pot

1 level teaspoon approx	2	30

Pour-Over & Cook-In Sauces — 1 sachet

Apple	25	110
Barbecue	30	135
Beef Seasoning	25	135
Bread	35	140
Cheddar Cheese	20	180
Cheese with Chives	25	150
Chicken Seasoning	25	130
Curry	25	125
Mushroom	15	95
Onion	25	115
Parsley	20	90
Spaghetti Bolognese	35	160
Sweet and Sour	25	115
White	20	95

CROSSE AND BLACKWELL

Bonne Cuisine Sauces — 1 sachet

Gravy Madeira	15	100
Sauce Au Poivre	20	155
Sauce Hollandaise	15	100

Cook in the Pot — 1 sachet

Beef Goulash	25	175
Beef Stroganoff	25	190
Chicken Chasseur	20	175
Chilli-con-Carne	25	175
Fish Bonne Femme	20	135
Lamb Ragout	30	175
Madras Curry	15	155
Sausage Casserole	25	145
Shepherds Pie	35	180

Dish of the Day — 1 sachet

Barbecue	35	210
Bolognese	40	230
Chilli	35	205
Garlic and Herb	35	300
Mild Mustard	20	140
Southern Style	35	300

CROSSE AND BLACKWELL – Continued

	Carbohydrate in grams	Calories
Tandori	35	300
Tomato and Herb	35	210

FRAY BENTOS

Beef Stock (1)	neg	25
Chicken Stock Cubes (1)	neg	35

GRANNY SMITH

Suet Dumpling & Pudding Mix*		
225g packet	135	1070
Yorkshire Pudding & Pancake Mix*		
125g packet	85	650

GREEN'S

Complete Batter Mix†		
99g sachet	80	380
Crispy Batter Mix*		
93g sachet	80	340
Pouch Batter Mix*		
127g sachet	105	530

HOMEPRIDE

Classic Chinese Sauces — 383g tins

Cantonese Sweet & Sour Sauce	105	455
Peking Aromatic Sauce	60	245
Peking Barbecue Sauce	85	365
Singapore Curry Sauce	35	390
Szechuan Spicy Sauce	80	400

Classic Curry — 383g tins

Dansak	45	340
Korma	45	305
Madras	35	295
Masala	35	315
Rogan Josh	40	325
Vindaloo	40	420

Coat and Cook — 1 sachet

Barbecue	25	75
Southern Fried	20	80

Cook-in-Sauce — 376g tins

Barbecue	60	300
Chilli Con Carne	55	280
Curry	40	420
Red Wine	30	255
Sauce for Beef Stroganoff	20	295
Sauce for Chicken Chasseur	30	185
Sauce for Chicken Provencale	30	140
Sweet and Sour	50	220
Tomato and Onion	40	200
White Wine with Cream	30	275

*when made according to instructions
†before additions

HP FOODS

	Carbohydrate in grams	Calories
Gravy Browning,		
1 level teaspoon approx	2	5

J A SHARWOOD
Sauces — 10oz/284g tins

Dhansak Sauce.............................	25	240
Korma Curry Sauce	20	355
Madras Curry Sauce........................	20	295
Masala Sauce...............................	35	320
Rogan Josh Curry Sauce	20	270
Vindaloo Curry Sauce	25	230

KNORR
Aromat

1 level teaspoon approx	1	10
Beef Cube (1)	3	35
Beef Stock Powder		
1 level teaspoon approx	1	10
Chicken Cube (1).............................	2	35
Chicken Stock Powder		
1 level teaspoon approx	1	10
Gravy Cube (1)	7	40
Ham Cube (1).................................	2	30
Lamb Cube (1)................................	3	35
Vegetable Cube (1)...........................	2	35

Sauces — 1 sachet

Apple*.......................................	25	100
Bread*.......................................	30	135
Cheese*	15	135
Chilli*	30	180
Garlic*.......................................	20	160
Goulash*....................................	25	170
Onion*	20	100
Parsley*	15	70
Red Wine*	20	120
Savoury White*..............................	15	75
Spaghetti*	30	155
White Wine*.................................	25	175

Stuffing Mixes — 1 sachet

Apricot and Sultana	55	295
Cider Apple and Herbs*	60	360
Garlic and Herbs*	60	370
Hazelnut and Herbs*........................	55	385
Muesli	60	330
Sage and Onion*	60	365

LEA AND PERRINS
Curry Concentrate

1 level teaspoon approx	n/a	10

*when made according to instructions
†before additions

26

MARKS AND SPENCER

Sauces - 425g tins

	Carbohydrate in grams	Calories
Bolognese	20	310
Cream and Mushroom	35	345
Medium Curry Cooking Sauce	35	175
Napoletana	30	225
Red Wine Cooking Sauce	25	235
Sweet and Sour Cooking Sauce	35	165

McCORMICK FOODS

Mixes — 1 sachet

Brown Gravy Mix	2	95
Chicken Gravy Mix	2	95
Herb Flavour Brown Gravy	3	85
Mushroom Gravy Mix	3	75
Turkey Gravy Mix	2	85

OXO

Chicken Oxo Cubes (1)	1	13
Red Oxo Cubes (1)	1	15

PAXO

Bread Sauce Mix		
99g packet	75	340
Parsley and Thyme Stuffing Mix		
85g packet	60	280
Sage and Onion Stuffing Mix		
85g packet	65	290

QUAKER

Dinner Jackets — 250g jars

Bacon & Mushrooms in Tomato Sauce	35	315
Chicken & Eastern Spice in Yogurt Sauce	25	470
Ham & Sweetcorn in a Creamy Sauce	30	550
Mexican Chilli in a Creamy Sauce	40	495

QUORN

Sauce Mixes — 1 sachet

Bread*	25	115
Cheese*	15	105
Onion*	20	80
Parsley*	20	90
Savoury White*	15	85

SAFEWAY

Sauce Mixes — 1 packet

Beef Bourguignon	25	125
Bread	20	95
Chicken Chasseur	30	145
Chilli Con Carne	30	140

*when made according to instructions

	Carbohydrate in grams	Calories
Onion	25	110
Parsley	15	75
Sausage Casserole	30	130
Sweet & Sour	35	160
Traditional Beef Casserole	25	110
Traditional Chicken Casserole	25	120
White	15	95

SAINSBURY

	Carbohydrate in grams	Calories
Batter Mix		
128g packet	100	440
Bolognese Cook in Sauce		
298g tin	20	285
Curry Cook in Sauce		
385g tin	65	335
Passata		
500g tin	30	150
Red Wine Cook in Sauce		
385g tin	25	155
Sweet/Sour Cook in Sauce		
385g tin	60	270
White Wine Cook in Sauce		
385g tin	20	215

SCHWARTZ

Spice 'n' Easy — 1 packet	Carbohydrate in grams	Calories
Beef Casserole	20	110
Biriani	20	115
Chicken Casserole	25	120
Chicken Chasseur	30	145
Chicken Italienne	25	110
Chilli Chicken	20	110
Chilli con Carne	30	130
Chop Suey	15	85
Farmhouse Sausage Casserole	30	150
Goulash	30	135
Lasagne	25	120
Madras Curry	25	140
Shepherd's Pie	25	115
Spaghetti Carbonara	20	140
Spaghetti Sauce	30	125
Sweet and Sour	30	130
Tandoori Chicken	15	95

SHIPPAMS

Sauces — 270ml jars	Carbohydrate in grams	Calories
Hot Taco Sauce	25	110
Mild Taco Sauce	25	110

	Carbohydrate in grams	Calories
TESCO		
Batter Mix†		
130g packet........................	95	430
Bolognaise Sauce		
15oz/425g tin	30	415
Casserole Mixes — 1 packet		
Beef Stroganoff†........................	35	165
Chicken Chasseur†........................	30	180
Goulash†........................	40	155
Madras Curry†........................	35	145
Sage and Onion Stuffing		
85g packet	65	295
VIOTA		
Yorkshire Pudding		
127g packet........................	95	495
WAITROSE		
Sauces — 425g tins		
Arrabiata........................	20	140
Bolognese........................	20	300
Napoletana........................	15	115
WHITWORTHS		
Quick Batter Mix		
17oz/500g packet	390	1690
Yorkshire Pudding and Pudding Mix		
9oz/255g packet........................	200	890
WHOLE EARTH		
Italiano		
454g jar	50	275

†before additions

Dairy Products & Substitutes

CHEESE

There is very little variation in the carbohydrate and calorie values for cheese products. Below is a useful guide:

	Carbohydrate in grams	Calories
Cheese Slices (1)	neg	70
Cheese Spread with		
Blue Cheese/Celery/Chives/Crab/		
Ham/ Onion/Pineapple/Shrimp	neg	70-90
Cheese Triangles (1)	neg	40
Cream Cheese 1oz	neg	130
Full Fat Processed Cheese 1oz	neg	100
Full Fat Soft Cheese 1oz	neg	120
Lactic Cheese 1oz..............................	neg	90

CHEESE WITH ADDITIVES

Cheddar Cheese with –		
Beer & Garlic 1oz.............................	neg	130
Ham & Mustard 1oz..........................	neg	110
Herbs & Garlic 1oz...........................	neg	120
Port & Blue Stilton 1oz......................	neg	135
Port Wine 1oz	neg	125
Sweet Pickle 1oz	1	105
Walnuts 1oz	neg	120
Double Gloucester Cheese with –		
Blue Stilton 1oz..............................	neg	125
Caerphilly & Onion 1oz......................	neg	105
Mustard Pickle 1oz..........................	1	120
Onion & Chives 1oz	neg	110
Sage Derby Cheese 1oz	neg	120

Useful brand names: **Admirals, Ilchester, St. Ivel.**

APPLEWOOD
Smoked Cheddar Cheese rolled in Paprika

170g wedge...................................	2	730

DAIRY CREST
Lymeswold Country Recipe – 75g packet

Apple..	5	230
Herbs & Garlic...............................	2	240
Onion & Watercress..........................	2	215
Pineapple & Kirsch..........................	5	220
Spring Onion & Dill..........................	2	240

KRAFT
Philadelphia Cheese – 3oz/85g block

all varieties	<3	275

YOPLAIT
Petits Filous

	Carbohydrate in grams	Calories
60g pot......................................	8	85

CREAM

There is very little variation in the carbohydrate and calorie values for Cream. Below is a guide for all the popular brands:

	Carbohydrate in grams	Calories
Clotted Cream		
5fl.oz/142ml pot..........................	3	840
Cream for Coffee		
14g pot....................................	neg	20
Double Cream		
(Chilled, Fresh or Long Life)		
5fl.oz/142ml pot..........................	4	630
Half Cream		
5fl.oz/142ml pot..........................	6	200
Non Dairy Cream		
5fl.oz/142ml pot..........................	9	400
Single Cream		
(Chilled, Fresh or Long Life)		
5fl.oz/142ml pot..........................	6	285
Sour Cream		
5fl.oz/142ml pot..........................	6	285
Sterilised Cream		
6oz/170g tin..............................	7	420
Whipping Cream		
(Chilled, Fresh or Long Life)		
5fl.oz/142ml pot..........................	4	510

PLAMIL
Delice Cream Substitute

6oz/170g packet...........................	6	135

VAN DEN BERGHS
Elmlea Single

5fl oz/142ml carton	5	280
10fl oz/284ml carton......................	10	555
Elmlea Whipping		
5fl oz/142ml carton	3	470
10fl oz/284ml carton......................	6	940

MILKS & MILK DRINKS

	Carbohydrate in grams	Calories
Dried Milk		
1 pint when made up......................	25	280
Evaporated Milk		
170g tin.....................................	20	270
410g tin.....................................	40	650
Instant Milk		
1 level teaspoon	2	25
DAIRY CREST		
Flite – 200ml carton		
Banana/Strawberry.........................	15	120
Chocolate	16	125
EDEN VALE		
Supershake — 180ml carton		
all flavours	22	135
EXPRESS		
Stripes Flavoured Milks – 200ml carton		
Banana/Passion Fruit.......................	16	110
Chocolate	20	120
Raspberry/Strawberry	16	110
Stripes Flavoured Milks – 500ml bottle		
Banana/Passion Fruit.......................	40	270
Chocolate	50	305
Raspberry/Strawberry	40	270
MARKS AND SPENCER		
Milk Shakes – 180ml pack		
Chocolate	25	155
RAINES DAIRY FOODS		
Creamed Smatana		
500ml pack	25	660
Standard Smatana		
500ml pack	25	600
WAITROSE		
Milk Shakes – 180ml pack		
Chocolate	24	155
Fudge	25	195
Strawberry	23	155

MILK SUBSTITUTES

	Carbohydrate in grams	Calories
CADBURY		
Coffee Compliment		
1 rounded teaspoon........................	1	10
CARNATION		
Coffee Mate		
1 rounded teaspoon........................	1	10
Mellora		
9g of powder	6	40
GRANOSE		
Granose Soyamilk Carob Flavour		
500ml carton	17	295
ITONA		
Soya Plantmilk		
400ml pack...................................	20	560
PLAMIL		
Soya Milk		
500ml carton	18	515
PROVAMEL		
Soya Drink-Carob		
500ml carton	24	270
SAFEWAY		
Soya Milk (sweetened)		
500ml carton	30	230

YOGURT

There is very little variation in the carbohydrate and calorie values for Natural Set Yogurt (full fat) and Whole Milk Natural Yogurts from one manufacturer to another. We therefore give below a useful guide for all the popular brands:

	Carbohydrate in grams	Calories
Natural Set Yogurt (full fat)		
150g pot	9	165
Whole Milk Natural Yogurt		
140g pot	10	105
CHAMBOURCY		
Nouvelle Yogurts – 150g pot		
Black Cherry	24	120
Peach & Passion Fruit	23	120
Peach and Redcurrant	28	140
Raspberry	19	110
Strawberry	21	115
Real French (Bonjour) – 125g pot		
all flavours	17	90-100
Robot Yogurts – 142g pot		
all flavours	18-20	110
COOL COUNTRY		
Fruit Yogurt — 142g pot		
all flavours	22	115
Jackpots — 113g pack		
all flavours	18	95
Surprises — 150g pot		
all flavours	26	145
DAIRY CREST		
Thick 'n' Creamy – 150g pot		
Exotic Fruits	26	175
Fruits of the Forest	26	175
Rhubarb	25	170
Strawberry & Vanilla	24	170
Very Low Fat Pasteurised Fruit Yogurt		
125g pot, all flavours	18	90
DUNSTERS FARM		
Low Fat Yogurt – 150g pot		
Banana	20	130
Hazelnut	20	175
Strawberry	19	130
EDEN VALE		
French Style Yogurt – 125g pot		
all flavours	15	110

EDEN VALE – Continued

	Carbohydrate in grams	Calories
Gold Ski – 150g pot		
all flavours	28	180
Munch Bunch Yogurt – 125g pot		
Apple	33	155
Banana	24	125
Blackberry	23	120
Chocolate	33	155
Fudge/Sherbert Lemon	22	115
Raspberry	24	125
Strawberry	25	125
Original Ski – 150g pot		
all flavours	25	140

EXPRESS (MILKMAN)

	Carbohydrate in grams	Calories
Fruit Yogurt – 150g pot		
Black Cherry	28	140
Peach Melba/Raspberry/Strawberry	25	130

FAGE

	Carbohydrate in grams	Calories
Total Greek Yogurt		
Fruit Flavours 175g tub	7	220
Sheep's Milk 225g tub	9	210
Strained Cow's Milk 225g tub	9	305

LITTLEWOODS

	Carbohydrate in grams	Calories
French Style – 150g pot		
all flavours	26	155
Low Fat – 150g pot		
all flavours except Banana	25-27	130
Banana	32	145

LOSELEY

	Carbohydrate in grams	Calories
Low Fat Yogurt – 150g pot		
Hazelnut	21	130
Strawberry	21	105

MARKS AND SPENCER

	Carbohydrate in grams	Calories
French Style Yogurt – 150g pot		
all flavours	23	155
Low Fat Yogurt – 150g pot		
Apricot and Guava	30	165
Apricot and Passion Fruit	30	150
Black Cherry Double Decker	21	190
Nectarine & Orange	29	150
Peach Melba	26	140
Raspberry & Passion Fruit	28	160
Raspberry Ripple	32	190
Rhubarb	23	150
Strawberry	29	155
Sunfruit	29	160
Toffee	27	170

MARKS AND SPENCER – Continued

	Carbohydrate in grams	Calories
Thick & Creamy – 150g pot		
all flavours	29	160

MILRAM

	Carbohydrate in grams	Calories
Low Fat Yogurt		
with Compote of Fruit – 150g pot		
all flavours	23	125

MORRISONS

Low Fat Yogurt – 150g pot		
Black Cherry/Blackcurrant	21	135
Gooseberry/Muesli	26	150
Mandarin/Peach Melba	21	135
Raspberry/Strawberry	21	135

RAINES DAIRY FOODS

Mr Men Yogurt – 150g pot		
Banana	28	145
Black Cherry/Strawberry	27	140
Chocolate	29	150
Fudge/Jaffa Orange	29	145
Peach Melba	30	150
Raspberry	26	135

SAFEWAY

Funtime Yogurts – 150g pot		
Banana/Blackcurrant	27	140
Fudge	29	145
Strawberry	26	135
Low Fat Yogurts – 150g pot		
Apricot and Mango	25	130
Banana/Blackcherry	28	145
Blackcurrant/Gooseberry	27	140
Coconut	35	180
Elderberry and Cherry	25	130
Hazelnut	25	150
Jaffa Orange	29	145
Kiwi Fruit/Lemon	27	140
Lychee	28	145
Mandarin/Peach & Papaya	27	140
Muesli	27	155
Passion Fruit & Melon	26	135
Peach and Redcurrant	27	140
Peach Melba	32	155
Pear & Raspberry/Pineapple	26	135
Plum	29	145
Plum and Walnut	27	160
Raspberry/Rhubarb	28	145
Raspberry & Passion Fruit	27	140
Tropical Fruit	30	150

SAFEWAY - Continued

	Carbohydrate in grams	Calories
Velvet Yogurt - 150g pot		
Blackcherry/Strawberry flavours	28	150
Tropical.....................................	31	160

SAINSBURY

	Carbohydrate in grams	Calories
Low Fat Yogurts - 150g pot		
Black Cherry	25	135
Fruits of the Forest	27	145
Hazelnut	23	150
Peach Melba	27	145
Rhubarb..................................	27	145
Strawberry	22	130
Mr Men Yogurts - 125g pot		
Banana/Peach	22	120
Black Cherry	20	115
Chocolate................................	24	125
Fudge	25	130
Strawberry	22	120
Original French Recipe - 125g pot		
all flavours...............................	20	100
Thick & Creamy Yogurt - 150g pot		
all flavours...............................	31	180

SPELGA

	Carbohydrate in grams	Calories
Low Fat Yogurts - 142g pot		
Apple/Raspberry/Strawberry..............	24	135
Apricot	26	145
Black Cherry	25	145
Hazelnut	23	150
Manderin	23	135
Muesli	25	150
Peach Melba	28	150
Pear Melba	27	150
Pineapple	26	145

STAPLETON FARM

	Carbohydrate in grams	Calories
Bulgarian Recipe Breakfast Yogurt		
125 pot	8	95
Greek Style Yogurt		
180g pot.................................	12	230
Live Fruit Yogurt		
142g pot.................................	24	160

ST IVEL

	Carbohydrate in grams	Calories
Prize Italiano - 90g pot		
all flavours...............................	15	125
Rainbow - 125g pot		
all flavours...............................	17	90
Real - 125g pot		
all flavours...............................	17	105

SUDMILCH

	Carbohydrate in grams	Calories
Fruit Basket		
150g pot...............................	25	135
250g pot...............................	45	225
Frutti Very Low Fat Fruit Yogurt		
125g pot...............................	17	80

TESCO

Low Fat Yogurts – 150g pot		
Apricot/Blackberry & Apple...............	28	150
Banana/Coconut............................	27	145
Black Cherry................................	30	155
Blackcurrant................................	28	150
Chocolate/Toffee	30	160
Fruits of the Forest	31	160
Hazelnut.....................................	22	155
Orange/Passion Fruit & Melon.............	22	125
Pineapple	22	125
Peach Melba	29	155
Plum	23	130
Raspberry...................................	28	145
Rhubarb.....................................	25	135
Strawberry..................................	24	135
Real French Set Yogurt – 125g pot		
all flavours..................................	16	100

WAITROSE

Creamy Yogurt – 125g pot		
all flavours..................................	25	175-185
Yogurt – 150g pot		
Apricot/Banana............................	24	135
Blackcherry.................................	28	145
Blackberry & Apple........................	24	135
Blackcurrant/Gooseberry	24	135
Champ Rhubarb	27	140
Chocolate...................................	26	150
Hazelnut.....................................	21	135
Morello Cherry	24	135
Passion Fruit & Melon	24	135
Peach Melba	27	140
Pineapple & Coconut.......................	21	130
Raspberry...................................	24	135
Strawberry..................................	22	120
Victoria Plum	22	130

YOPLAIT

Breakfast Yogurt – 140g pot		
all flavours..................................	23	145
Whole Milk Fruit Yogurts – 140g pot		
all flavours..................................	30	135

YOPLAIT – Continued

	Carbohydrate in grams	Calories
YOP Drinking Yogurt		
200ml bottle	25	165
750ml bottle	100	625

Desserts

LOW SUGAR

	Carbohydrate in grams	Calories
AMBROSIA Light Rice		
439g can	60	335
150g pot	21	115
BIRDS Sugar Free Angel Delight – 49g packet		
all flavours before making up	32	225-235
when made up with —		
half pint semi-skimmed milk approx	45	355-365
half pint skimmed milk approx	45	320-330
half pint full fat milk approx	45	415-425
GRANOSE Soya Dessert — 525g carton		
all flavours approx	55	400
HEINZ WEIGHT WATCHERS Rice Pudding		
440g tin	55	310
ITONA Brown Rice Pudding		
400ml tin	40	360
LYONS MAID Weight Watchers Reduced Calorie		
Ice Cream 1 scoop	7	65
MARKS AND SPENCER Fruit Fool – 113g pot		
Gooseberry	24	180
Rhubarb	16	150
Strawberry	19	165
MILRAM Delight – 150g pot		
all flavours	24	210
Light & Airy Quark Dessert – 125g packet		
all flavours	23	180

* When made acording to instructions

MODERN HEALTH PRODUCTS
Mr Merry Jelly Mix*
   28g packet   20   85

PROVAMEL
Soya Dessert – 525g packet
   Carob   60   395
   Vanilla......................................   75   450

SOJAL
Frozen Dessert – 1 scoop
   all flavours...................................   7   90

VITARI
Frozen Fruit Desserts – 100ml pot
   Apple/Passion Fruit/Strawberry   16   65

*when made according to instructions

Dressings, Pickles, Sauces

There is no reason why diabetics cannot use the manufactured Dressings, Pickles and Sauces. However, it is important to bear in mind that they are usually a major source of sugar and in the case of dressings, fat as well. Providing only small amounts are taken at any one time, this should not be a bar to their use.

DRESSINGS

	Carbohydrate in grams	Calories
Basic Oil and Vinegar type dressings		
1 level tablespoon approx....................	neg	80
Cheese and Cream dressings		
1 level tablespoon approx....................	neg	80-100

HEINZ

All Seasons Dressings – all flavours		
1 level tablespoon approx	2-3	40-45

WHOLE EARTH

Salad Dream Creamy Nut Dressing		
1 level tablespoon	4	25

PICKLES

Most Pickles and Relishes provide approximately 5g CHO and 20-30 calories per level tablespoon. Chutneys contain a little more sugar and usually contain between 5-10g CHO and 30 calories per level tablespoon.

DOWN TO EARTH WHOLEFOODS

Sugar Free Chutney	Carbohydrate in grams	Calories
Apricot & Date		
1 level tablespoon	7	20
Lemon & Apple		
1 level tablespoon	7	15
Mango & Orange		
1 level tablespoon	6	15
Pineapple & Ginger		
1 level tablespoon	6	15

WHOLE EARTH

No Sugar Added range		
Corn Relish, 1 level tablespoon	4	30
Cucumber Relish, 1 level tablespoon	3	15
Tomato Relish, 1 level tablespoon	3	25

SAUCES

The following is a useful guide:

	Carbohydrate in grams	Calories
Apple Sauce		
1 level tablespoon approx.	3	10
Brown Sauce		
1 level tablespoon approx.	5	20
Cranberry Sauce		
1 level teaspoon approx.	2	10
Creamed Horseradish Sauce		
1 level teaspoon approx.	1	10
Fruity Sauce		
1 level tablespoon approx.	5	20
Horseradish Sauce		
1 level teaspoon approx.	neg	5
Mayonnaise		
1 level tablespoon approx.	neg	100
Mint Jelly		
1 level teaspoon approx.	5	15
Mint Sauce		
1 level teaspoon approx.	neg	5
Redcurrant Jelly		
1 level teaspoon approx.	4	15
Salad Cream		
1 level tablespoon approx.	3	50
Tartare Sauce		
1 level tablespoon approx.	3	40
Tomato Ketchup		
1 level tablespoon approx.	5	20
HEINZ		
Apple Sauce		
128g tin	23	85
PEARCE DUFF		
Apple Sauce		
190g pot	42	160
WHOLE EARTH		
Kensington Sauce,		
1 level tablespoon	5	20

Fruit Drinks

UNSWEETENED

There is very little variation in the Carbohydrate and Calorie values for Unsweetened Fruit Juices. We give below an approximate guide which covers all the popular brands.

	Carbohydrate in grams	Calories
Apple Juice Unsweetened		
200ml carton	25	90
1 litre carton	130	400
Grapefruit Juice Unsweetened		
200ml carton	20	80
1 litre carton	90	400
Orange Juice Unsweetened		
200ml carton	20	80
1 litre carton	120	430
Pineapple Juice Unsweetened		
200ml carton	25	90
1 litre carton	120	450
Tomato Juice Unsweetened		
1 litre carton	40	190

ADAMS FOODS
Just Juice — 1 litre cartons

Banana and Lemon	120	550
Grape and Blackcurrant	130	520
Orange and Apricot	105	385
Ruby Red Grapefruit	90	320

BOOTS
Carbonated Apple Juice

1 litre pack	100	390

BRITVIC
Apple Juice		
170ml can	22	70
Grapefruit Juice		
4oz/113ml bottle	16	60
6oz/170ml can	25	95
Orange Juice		
4oz/113ml bottle	14	55
6oz/170ml can	20	75
Pineapple Juice		
4oz/113ml bottle	16	60
6oz/170ml can	23	85
Tomato Juice		
6oz/170ml can	11	45
Tomato Juice Cocktail		
4oz/113ml bottle	8	30

BRITVIC – Continued

	Carbohydrate in grams	Calories
Tropical Fruit Juice		
113ml bottle	15	55

CAMPBELLS
Tomato and Vegetable Juice

200ml carton	8	40
500ml carton	20	100

COCA COLA
5 Alive Lite

200ml carton	10	40
1 litre carton.....................................	50	210

DEL MONTE
Orange Apple Passionfruit Juice

200ml carton	20	80
1 litre carton.....................................	100	400
Orange Pineapple Juice		
200ml carton	22	90
1 litre carton.....................................	110	450
Presse		
750ml carton	75	315

FOOD BROKERS
Drink 10

700ml bottle	85	370

GREEN GATE FOODS
Natures Wonder

200ml carton	24	110
1 litre carton.....................................	120	550

HP BULMER
Kiri Apple Juice

200ml bottle	20	75
750ml bottle	75-80	280

HUNTS
Tomato Juice Cocktail

107ml bottle	4	20
Unsweetened Orange Juice		
107ml bottle	10	40

LIBBY
"C" Drinks – 200ml carton

Apple/Pineapple............................	24	90
Blackcurrant	22	85
Grapefruit C (reduced calories)		
929ml bottle	78	300
Grapefruit Juice, Unsweetened		
525ml tin.....................................	42	165
454ml bottle	36	140

	Carbohydrate in grams	Calories
Orange C (reduced calories)		
929ml bottle	70	260
MARKS AND SPENCER		
Apple & Mango Juice		
200ml carton	22	85
Apple Sparkle		
250ml can	28	115
70cl bottle	80	325
Mandarin Juice		
500ml pack	45	185
Orange Juice, frozen		
6fl.oz/170ml carton	17	70
Orange Juice Plus		
980ml bottle	60	225
SAFEWAY		
Long Life Juice – 1 litre carton		
English Apple................................	120	400
Red/White Grape	145	550
Sparkling Juice - 75cl bottle		
Apple...	90	340
Red/White Grape	90	355
SCHWEPPES		
Appletise		
200ml bottle	23	85
Natural Orange Juice		
113ml bottle	14	55
180ml bottle	23	85
Pineapple Juice		
113ml bottle	14	55
180ml bottle	23	85
Tropical Spring		
180ml split	15	55
250ml can	20	80
SHLOER		
Sparkling Drinks - 200ml bottles		
Apple Juice	20	70
Red Grape Juice............................	26	100
Sparkling Drinks - 700ml bottles		
Apple Juice	65	245
Red Grape Juice............................	95	345
Sparkling Apple Juice		
250ml can	24	90
Sparkling Drinks — 250ml cartons		
Apple Juice	24	90
Red Grape Juice............................	33	125

SHOWERINGS

	Carbohydrate in grams	Calories
Zapple Sparkling Apple Juice		
180ml bottle	21	80

ST IVEL

Mr Juicy – 1 litre carton		
Apple	100	390
Grapefruit	75	300
Orange	90	380
Pineapple	105	400
Mr Juicy – 200ml carton		
Apple	20	80
Grapefruit	15	60
Orange	18	80
Pineapple	21	80
Real Juices – 1 litre carton		
Apple	115	420
Exotic	105	470
Grapefruit	90	310
Mediterranean	95	350
Orange	105	380
Pineapple	110	400

STUTE FOODS

Red/White Grape Juice		
200ml bottle	30	120
1 litre bottle/carton	150	590
Vegetable Juice		
500ml bottle/carton	10	45

THE TAUNTON CIDER COMPANY

Blackcurrant & Apple Piermont		
250ml can	15	55
Piermont		
250ml can	15	55

WALLS

100% Juice Lolly	8	35

WHOLE EARTH

Soft Drinks – 250ml bottle		
Cola	27	105
Orange Soda	27	100
Real Lemonade	28	105

Hot Beverages

LOW SUGAR

	Carbohydrate in grams	Calories
CARNATION Sugar Free Hot Chocolate Drink 1 sachet	11	65
RIDPATH PEK Barley Cup 1oz	15	80

Instant Meals & Quick Snacks

BATCHELORS

	Carbohydrate in grams	Calories
Slim -A-Meal – 1 pack		
Beef Risotto	45	250
Chicken Risotto	45	240
Chow Mein	40	240
Paella	50	250
Vesta Meals – serves 2 pack		
Beef Curry and Rice	170	950
Beef Risotto	115	755
Beef Madras and Rice	170	925
Chicken Curry and Rice	160	865
Chicken Masala	165	850
Chicken Supreme	145	940
Chop Suey	185	1020
Chow Mein	110	680
Paella	110	640
Prawn Curry	155	740
Shanghai Beef Noodles	110	675
Spicy Risotto	125	640
Sweet & Sour Chicken	205	1020

BOOTS

	Carbohydrate in grams	Calories
Shapers – 1 pot		
Beef Flavour Chow Mein	35	205
Beef Flavour Risotto	45	220
Rice with Beef	50	245
Rice with Chicken	50	250

CROSSE AND BLACKWELL

	Carbohydrate in grams	Calories
"Snackatak" – 1 sachet		
Chicken Curry & Rice	50	270
Chilli-con-Carne	49	300
Farmhouse Hot Pot	51	290
Pasta Bolognese	48	275

GOLDEN WONDER

	Carbohydrate in grams	Calories
Pot Casserole — 1 pot		
Beef*	35	195
Goulash*	35	195
Pot Fish – 1 pot		
Cod in Parsley*	40	210
Cod in Mushroom*	45	205
Pot Noodle – 1 pot		
Beef and Tomato*	45	290
Cheese and Tomato*	40	265
Chicken and Mushroom*	40	290
Chow Mein*	40	290
Spicy Curry*	45	310
Sweet and Sour*	45	270

* when made up according to instructions

GOLDEN WONDER – Continued

	Carbohydrate in grams	Calories
Pot Rice – 1 pot		
Chicken Curry*	45	215
Chicken Risotto*	40	215
Savoury Beef*	40	215
Pot Spaghetti – 1 pot		
Bolognaise*	40	200

KP

	Carbohydrate in grams	Calories
Quick Lunch – 1 pot		
Bolognaise	27	150
Chow Mein	28	160
Curry with Rice	29	145
Risotto	28	150

TESCO

	Carbohydrate in grams	Calories
Beef Curry with Rice (2 servings)		
740g pack	170	900
Chicken Curry with Rice (2 servings)		
740g pack	165	860

*when made according to instructions

Jams, Pastes, Spreads

There is very little variation between brands of Peanut Butter, except between sugar-free and sugar-added varieties. Below is a list which is a sufficiently accurate guide for every day use:

	Carbohydrate in grams	Calories
Peanut Butter		
Crunchy and Smooth 1oz	4-7	175

Popular Brands: **Safeway, Sainsbury and Sunpat.**

	Carbohydrate in grams	Calories
Peanut Butter (No added Sugar Varieties)		
Crunchy and Smooth 1oz	3-6	175

Popular Brands: **Boots, Granose, Lifecycle, Prewetts, Sunwheel, Whole Earth.**

BOOTS

Savoury Spread 1oz	4	60
Shapers Reduced Calorie Spread		
all flavours 1oz	neg	35

COUNTRY BASKET

No Added Sugar Jam –		
all flavours 1oz	8	30

ETHOS (NO-SUGAR ADDED)

Jam all flavours 1oz	9	30
Marmalade 1oz	9	30

GRANOSE

Sandwich Spreads		
Cereal 1oz	4	65
Mushroom 1oz	2	95
Olive 1oz	2	90
Tastex 1oz	5	60

HEDGEHOG FOODS

All Fruit Spread –		
all flavours 1oz approx	10	40

HEINZ

Spreads – 1oz		
Celery Corn & Apple/Cucumber	5	55
Sandwich	5	60
Tomato & Onion	8	65
Toast Toppers – 128g tins		
Chicken & Mushroom	8	70
Curried Chicken	10	95

	Carbohydrate in grams	Calories
Ham and Cheese	9	180
Mushroom and Bacon	8	165
Turkey and Ham	9	110

HEINZ WEIGHT WATCHERS
Reduced Sugar Jams & Marmalade

all flavours 1oz	10	35

LEDBURY PRESERVES
Del 'Ora Jams & Marmalades

all flavours 1oz	12	45

LIFECYCLE
No Added Sugar Jams & Marmalade

all flavours 1oz	9	35
Pear & Apricot Spread 1oz	16	70
Pear & Black Cherry Spread 1oz	16	70
Pear & Strawberry Spread 1oz	16	70

NATURE'S STORE
Conserves & Marmalade

all flavours 1oz	10	35

ROBERTSON TODAY'S RECIPE
Jams and Marmalade

all flavours, 1oz	14	55

Pure Fruit Spread

all flavours 1oz	9	35

SAFEWAY
No Added Sugar Jams & Marmalade

all flavours 1oz	10	40
Savoury Spread 1oz	neg	65

SAFFRON WHOLE FOODS
'No added Sugar' Marmalade and Preserves

all flavours, 1oz	8	30

SUNWHEEL FOODS

Hazelnut Spread 1oz	4	175
Pear 'n' Apple Spread 1oz	17	75
Sesame Spread 1oz	5	160
Sunflower Spread 1oz	6	165

THURSDAY COTTAGE
Marmalade

all flavours 1oz	11	40

Reduced Sugar Jams

all flavours 1oz	13	50

WAITROSE
Reduced Sugar Jams

	Carbohydrate in grams	Calories
all flavours 1oz	10	35

WELSH LADY
No Added Sugar Preserves

all flavours 1oz	10	45

WHOLE EARTH

American Style Peanut Butter 1oz	7	170
Jams and Marmalade		
all flavours 1oz	10	40
Pear & Apple Spread		
with Orange & Lemon 1oz	20	70
Sweet 'n' Fruity Spreads		
all flavours 1oz	14	55
Three Nut Butter 1oz	4	190

Meats, Meat Products

There is very little variation in the carbohydrate and calorie values for certain canned/chilled meats from one manufacturer to another. Below is a useful guide per ounce for all the popular brands:

	Carbohydrate in grams	Calories
Brisket Beef	neg	60
Chopped Ham	neg	50
Chopped Ham & Pork	neg	90
Chopped Pork	neg	80
Haslet	5	80
Lambs Tongue	neg	70
Lunch Tongue	neg	70
Ox Tongue	neg	70
Pork Luncheon Meat	2	100
Pork Tongue	neg	70

BOWYERS
Chopped Ham Loaf

4oz pack	3	300
Faggots (1)	24	370

BRAINS
Faggots in Rich Sauce

184g pack	15	300
369g pack	25	600
539g pack	40	875

CO-OP
Faggots in Sauce

13oz/370g pack	40	660
19oz/540g pack	75	1115
Faggots without Sauce		
1 from pack of 6	9	115

CROSSE AND BLACKWELL
Ham & Tongue Roll

5oz/142g tin	13	385

ICELAND
Bacon Rockets

when grilled (1)	19	175
Beef Burgers (1)	2	105
Beefy Bats		
when grilled (1)	23	195
Lamb Saucers		
when grilled (1)	25	260
Relish Burgers (1)	1	245

MATTESSON WALLS

	Carbohydrate in grams	Calories
Pre-Packed Meats – 4oz/113g packs		
Pork & Pepper Loaf.........................	6	295

MILLERS

Roast Faggots (1)	21	265

ROBIRCH

Pre-Packed Meats – 4oz packs		
Stuffed Pork Loaf..........................	18	270
Savoury Faggots (1)	11	180

ROSS

Faggots in Rich Sauce 2's		
5.5oz/185g pack............................	20	350

SAFEWAY

Faggots in Rich Sauce (frozen)		
pack of 4 (368g)	45	760
pack of 6 (539g)	65	1130

TESCO

Faggots in Rich Sauce		
450g pack..................................	60	795
Pre-Packed Meats – 4oz packs		
Gala Slices.................................	3	275
Pork Roll & Egg	4	300
Pork Roll with Stuffing	5	340

W A TURNER

4 Faggots in Rich Sauce		
13oz/369g pack	50	750
6 Faggots in Rich Sauce		
19oz/539g pack	70	1095

Pancakes

SAVOURY

	Carbohydrate in grams	Calories
BEJAM		
Chinese Spring Rolls (1)	15	165
Curry Spring Rolls (1)	16	155
BIRDS EYE		
Pancakes if shallow fried –		
Cheese and Ham (1)	14	160
Chicken and Mushroom (1)	14	150
Minced Beef (1).............................	12	130
FINDUS		
Crepes		
Asparagus with Ham (1)	11	120
Beef Burgundy (1)...........................	15	120
Chicken with Mushroom Sauce (1)	17	165
Swiss Cheese with Ham (1)................	12	155
Pancakes		
Cheddar Cheese (1)	13	110
Chicken and Bacon (1)	17	80
Chicken Curry (1)...........................	15	95
Minced Beef (1).............................	15	90
Smoky Bacon (1)	16	80
Steak and Kidney (1)	15	80
GORCY OF FRANCE		
Marie Crepes		
Ham & Bolognaise (1)......................	23	185
Ham & Cheese (1)	19	165
Mushroom (1)...............................	20	150
MARKS AND SPENCER		
2 Cheese and Ham Pancakes		
227g pack..................................	25	500
2 Mushroon Pancakes		
227g pack..................................	30	390
Crispy Pancake Rolls (1)........................	15	140
MR CHANG'S		
Chinese Spring Rolls		
1 from pack of 4, when cooked.............	12	105
ROSS		
Chinese Spring Rolls (1)	25	140
SAFEWAY		
Chicken Spring Roll (1)	16	130
Vegetable Spring Roll (1)	18	125

SAINSBURY
Cheese, Mushroom & Ham Crepes
  when cooked (1) 19 210
Spring Rolls when cooked (1) 15 140

SHIPPAMS
Old El Paso Taco Shells (1) 7 60

WAITROSE
Pancakes – 180g packs
  Cheese/Ham/Mushroom 25 290

SWEET

	Carbohydrate in grams	Calories
MARKS AND SPENCER		
Scotch Pancakes (1)..........................	9	65
Sultana and Syrup Pancakes (1)	20	105
SAINSBURY		
Lemon & Raisin Pancakes (1)................	18	90
SUNBLEST TEATIME		
Scotch Pancakes (1)..........................	15	90
TESCO		
Pancakes (1)..................................	16	85
Sultana and Syrup Pancakes (1)	17	100
Syrup Pancakes (1)	15	100

Pasta

	Carbohydrate in grams	Calories
BATCHELORS		
Super Noodles — 1 sachet		
Barbecue Tomato	80	415
Chicken	70	360
Mild Curry	80	375
CO-OP		
Spaghetti in Tomato Sauce		
8oz/227g tin	30	140
15oz/425g tin	60	255
CROSSE AND BLACKWELL		
Alphabetti Spaghetti with Tomato Sauce		
15oz/425g tin	55	260
Spaghetti Rings with Tomato Sauce		
15oz/425g tin	55	260
Straight Spaghetti in Tomato Sauce		
15oz/425g tin	55	245
Wholewheat Spaghetti		
15oz/425g tin	60	280
Wholewheat Spaghetti Rings		
15oz/425g tin	55	250
Wholewheat Spaghetti Spirals		
15oz/425g tin	55	265
Pasta Choice — 95g packs		
all varieties	70	335
HEINZ		
Haunted House		
7.58oz/215g tin	35	155
Invaders		
7.58oz/215g tin	30	140
Noodle Doodles		
7.58oz/215g tin	30	130
Spaghetti Hoops in Tomato Sauce		
7.58oz/215g tin	30	140
Spaghetti in Tomato Sauce		
7.58oz/215g tin	35	150
Weight Watchers		
No Added Sugar Spaghetti		
215g tin	25	115
440g tin	50	235
Wholewheat Pasta Shells in Tomato Sauce		
7.58oz/215g tin	30	140
ICELAND		
Canneloni		
311g pack	50	500

	Carbohydrate in grams	Calories
Ravioli		
per pack	45	370
Spaghetti Bolognese		
361g pack	30	930
ROYAL NORFOLK		
Spaghetti in Tomato and Cheese Sauce		
15.2oz/430g tin	55	280
Spagheti Rings in Tomato and Cheese Sauce		
15.2oz/430g tin	55	280
SAFEWAY		
Spaghetti in Tomato Sauce		
213g tin	25	125
15oz/425g tin	65	255
Spaghetti Rings in Tomato Sauce		
425g tin	55	250
SAINSBURY		
Spaghetti Numberelli/Rings		
212g tin	30	130
425g tin	55	255
Straight Spaghetti		
212g tin	30	130
425g tin	55	255
Wholewheat Spaghetti		
15oz/425g tin	40	190
TESCO		
Spaghetti in Tomato Sauce		
213g tin	30	130
425g tin	55	260
Spaghetti Letters/Rings in Tomato Sauce		
425g tin	55	260
WAITROSE		
Spaghetti in Tomato Sauce		
8oz/227g tin	30	125
15oz/425g tin	55	235
Spaghetti Rings in Tomato Sauce		
8oz/227g tin	30	140
15oz/425g tin	50	260

PREPARED DISHES

	Carbohydrate in grams	Calories

BIRDS EYE
MenuMaster Range –
Fish Dishes – 1 packet

	Carbohydrate in grams	Calories
Mariners Pasta Gratin......................	35	355
International Meals – 1 packet		
Lasagne...	45	435
Spaghetti Bolognese........................	55	370
Traditional Meals – 1 packet		
Macaroni Cheese with Itam	40	490

BUITONI
Canelloni

14.1oz/400g can..........................	60	390
330g pack....................................	55	550
Lasagne		
300g pack....................................	55	530
Ravioli		
14.1oz/400g can..........................	60	330
Wholewheat Ravioli		
14.1oz/400g tin............................	60	340

EDEN VALE
Pasta Salad

8oz/227g pack..............................	35	450

FINDUS
Cannelloni

350g pack....................................	45	420
Lasagne		
10oz/284g pack	35	345
20oz/568g pack	75	690
Lean Cuisine Range – 1 packet		
Beef & Pork Cannelloni	25	235
Spaghetti Bolognese........................	35	245

HEINZ
Invaders with Meteors

15.5oz/440g tin	65	395
Macaroni Cheese		
7.41oz/210g tin	25	225
Ravioli in Beef & Tomato Sauce		
7.58oz/215g tin	30	165
Ravioli in Tomato Sauce		
7.58oz/215g tin	30	165
Spaghetti Bolognese		
7.41oz/210g tin	30	175

KATIE'S KITCHEN
Macaroni Cheese

16oz/450g pack	65	715

	Carbohydrate in grams	Calories
Tagliatelle		
16oz/454g pack	55	600
LOCKWOODS		
Macaroni Cheese		
7.58oz/215g tin	25	250
15oz/425g tin	50	498
MARKS AND SPENCER		
Canneloni (frozen)		
(Serves 2) 567g pack	80	755
Chicken and Pasta Bake		
(Serves 1) 283g pack	35	420
Lasagne (frozen)		
(Serves 1) 283g pack	50	385
Family Size) 907g pack	155	1235
Seafood Pasta		
(Serves 2) 570g pack	35	690
Spaghetti Bolognaise (frozen)		
23oz/650g pack	110	790
McVITIE'S FROZEN FOODS		
Mama Mia's Pasta		
Cannelloni		
350g pack....................................	55	470
Chicken Lasagne		
380g pack....................................	65	485
Ham & Mushroom Lasagne		
390g pack....................................	55	440
Lasagne		
390g pack....................................	55	480
Seafood Lasagne		
390g pack....................................	55	440
MR CHANG'S READY MEALS		
Chicken Chow Mein		
8oz/227g pack...............................	50	330
SAFEWAY		
Fish Lasagne		
550g pack....................................	60	650
Macaroni Cheese		
213g tin......................................	25	250
425g tin......................................	50	500
Macaroni Cheese with Ham (frozen)		
298g pack....................................	45	500
Ravioli		
200g tin......................................	30	160
400g tin......................................	55	320
Vegetable Lasagne		
550g pack....................................	65	555

SPAGHETTI HOUSE
Chilled Meals –

	Carbohydrate in grams	Calories
Cannelloni di Carne		
300g pack	40	480
520g pack	65	835
Cannelloni Vegetariani		
300g pack	45	420
520g pack	75	765
Cappelletti Tricolore		
285g pack	60	460
515g pack	105	800
Conchigli alla Palermitana		
300g pack	60	420
Fusilli al Tonno		
515g pack	90	655
Lasagne Bolognese		
300g pack	40	380
520g pack	65	690
Lasagne Verdi		
300g pack	40	400
520g pack	70	660
Lasagne Veg V		
300g pack	45	365
520g pack	65	620
Lasagne Vegetariane		
300g pack	35	310
Penne all' Arrabbiata		
300g pack	65	365
Rigatoni all' Amatriciana		
520g pack	110	690
Tortelloni Aurora		
300g pack	50	400

TESCO
Lasagne

	Carbohydrate in grams	Calories
(Serves 1) 330g pack	40	410
(Serves 2) 600g pack	80	820
Spaghetti Bolognese		
(Serves 1) 300g pack	45	285

WAITROSE
Cannelloni Bolognese

	Carbohydrate in grams	Calories
283g pack	45	405
Lasagne		
9oz/225g pack	30	380
18oz/510g pack	60	755
Pasta & Tuna Bake		
425g	35	505
Ravioli		
400g tin	65	335
800g tin	125	665
Spinach Cannelloni		
283g pack	35	475

Tagliatelle Carbonara
  454g pack..................................... 55   475
Tagliatelli Nicoise
  425g pack..................................... 40   725

Pastry, Pastry Goods

PASTRY

	Carbohydrate in grams	Calories
BEJAM		
Puff Pastry		
1 kilo pack....................................	565	5360
Short Crust Pastry		
1 kilo pack....................................	645	5600
DORSET		
Puff Pastry		
12oz/340g pack	115	1380
Short Pastry		
6oz/170g pack...............................	80	725
GRANNY SMITH		
Short Pastry Mix*		
225g pack....................................	165	1330
450g pack....................................	330	2685
GREENROSE FROZEN FOODS		
Wholemeal Puff Pastry		
13oz/370g pack	130	1330
JUS-ROL		
Puff Pastry		
215g pack....................................	85	830
370g pack....................................	145	1425
454g pack....................................	180	1750
Shortcrust Pastry		
215g pack....................................	100	950
370g pack....................................	175	1635
Shortcrust Shells (1)	10	100
Vol-au-Vent		
Cocktail (1)	4	40
Kingsize (1)	18	180
Medium (1)	7	70
McDOUGALLS		
Flaky Pastry		
16oz/454g pack	230	2455
Shortcrust Pastry		
16oz/454g pack	250	2220
Suet Pastry		
16oz/454g pack	230	2270
PALETHORPES		
Puff Pastry		
250g pack....................................	90	995
500g pack....................................	180	1985

*when made according to instructions

PALETHORPES – Continued

	Carbohydrate in grams	Calories
Shortcrust Pastry		
250g pack......................................	115	1095
500g pack......................................	230	2190
SAFEWAY		
Puff Pastry (fresh)		
250g pack......................................	95	995
Puff Pastry (frozen)		
13oz/369g pack	135	1570
Short Pastry Mix		
16oz/454g pack	250	2240
Shortcrust Pastry (frozen)		
13oz/369g pack	205	1830
SAINSBURY		
Fresh Wholemeal Pastry		
250g pack......................................	85	950
Puff Pastry		
250g pack......................................	95	990
Shortcrust Pastry		
250g pack......................................	110	1115
500g pack......................................	215	2225
Shortcrust Pastry Mix		
16oz/454g pack	280	2270
SAXBY'S		
Puff Pastry		
16oz/454g pack	175	n/a
Short Pastry		
16oz/454g pack	190	n/a
TESCO		
Flaky Pastry		
450g pack......................................	180	2515
Shortcrust Pastry		
450g pack......................................	270	2215
WAITROSE		
Puff Pastry (frozen)		
454g pack......................................	160	1730
WHITWORTHS		
Pastry Mix		
8oz/226g pack................................	130	1140

PASTRY GOODS

	Carbohydrate in grams	Calories
ADAMS PORK PRODUCTS		
Chicken and Sweetcorn Pastry (1)	35	405
Hand-Raised Pork Pies — 1lb	105	1645
Lincolnshire Pork Pie		
7oz................................	46	780
1lb	105	1710
Lincolnshire Traditional Pasties		
1 from pack of 4	18	220
Individual	42	495
Picnic Pork Pies		
1 from pack of 2	21	325
BEJAM		
Chicken Florentine En-Croute (when baked)		
12oz/340g pack	90	835
Chicken Pie (when baked)		
Individual 5oz	32	385
Cornish Pasties (as sold)		
Traditional (1)........................	70	505
Pork Pies (as sold)		
Buffet (1)	22	350
Traditional (1)........................	35	625
Quiche Lorraine (as sold)................	24	340
Sausage Rolls (when baked)		
Party Size (1)	7	80
Steak & Kidney Pie (when baked)		
Individual 5oz	32	390
Turkey & Ham Buffet Pies (as sold) (1).......	23	310
Turkey Asparagus En-Croute (when baked)		
12oz/340g pack	90	820
BIRDS EYE		
Cheese Egg and Bacon Flan		
11oz/312g pack	65	1000
Chicken Pie		
Serves 1	33	410
Serves 2-3	80	1080
Flaky Bake Pies –		
Seafood.............................	36	465
Steak & Mushroom	30	455
Minced Beef & Veg. Pie		
Serves 1	30	325
Steak and Kidney Pie		
Serves 1	32	370
Serves 2-3	90	1120
BOWYERS		
Chilled Products		
Bacon & Cheese Lattice Flan (1)	27	325
Bacon and Chutney Snack (1)...............	18	240

	Carbohydrate in grams	Calories
Beef and Kidney Pie		
175g	47	580
Family size	85	1150
Beef and Onion Snack (1)	17	255
Cheese & Onion Pasty (1)	35	395
Cheese & Onion Pasty baked (1)	40	410
Chicken and Ham Pie (1)	40	415
Chicken and Mushroom Pie		
Family size	90	910
Chicken Bacon & Mushroom Lattice Flan (1)	10	265
Cornish Pasty (1)	38	385
Farmhouse Pie 4oz piece	22	430
Gala Pie 4oz piece	25	420
Gala Pie		
Presliced	23	370
with Egg 4oz piece	25	430
Gold Seal Steak & Kidney Pie (1)	40	500
Ham & Mushroom Lattice Flan (1)	28	290
Meat & Vegetable Pie (1)	50	575
Minced Beef Pie		
Family size	90	1295
Individual	38	525
Pork Pies		
Buffet 70g	20	300
Individual 140g	38	640
Raised 530g	125	2305
Pork Pie with Egg 530g	125	2385
Quiche – 4oz piece		
Cheese & Ham	15	260
Cheese & Onion	14	205
Spanish	13	200
Sausage Rolls		
Individual (1)	17	275
Jumbo (1)	35	490
Turkey & Ham Buffet Pie (1)	13	185
Frozen Products		
Chicken & Ham Pie (1)	33	335
Chicken & Mushroom Pie		
Heat & Eat 130g	25	390
Ready to Bake 130g	24	360
Cornish Pasty		
Buffet 60g	15	160
Heat & Eat 5oz	40	385
Curried Mince Pie (1)	33	445
Minced Beef Baked		
Heat & Eat 130g	33	445
Ready to Bake 5oz	33	440
Steak & Kidney Pie		
Heat & Eat 5oz	40	330
Ready to Bake 5oz	35	300

BUXTED

Pies – 680g	Carbohydrate in grams	Calories
Chicken	75	830
Chicken & Mushroom	70	810

CO-OP
Chilled

Cornish Pastie (1)	38	370
Meat and Potato Pie (1)	40	335
Minced Beef and Onion Pie (1)	38	345
Pork Pie		
Large 1lb/454g	95	1410
Small 4oz	30	400
Steak and Kidney Pie (1)	37	330
Family Pies (frozen) — 1lb/454g		
Chicken and Vegetable	135	1265
Minced Beef and Onion	145	1400
Steak and Kidney	135	1400
Sausage Rolls		
King size (1)	13	155
Party size (1)	5	60

DORSET

Cheese and Onion Flan		
5oz/142g	30	400
Cheese Egg and Bacon Flan		
5oz/142g	30	400
Chicken and Mushroom Pie		
5oz/142g	35	350
Chicken and Pea Pie		
5oz/142g	33	345
Chicken Roll		
2oz/57g	11	155
Cornish Pasty		
Small 89g	23	260
Dorset	23	260
Minced Beef and Onion Pie		
5oz/142g	36	385
Minced Beef and Vegetable Pie 128g	29	310
Pasty — 88g		
Curried Beef and Onion	20	255
Dorset	23	260
Quiche Lorraine		
4oz/113g	20	275
Sausage Rolls		
Cocktail (1)	5	60
Cocktail Low Fat (1)	5	45
Kingsize (1)	15	195
Large (1)	12	150
Party size (1)	8	95
Steak and Kidney Pie		
5oz142g	36	390

DORSET - Continued	Carbohydrate in grams	Calories
Steak and Kidney Pudding 156g.............	39	370
Steak and Mushroom Pie		
5oz/142g.....................................	37	365
Turkey Pie		
5oz/142g.....................................	36	355
Wholemeal Savoury Flans - 625g		
Broccoli Cheese & Smoked Bacon........	34	405
Cottage Cheese & Smoked Salmon......	32	455
Farmhouse with Tomato & Apple........	32	435

FINDUS
Egg Cheese & Bacon Flan 380g	80	910
French Mushroom Flan 380g	90	855
French Onion Flan 380g	95	880

FRAY BENTOS
Chicken and Mushroom Pie		
425g tin......................................	70	830
Steak & Ale Pie		
425g tin......................................	60	870
Steak & Ale Pudding		
425g tin......................................	50	935
Steak and Kidney Pie		
213g tin......................................	30	470
425g tin......................................	55	935
Steak and Kidney Pudding		
213g tin......................................	45	455
425g tin......................................	85	905
Steak & Vegetable Pie		
213g tin......................................	30	390
425g tin......................................	60	775
Steak & Vegetable Pudding		
425g tin......................................	90	915
Turkey & Ham Pie		
425g tin......................................	60	815

FRESHBAKE FOODS
Cheese Egg & Bacon Flan		
1 from pack of 4	26	420
Family Pies — 440g (frozen)		
Minced Beef/Onion	125	1250
Steak/Kidney	115	1310
Minced Beef and Onion Pie 5oz.............	30	385
Steak and Kidney Pie 5oz	30	385
Steak/Kidney Pudding (frozen)		
1 from pack of 4	36	400

GOBLIN
Meat Pudding		
142g	22	285
212g	30	425

GOBLIN – Continued

	Carbohydrate in grams	Calories
Steak and Kidney Pudding		
142g	22	285
212g	30	425

GORCY OF FRANCE
Marie Range – 400g

Quiche Lorraine	55	940
Quiche (Mushroom)	100	1060
Seafood Quiche	80	910

GREENROSE FROZEN FOODS
Wholemeal Harvest Range –

Savoury Pasties (1)	35	320
Savoury Rolls (1)	15	130
Steak & Kidney Pies (1)	32	365
Turkey & Leek Pies (1)	32	355

HOLLAND & BARRETT –
See ready Meals
Vegetarian Prepared Dishes

ICELAND

Broccoli Cheese & Port Flan		
500g	120	1555
Buffet Cornish Pasties (1)	18	190
Buffet Flans (1)	18	190
Buffet Pork Pies (1)	20	325
Cauliflower Cheese Flans		
Mini	33	430
1lb	95	1270
Cheese & Onion Flan		
1 from pack of 4	32	505
1lb	95	1400
Cheese Egg & Bacon Flan		
1 from pack of 4	32	505
1lb	95	1400
Chicken & Ham Buffet Pies (1)	20	310
Chicken & Sweetcorn Flan		
1 from pack of 4	31	475
1lb	85	1315
Cocktail Flan		
Broccoli Cheese & Bacon (1)	7	85
Chicken & Peppers (1)	7	80
Salmon (1)	7	80
Country Vegetable Flan		
1 from pack of 4	43	505
1lb	105	1360
Country Vegetable Pie 1lb	48	560
Mushroom Flan		
Mini	37	460
1lb	110	1390

	Carbohydrate in grams	Calories
Sausage Plait 411g............................	100	1085
Sausage Rolls		
Bite-size (1)...................................	6	80
Cocktail (1)...................................	7	95
Kingsize — 1 from pack of 10.............	12	155
Kingsize — 1 from pack of 20.............	14	165
Large (1).....................................	10	135
JUS-ROL		
Cocktail Sausage Rolls (1).....................	6	70
Cornish Pasties (1)	36	345
Sausage Rolls (1)...............................	20	190
KRAFT		
Cheese/Onion Pasties (1)......................	27	310
Country Beef & Vegetable Pie (1)	35	360
Country Chicken Pie (1)	35	390
Country Chicken & Vegetable Pie (1)........	38	390
Country Steak & Kidney Pie (1)	37	390
Ploughmans Pasty (1)...........................	35	440
Sausage Rolls		
Cheese Pastry (1)..........................	5	75
Cocktail/Party Size (1)	5	75
Giant (1).....................................	19	275
Kingsize (1)	12	175
Steak and Kidney Pudding 120g.............	34	340
Traditional Cornish Pasties (1)	35	365
LITTLEWOODS		
Cornish Pasty (frozen)		
1 from pack of 4	30	355
Cotswold Pasty (fresh)	95	775
Gala Egg Pie 1oz	6	100
Frozen Pies - 1 from pack of 2		
Cheese & Onion	40	400
Chicken & Mushroom.......................	35	415
Hotpot	17	225
Mince Beef & Onion.......................	35	455
Steak	35	450
Steak & Kidney.............................	35	460
Meat & Potato Pie (fresh)	45	495
Pork Pie -		
Buffet (1)....................................	23	320
Hand Raised	115	1760
Individual (1)................................	37	555
Sausage Rolls -		
Loose Cocktail..............................	7	110
1 from pack of 2	18	270
1 from pack of 6	7	110
1 from pack of 10 (frozen).................	17	140

	Carbohydrate in grams	Calories
Scotch Pies – (fresh)		
45g	22	230
142g	62	725
1 from pack of 2	60	710
1 from pack of 3	22	235
Steak Pie (fresh)	200	2470
Steak & Kidney Pie (fresh)		
Individual loose/pre-pack 177g	45	550
Large loose/pre-pack 474g	110	1400
LOCKWOODS		
Pies – 430g		
English Country Vegetable	60	430
French Country Vegetable	60	435
Potato & Onion	65	510
MARKS AND SPENCER		
Bacon, Egg & Sausage Flan	65	1110
Beef and Onion Pasties		
1 from pack of 2	35	330
Broccoli Quiche	80	870
Chicken & Leek Plate Pie	110	1300
Chicken & Mushroom Plate Pie	75	970
Chicken Pie – Shortcrust Ind	36	400
Cornish Pasties Puff Pastry		
Individual	33	370
1 from pack of 4	16	175
Cured Pork Pie		
1 from pack of 2	16	245
Individual	32	535
Lattice Sausage Rolls (1)	10	200
Melton Mowbray Pork Pie large	75	1390
Minced Beef Pie Traditional Small	32	575
Minced Beef Pie (Topcrust only)	70	1070
Mini Chicken & Ham Pies		
1 from pack of 4	10	175
Mini Pasties with Fresh Vegetables (1)	24	165
Pork & Egg Pie large	55	1350
Pork Pies Crisp Bake		
1 from pack of 4	18	280
Puff Pastry Sausage Rolls		
1 from pack of 6	12	135
Quiche Lorraine		
Individual	26	495
Standard	70	1210
Large	80	1410
Quiche with Cheese and Onion	60	1110
Quiche with Mushrooms	65	1090
Quiche with Tomato and Cheese	55	1055
Rich Pastry Steak & Kidney Pie	135	1620

	Carbohydrate in grams	Calories
Roast Chicken Plate Pie...................	105	1300
Roast Turkey & Ham Plate Pie............	90	1190
Scotch Pies (1)	17	375
Steak and Kidney Plate Pie	115	1450
Steak & Kidney Pudding		
Family size..........................	80	910
Turkey in Rich Pastry Pie..................	115	1510

MILLERS
Chicken and Bacon Pie		
Family (1)	100	1370
Individual (1)........................	27	385
Pork Pie		
Individual	26	425
Mini	16	215
Sausage Rolls		
Dorset Super Size	24	400
Standard............................	14	230
Steak and Kidney Pie		
Family	100	1360
Steak and Kidney Pudding		
Individual	34	415
Turnover Pasty (1)......................	38	470

OLAF FOODS
Bellarena Salmon Bake		
227g pack..........................	30	445

PETER'S SAVOURY PRODUCTS
Beef and Vegetable Pasty.................	43	435
Chicken and Mushroom Pie		
Deep Round	49	410
Standard Round.....................	41	375
Cornish Pasty		
Ridged	42	480
Semi Circular	41	425
Minced Beef and Onion Pie		
Oval	43	450
Round..............................	39	370
Pork Pie individual	37	510
Sausage Roll		
Giant	30	360
Large..............................	27	310
Steak and Kidney Pie		
Deep round	46	445
Oval	42	455
Standard round	38	385

PORK FARMS
Simple Simon Pork Pies (1)................	24	405

	Carbohydrate in grams	Calories
ROBIRCH		
Chicken & Mushroom Pie 197g	55	515
Cornish Pasty (1)	45	425
Cotswold Range –		
Chicken & Mushroom Pie (1)...............	45	440
Meat & Vegetable Pasty (1)	45	435
Minced Beef & Onion Pie (1)	45	460
Steak & Kidney Pie(1).......................	50	515
Grosvenor Pork Pie		
4oz/113g slice.............................	24	400
Meat and Potato Pie 199g	58	510
Minced Beef & Onion Pie		
162g	50	485
422g	100	1160
Pork Pies –		
Buffet (1)....................................	18	250
Family	115	1720
Individual (1)................................	40	485
Medium (1)	50	785
Picnic (1)....................................	85	1265
Sausage Roll –		
Large...	32	335
Small...	21	225
Steak & Kidney Pie		
203g	50	520
463g	110	1235
Steak & Kidney Pudding (1)	45	420
ROSS		
Chicken Pasties (1)...............................	20	240
Cornish Pasty (1)	20	240
Family Pies — 1lb		
Chicken......................................	105	1290
Minced Beef and Onion	110	1380
Steak and Kidney...........................	105	1290
Individual Cheese & Onion Quiche	29	465
Individual Pies		
Beef & Kidney Stewpot....................	40	490
Chicken & Vegetable......................	36	410
Chicken & Veg Stewpot...................	45	440
Steak and Kidney	35	450
Jumbo Traditional Pasties (1).................	40	405
Sausage Rolls		
1 from pack of 20.........................	11	150
Jumbo (1)...................................	24	255
Steak & Kidney Pudding (1)	35	305
SAFEWAY		
Chicken and Ham Pie (frozen)		
5oz/142g (1 from pack of 4)	25	360
16oz/454g...................................	95	1190

	Carbohydrate in grams	Calories
Cornish Pasty (chilled)		
Individual	40	365
Large	65	580
Meat & Potato Pie (chilled)		
Individual 5oz	40	410
Minced Beef & Onion Pie (chilled)		
Family 12oz	60	890
Individual 5oz	35	400
Quiche		
Cauliflower	80	980
Chicken & Asparagus	80	950
Country Vegetable	80	765
Espagne	75	980
Lorraine	70	915
Mushroom	80	1020
Smoked Salmon & Broccoli	70	760
Swiss Cheese & Ham	95	1470
Sausage Rolls (chilled)		
Large (1 from pack of 2)	20	300
Mini (1 from pack of 6)	10	145
Steak & Kidney Pudding (chilled)		
Large	95	1070
Small	40	430
Steak and Kidney Pie (frozen)		
5oz/142g (1 from pack of 4)	30	380
1lb	90	1190

SAINSBURY

	Carbohydrate in grams	Calories
Bacon & Cheese Flan (frozen)	29	390
Beef and Onion Pasties (1)	44	395
Beef and Vegetable Pasty (1)	29	315
Chicken Pie with Vegetables (frozen)		
1 from pack of 4	37	410
Cornish Pasties (frozen)		
1 from pack of 4	20	310
Crusty Bake Pork Pie		
2oz	15	210
4oz	30	420
Minced Beef Pies frozen (1)	35	475
Minced Beef and Onion Pie 15oz	145	1600
Premium Pork Pie (1)	26	400
Premium Steak Pie 5oz	29	360
Sausage Rolls (frozen)		
Cocktail (1)	6	105
Party Size (1)	4	60
Savoury Pie Beef and Vegetable 16oz	100	1050
Steak & Kidney Pie (frozen)	30	380
Steak & Kidney Pudding 6oz	31	385

SAXBY'S

	Carbohydrate in grams	Calories
Cheese, Ham & Onion Pasty (1)	44	525

SAXBY'S - Continued

	Carbohydrate in grams	Calories
Cornish Pasty (1)	35	355
Ham & Chicken Pie 1lb	105	1360
Hot Eating Pies -		
Chicken & Mushroom......................	65	515
Steak & Mushroom	42	420
Minced Beef & Onion Pie		
Individual	36	465
Pork Pies		
5oz..	40	495
10oz	75	1025
1lb	115	1620
Sausage Rolls		
1 from pack of 2	19	250
Steak and Kidney Pies		
Family	125	1690
Individual	55	580
Steak & Kidney Pudding Large..............	130	1100
Traditional Cornish Pasty	60	380
Turkey Ham & Stuffing Pie 270g............	65	850

TESCO
Chilled Products

	Carbohydrate in grams	Calories
Beef and Onion Pie Small	36	440
Beef Steak Pie		
Family 16oz/454g...........................	120	1180
Cheese and Onion Flan 168g................	35	550
Chicken and Vegetable Pie		
Individual 145g.............................	40	450
Large 500g	125	1435
Cornish Pasty 150g	39	445
Meat and Potato Pie		
Individual 145g.............................	38	435
Minced Beef and Onion Pie		
Large 370g.................................	90	1030
Pork Pies		
Buffet......................................	21	280
Countrystyle		
280g....................................	75	1085
492g....................................	135	1910
Countrystyle Lattice Pork 362g...........	90	1325
Nottinghamshire Pork Pie 170g...........	48	675
Pork and Egg		
1oz......................................	7	105
450g.....................................	120	1545
Traditional Pork Pie 140g................	35	610
Traditional Pork Pie 300g................	75	1300
Sausage Rolls		
Large	50	595
Small	17	250
Steak and Kidney Pie Individual.............	42	510
Steak and Kidney Pudding Large............	70	685

TESCO - Continued

Frozen Products

	Carbohydrate in grams	Calories
Minced Beef and Onion Pie		
Individual 140g	38	400
Large 370g	140	1420
Premium Steak Pie		
Small 128g	35	380
Family 510g	115	1445

TIFFANY

	Carbohydrate in grams	Calories
Cornish Pasties		
1 from pack of 2, 4 or 6	32	270
Family Pies — 1lb		
Beef and Vegetable	110	1115
Chicken and Vegetable	110	1115
Minced Beef and Onion	110	1135
Individual Oval Pies		
Beef and Vegetable	31	295
Chicken and Vegetable	31	290
Minced Beef and Onion	28	320
Steak and Kidney	30	295
Individual Round Pies		
Chicken and Mushroom	34	330
Cottage	21	270
Minced Beef and Onion	34	325
Steak and Kidney	27	300
Sausage Rolls		
1 from pack of 2, 4 or 6	15	140
"Upper Crust" Individual Pies –		
(1 from pack of 2) 170g each		
Chicken	35	430
Haddock Prawn & Mushroom	35	410
Ham Leek & Cheese	50	480
Steak & Mushroom	35	405
Turkey & Game	35	410
"Upper Crust" Pies		
Chicken and Asparagus 1oz	6	75
per pie	150	1760
Ham Leek and Cheese 1oz	6	75
per pie	160	1780
Steak and Mushroom 1oz	6	70
per pie	140	1610
Tuna and Mushroom 1oz	6	65
per pie	150	1560

TYNE BRAND

	Carbohydrate in grams	Calories
Steak and Kidney Pie		
432g tin	65	835
Steak and Kidney Pudding		
206g tin	40	490
447g tin	85	960

TYNE BRAND – Continued

	Carbohydrate in grams	Calories
Steak and Mushroom Pie		
404g tin	65	815
WAITROSE		
Chicken Ham & Mushroom Pie		
5oz	30	335
425g	110	1215
Chunky Chicken, Bacon & Ham Pie		
425g	100	1285
Chunky Steak Pie	105	1720
Chunky Steak & Kidney Pie	115	1390
Cornish Pasty 170g	47	450
Family Pies – 1lb		
Chicken Ham & Mushroom	110	1170
Minced Beef	110	1220
Steak & Kidney	115	1120
Steak Mushroom & Red Wine	100	1090
Ham & Cheese Quiche Small	20	270
Minced Beef Pies small	33	400
Minced Beef/Onion Pie		
Individual 5oz	30	390
Large 14oz	95	1210
Pork Pies –		
1lb	105	1610
Individual	31	500
Mini	18	240
Quiche – 14oz		
Broccoli & Swiss Cheese	65	795
Ham & Swiss Cheese	65	845
Sausage Rolls		
1 from pack of 2	20	295
Steak and Kidney Pie		
Individual	30	410
small	28	340
WALTER HOLLAND		
Cheese & Onion Pie		
1 from pack of 4	55	465
Chicken & Mushroom Pie		
1 from pack of 4	50	470
Cornish Pasty		
Individual	37	400
1 from pack of 4	35	325
Meat Pie		
1 from pack of 4	40	350
Mini Pork Pie		
1 from pack of 10	25	200
Pork Pie – 5oz		
1 from pack of 4	50	435
Potato and Meat Pie		
1 from pack of 4	55	390
Sausage Rolls (1)	17	165

WALTER HOLLAND – Continued

	Carbohydrate in grams	Calories
Steak and Kidney Pie		
1 from pack of 4	55	435
Steak and Kidney Pudding		
1 from pack of 4	55	360

W A TURNER

	Carbohydrate in grams	Calories
Chicken & Vegetable Roll (baked)		
354g pack....................................	100	1065
Minced Beef Roll (baked)		
354g pack.....................................	95	1160
Steak & Kidney Roll (baked)		
354g pack.....................................	90	1040
Wholemeal Vegetable Roll (baked)		
354g pack....................................	95	1010

Patés

BOWYERS	Carbohydrate in grams	Calories
Ardennes Paté 1oz	neg	105
Brussels Paté 1oz	neg	105

CULROSE
Pork and Liver Paté

4oz/113g pack	neg	320
6oz/168g pack	neg	480

GRANOSE

Soya Bean Paté 1oz	2	40
Vegetable Paté		
142g pack	5	335

JOHN WEST
Dressed Crab

42g pot	2	60
Pressed Cod Roes		
7oz/198g pot	4	205
12oz/340g pot	7	355
Salmon Paté		
42g pot	neg	90

MARKS AND SPENCER
Beef Spread

5oz/142g pot	3	425
Country Style		
8oz/227g pot	2	425
Ham Spread		
5oz/142g pot	2	425

MATTESSON WALLS
Patés — 4oz packs

Ham and Tongue	2	235
Liver	3	360
Liver and Bacon	2	345
Liver and Ham	1	340

PLUMROSE
Farmhouse Spreading Paté - 32g pack

Chicken with Herbs	2	105
Ham	neg	100
Luxury Liver	2	95
Savoury Beef	1	90
Farmhouse Spreading Paté - 95g pack		
Chicken with Herbs	3	310
Ham	1	300
Luxury Liver	5	230
Mackerel	5	135

PLUMROSE - Continued

	Carbohydrate in grams	Calories
Salmon	5	135
Savoury Beef	3	270

PRINCES
Patés — 3.35oz/95g packs

Chicken Liver	5	310
Pork Liver	5	300
Smoked Ham	7	310
Turkey	6	315

ROBIRCH

Liver Sausage 1oz	5	65

SUTHERLAND
Salmon Paté

35g pot	1	45
53g pot	2	70

Pizzas & Pizza Bases

	Carbohydrate in grams	Calories
BEJAM		
Pizzas – when grilled		
5" Cheese & Tomato	30	235
5" Ham & Mushroom	30	225
BIRDS EYE		
Ham and Mushroom Luxury Pizza 325g	90	630
Tomato and Cheese Luxury Pizza 300g	80	550
BUITONI		
Pizzas – 390g		
Bologna	90	870
Napoli	100	760
Roma	90	835
Venezia	90	870
CO-OP		
Cheese Pizza 170g	58	425
Cheese Pizza Deluxe 270g	82	635
Cheese Pizza with Ham 184g	60	430
Cheese Pizza with Mushroom 184g	55	420
Pizza House (frozen) — 1 from pack of 4		
Cheese and Onion	26	225
Cheese and Tomato	29	245
Ham and Mushroom	24	210
FINDUS		
Crispy Base Pizza		
Cheese and Tomato		
8oz/227g pack	75	475
Ham		
10oz/283g pack	70	480
Crusty Bun Pizzas		
1 from pack of 4	32	230
French Bread Pizza — 6oz/180g		
Bacon Peppers and Mushroom	50	345
Italian Style Sausage	50	330
Savoury Barbecue Beef	50	400
Tomato and Cheese	55	410
GRANNY SMITH		
Pizza Base Mix*		
140g pack	115	595
HALDANE FOODS - HERA		
Complete Pizza Mix		
241g pack	155	800

* when made up according to instructions

	Carbohydrate in grams	Calories
ICELAND		
Baked Bean Pizza (1)	36	280
Cheese & Onion Pizza (1)	28	200
Cheese & Tomato Pizza (1)	33	255
Funsize Pizza (1)	20	140
Ham & Mushroom Pizza (1)	33	305
Italiano Pizza 364g	100	985
Marinara Pizza 340g	90	865
Pizza Fingers (1)	12	90
Tomato & Cheese Pizza 330g	110	1000
Vegetable Pizza 340g	105	925
MARIETTA FROZEN FOODS		
Chicken Bella Curry Pizza 5"	30	260
Chicken Suprema Pizza 5"	30	270
French Bread Pizza (1)	45	325
Ham & Mushroom Pizza		
5"	30	230
7"	65	475
Margherita Pizza 9"	95	865
Onion & Cheese Pizza		
5"	30	260
7"	60	470
Romana 9"	85	810
Seafood Pizza 5"	30	220
Special Topping Pizza		
5"	35	300
7"	70	610
Tomato & Cheese Pizza		
5"	30	250
7"	55	440
Tomato/Beef Saucers		
Fun Size	15	130
MARKS AND SPENCER		
American Pizza –		
Pepper/Mushroom 400g	55	840
American Style Pizza –		
Cheese & Tomato 400g	80	850
Margherti Pizza		
1 from pack of 6	28	255
Mini Pizzas		
1 from pack of 10	14	135
Tomato Cheese and Onion Pizza		
1 from pack of 6	27	240
McCAIN PIZZAS		
Snack Size Pizza		
Beefburger	26	215
Cheese and Onion	24	175
Cheese and Tomato	25	190
Ham and Mushroom	25	185

McCAIN PIZZAS – Continued

	Carbohydrate in grams	Calories
Salami	30	175
Seafood	30	205
Smokey Bacon & Sweetcorn	25	175

McVITIE'S FROZEN FOODS
Pizza Grills
	Carbohydrate in grams	Calories
Cheese and Onion (1)	21	180
Ham and Mushroom (1)	21	185
Tomato and Cheese (1)	21	190

Quarter Pounders
	Carbohydrate in grams	Calories
Tomato and Cheese (1)	40	310
Tomato Cheese and Onion (1)	40	300

ROSS
	Carbohydrate in grams	Calories
French Bread Pizza	45	380

Pizzas – Individual Size
	Carbohydrate in grams	Calories
Cheese and Onion	32	190
Cheese and Tomato	30	200
Ham Mushroom & Cheese	28	200
Wholemeal Tomato and Cheese	30	210

SAFEWAY
	Carbohydrate in grams	Calories
Cheese and Onion Pizza (frozen) 310g	75	725
Cheese/Onion Pizza (frozen)		
1 from pack of 4 (95g)	30	220
Cheese and Tomato Pizza (frozen) 300g	75	740
Cheese & Tomato with Crispy Bacon (frozen)		
1 from pack of 4 (95g)	30	220
Luxury Cheese and Tomato with		
Vegetables Meat and Fish 575g	175	1335
Pizza Bread		
1 from pack of 4	60	260
Tomato and Cheese Pizza with		
Ham and Mushroom Deep Pan 430g	130	855
Pepperoni and Peppers 430g	130	855
Pineapple and Ham 500g	150	990
Wholemeal Bread		
1 from pack of 2 or 4	60	260

SAINSBURY
	Carbohydrate in grams	Calories
Cheese and Tomato Pizza 198g	60	505
Italian Style 400g	105	840
Pan Baked		
Bacon & Sweetcorn 265g	66	545
Cheese & Tomatoes 450g	135	970

TESCO
	Carbohydrate in grams	Calories
Cheese and Mushroom Pizza 165g	65	440
Cheese and Tomato Pizza		
280g	100	710
Italiana Pizza 215g	65	510

TESCO - Continued	Carbohydrate in grams	Calories
Pizza Snacks, Mushroom 130g	40	285
Pizza Base Mix†		
140g pack	105	510
TIFFANY		
Cheese and Tomato Pizza 5"	29	225
Cheese Onion and Tomato Pizza 5"	30	215
WAITROSE		
French Bread — 1 from pack of 2		
Ham and Mushroom Pizza	50	335
Tomato and Cheese	38	325
Pizza Compagnola	95	680
Pizza Marinara	100	720
Pizza Pepperoni	100	745

† before additions

Potato Products

There is very little variation in the carbohydrate and calorie values for frozen chips and a useful guideline is given below to cover all the popular brands:

	Carbohydrate in grams	Calories
Crinkle Cut/Straight Cut Chips 1oz	6	40
Oven Chips 1oz................................	7	50-60

BATCHELORS
Potato Saucery — 1 sachet

Cheddar Cheese	70	315
Country Onion	75	330

BEJAM
American Fries

when deep fried 1oz	9	70
Crispy Potato Waffles (1)	16	95
Potato Croquettes (1)...........................	6	40
Steak Fries 1oz...............................	6	45

BIRDS EYE

Alphabites* - 1oz...........................	9	60
Country Potato Bake		
1 packet	45	435
Crispy Potato Fritters* 1oz	7	60
Croquette Potatoes* (1)	8	50
Potato Waffles* (1)	15	115

CADBURY
Smash

2.4oz/68g pack	50	200
4.62oz/131g pack	90	390

CO-OP
Dried Instant Potato

85g pack	50	225
170g pack................................	100	450
Potato Croquettes (1)........................	7	30
Potato Salad		
227g pot.................................	35	280

EDEN VALE
Potato & Chive Salad

8oz/227g pot	38	235

*when baked/grilled

	Carbohydrate in grams	Calories
FINDUS		
Potato Croquettes* (1).....................	15	70
Saute Potatoes* 1oz...........................	6	30
Swiss Style Potato Cakes* (1)...............	9	40
FRESHBAKE FOODS		
Roundas – Potato with		
Beans (1).....................................	23	120
Chicken Supreme (1).......................	18	125
Cod in Sauce (1).............................	18	120
Ham & Cheese (1).........................	15	155
Minced Beef (1)............................	18	145
GOBLIN		
Potato Salad		
160g tin......................................	30	350
HEINZ		
Potato Salad		
210g tin......................................	35	355
JUS-ROL		
Frozen Potato Croquettes (1)................	7	35
Pommes Noisettes (1).........................	1	10
KATIE'S KITCHEN		
Potato Savoury		
16oz/454g pack............................	45	700
LITTLEWOODS		
Potato Celery & Dill Salad		
227g pack....................................	30	350
LOCKWOODS		
Potato Salad		
240g pack....................................	40	430
MARKS AND SPENCER		
Creamy Potato Gratin		
454g pack....................................	65	635
Leek/Carrot Jackets		
1 from pack of 2	20	240
Mushroom Jackets		
1 from pack of 2	15	250
Potato & Cheese Farl (1).....................	21	100
Potato Croquettes (1).........................	13	90
McCAIN		
Beefeater Fast Fries 1oz	7	35
Beefeater Crispy Grooves 1oz	6	35

*when baked/grilled

	Carbohydrate in grams	Calories
Hash Browns 30g	7	45
Oven Croquettes 45g	7	70
String Fellows 1oz	8	60

ROSS

Bubble and Squeak 1oz	4	20
Crispy Crosses 1oz	6	50
Croquettes (1)	7	35
Duchesse Potatoes 1oz	5	30
Hash Browns 1oz	5	20
Jacket Scallops 1oz	5	30
Jacket Wedges 1oz	5	35
Noisettes 1oz	7	50
Oven Crunches 1oz	6	45
Roast Potatoes 1oz	5	30
Waffles (1)	7	55

SAFEWAY

Instant Mashed Potato (Dried)		
serves 2-3/71g pack	45	190
serves 5-6/142g pack	85	380
Potato & Chive Salad		
250g pack	45	475
Spicy Potato Salad		
8oz/227g pack	40	460

SAINSBURY

Instant Potato (Dried)		
2.3oz/68g pack	45	190
Oven-bake Potato Croquettes (1)	6	50

TESCO

Cheesey Potato Bake		
(Serves 2) 454g pack	50	565
Instant Potato Mix		
140g pack	85	370
Potato Salad with Chives		
250g pot	40	290
Potato Salad in Reduced Calorie Dressing		
150g pot	25	140

WAITROSE

Potato Dauphinoise		
11oz/312g pack	40	445

WHITWORTHS

Scalloped Potatoes - 145g pack		
with Au Gratin Sauce	105	530
with Savoury White Sauce	105	545
with Sour Cream and Chive	100	570

*when baked/grilled

YEOMAN

	Carbohydrate in grams	Calories
Instant Mashed Potato		
90g pack	60	250
177g pack	120	500
Instant Mashed Potato – No Added Salt		
177g pack	120	500
Mashed Potato – 130g pack		
with Chopped Onion	90	370
with Full Cream Milk	100	375

Ready Meals

PREPARED FISH DISHES

	Carbohydrate in grams	Calories
BEJAM		
Jumbo Fish Finger & Chips (baked)		
11oz/312g pack	60	480
BIRDS EYE		
Prawn Curry with Rice		
1 packet	55	350
FINDUS		
Prawn Curry with Rice – 1 serving pack		
Prawns	14	155
Rice	50	200
LITTLEWOODS		
Cod & Mushroom Crumble (frozen)		
400g pack..................................	55	470
Cod & Prawn Crumble (frozen)		
400g pack..................................	55	500
McCAIN		
Menu Classics –		
Seafood Newburg		
320g pack	20	230
Oven Meals –		
Cod & Chips		
290g pack	55	480
W A TURNER		
Cod in Batter Oven Chip Meal		
298g pack..................................	65	570

PREPARED MEAT/POULTRY DISHES

	Carbohydrate in grams	Calories
BEJAM		
Chicken & Chips (baked)		
8.5oz/240g pack............................	65	510
Chicken Cordon Bleu (2 servings)		
12oz/340g pack	110	1000
Chicken Kiev (2 servings)		
12oz/340g pack	90	1300
Jumbo Burger & Chips (baked)		
10oz/284g pack	35	475
Stir Fry Meals – 12oz/340g pack		
Chinese Chicken............................	40	280
Indian Chicken	45	335
BIRDS EYE		
MenuMaster International Meals – 1 packet		
Beef Curry with Rice	60	380
Chicken Curry with Rice	65	400
Chicken Supreme with Rice	60	460
Chilli Con Carne with Rice	55	375
BUXTED		
Chicken & Fries (baked)		
10oz/283g pack	70	650
CROSSE AND BLACKWELL		
Beef Curry with Separate Rice		
10oz/284g tin	55	385
15oz/425g tin	85	575
Chicken Curry with Separate Rice		
10oz/284g tin	55	315
15oz/425g tin	80	475
London Grill		
10oz/284g tin	40	445
15oz/425g tin	60	670
FINDUS		
Beef Curry with Rice 1 serving pack		
Meat...	12	200
Rice	50	200
Beef Oriental		
298g pack	45	315
Chicken Curry with Rice 1 serving pack		
Chicken......................................	13	200
Rice	50	200
Lean Cuisine Range – 1 packet		
Beef Julienne	35	250
Chicken A L'Orange	30	270
Chicken & Oriental Vegetables	40	260
Chicken Cacciatore	25	260
Glazed Chicken............................	25	270

	Carbohydrate in grams	Calories
ICELAND		
Bangers & Mash		
per pack.........................	90	925
Bangers Beans & Mash		
per pack.........................	100	990
Rump Steak Platter		
340g pack.....................	40	450
Sliced Beef Dinner		
340g pack.....................	45	470
Sliced Chicken Dinner		
340g pack.....................	65	680
Sliced Lamb Dinner		
340g pack.....................	35	450
Sliced Pork Dinner		
340g pack.....................	15	360
Sliced Turkey Meal		
340g pack.....................	30	305
KATIE'S KITCHEN		
Beef Stew & Dumplings		
16oz/454g pack	75	800
MARKS AND SPENCER		
Bangers & Mash		
10oz/283g pack	50	415
Steak & Kidney Pie Meal		
12oz/369g pack	55	715
McCAIN		
Menu Classics –		
Chinese Chicken		
296g pack	40	270
Chicken Italienne		
291g pack	40	260
Oriental Beef		
290g pack	30	280
Oven Meals –		
Chicken & Chips		
260g pack	50	445
Farmsteak Onion Ring & Chips		
265g pack	50	500
Ribsteak & Chips		
283.5g pack	45	560
MR CHANG'S READY MEALS		
Sweet & Sour Pork		
6oz/170g pack............................	35	350
ROBERT WILSON		
Chicken Curry		
392g tin........................	30	315

SAFEWAY

	Carbohydrate in grams	Calories
Mash & Bangers		
283g pack	**35**	**475**

TESCO

	Carbohydrate in grams	Calories
Bangers and Mash		
(Serves 2) 283g pack	**35**	**445**
Beef in Beer with New Potatoes		
(Serves 1) 300g pack	**30**	**335**
Beef Stroganoff		
(Serves 1) 325g pack	**55**	**525**
Crofters Pie		
(Serves 1) 330g pack	**40**	**375**

W A TURNER

	Carbohydrate in grams	Calories
Bangers & Mash (2 servings)		
24oz/682g pack	**60**	**970**
Oven Chip Meals – 1 packet		
Chicken Pie	**80**	**710**
Cottage Pie	**75**	**645**
Grill Steak	**60**	**670**
Sausage in Rich Sauce	**65**	**675**
Steak & Kidney Pie	**75**	**795**

VEGETARIAN PREPARED DISHES

ALLINSON

Vegetable Gourmet Ready Meals – 400g packs	Carbohydrate in grams	Calories
Ravioli Verdi	50	530
Vegetable Dhansak	40	230
Vegetable Sweet & Sour	60	470

BE-WELL NUTRITIONAL PRODUCTS

8 Amazing Grains Range – 1 serving sachet

Cereal Savour	145	665
Mixed Grain Vegetable Paella	90	440
Savoury Couscous	135	660
Sultan's Pilaf	100	505

Easy Beans range – 1 serving sachet

Bean Stew Mix	55	275
Lentil Curry Mix	40	220
Spaghetti Bean Bolognaise	60	300

BIRDS EYE

MenuMaster Vegetable Meals –

Vegetable Curry/Pilau Rice 1 packet	75	400
Vegetable Lasagne 1 packet	35	365

BOOTS

Lasagne 400g pack	60	415
Rissotto 400g pack	100	535
Vegetarian Soup Mix 1oz dry mix	20	95

Vegetarian Soup Mix – 1 packet

Spicy Vegetable Soup	40	235
Thick Green Bean	35	205
Thick Potato	35	205

FINDUS

Lean Cuisinne Range – 1 packet

Zucchini Lasagne	30	260

GRANOSE

Nuttolene

10oz/284g pack	30	850
15oz/425g pack	45	1270

HALDANE FOODS – HERA

Soup Mix – 125g packet

Farmhouse Vegetable	80	470
Minestrone	80	480

	Carbohydrate in grams	Calories
Tomato	75	455
Vegetable Goulash	65	470
Vegetable Cottage Pie		
(Serves 3) 213g pack	125	830
Tofeata Range		
Okara Patties (1)	20	240
Savoury Burger (1)	25	410
Spicy Burger (1)	38	350
Vegetable Cottage Pie		
(Serves 3) 213g pack	125	830
Vegetable Stew with Dumplings		
8oz/227g pack	150	780

HOLLAND & BARRETT
Flans – 450g		
Curried Lentil	135	1120
Potato, Cheese & Onion	125	1635
Quiche – 395g		
Brocolli & Cottage Cheese	70	655
Veg. Cheddar Mixed Pepper	70	810

ICELAND
Country Vegetable Pie		
400g pack	60	445
Vegetable Lasagne		
400g pack	45	430

MARKS AND SPENCER
Onion Bhajjis		
7oz/199g pack	23	420
Vegetable Casserole & Dumplings		
10oz/283g pack	35	305
Vegetable Samosas		
7oz/199g pack	60	480

PREWETT'S
Heat & Serve Main Meals – 400g packs		
Tortellini	45	335
Wholemeal Cannelloni	55	415
Wholemeal Lasagne	50	365
Wholemeal Ravioli	50	335
Vegetarian Meals – 400g packs		
Bolognese Sauce	30	175
Lentil Stew	55	280
Vegetable Curry	50	300
Vegetable Goulash	50	230

SAFEWAY
Onion Bhajia (1)	18	115
Vegetable Samosa (1)	9	85

VEGETARIAN FEASTS
Vegetarian Sausage Slice (1) 6 95

WAITROSE
Vegetable Moussaka
  1lb/454g pack 60 640
Vegetable Samosa 2oz 15 125

Rice Dishes

	Carbohydrate in grams	Calories
BATCHELORS		
Savoury Rice - 1 packet		
Beef/Chicken Flavour......................	100	435
Golden......................................	100	440
Mild Curry..................................	105	465
Mixed Vegetables	100	420
Mushroom	100	450
Special Chinese Fried.......................	100	635
Special Hawaiian Fried......................	110	660
Special Spicy Barbecue Fried..............	100	625
Special Indian Fried.........................	105	685
Special Sweet and Sour Fried	115	665
BAXTERS		
Scampi Dishes - 312g pack		
Americaine with Rice	55	340
Francaise with Rice..........................	55	355
Indienne with Rice	50	355
Provencale with Rice........................	50	295
Thermidor with Rice.........................	55	360
BIRDS EYE		
Chicken & Seafood Paella		
1 packet	45	270
KELLOGG		
Boil in the Bag Rice - 1 sachet		
all flavours...................................	85	365
ICELAND		
Beef Curry & Rice		
369g pack....................................	60	525
Chicken Curry & Rice		
369g pack....................................	60	465
Chilly Con Carne with Rice		
369g pack....................................	85	520
Prawn Curry with Rice		
375g pack....................................	40	265
Vegetable Chilli & Rice		
390g pack....................................	60	340
Vegetable Curry & Rice		
395g pack....................................	55	360
LOCKWOODS		
Rice Salad		
230g pack....................................	50	270

	Carbohydrate in grams	Calories
MARKS AND SPENCER		
Chicken Curry with Pilau Rice		
(Serves 1) 340g pack	40	330
Chinese Style Rice		
283g pack	60	430
Sweet & Sour Chicken with Rice		
(Serves 1) 354g pack	50	350
MR CHANG'S READY MEALS		
Special Fried Rice		
6oz/170g pack	50	270
SAFEWAY		
Beef Madras Curry (frozen)		
340g pack	65	560
Chicken Korma Curry (frozen)		
340g pack	70	500
Savoury Rice – 125g packs		
Chicken & Sweetcorn	100	445
Curry	100	430
Golden Vegetable	95	420
Mixed Vegetables	100	420
Mushroom & Peppers	100	430
Spanish Rice	95	420
Tomato	100	415
TESCO		
Rice & Vegetable Salad		
250g pack	70	340
Savoury Rice – 120g packets		
all flavours	90-95	400-420
WHITWORTHS		
Savoury Rice – 1 packet		
Beef Flavour	90	390
Curry	90	385
Mixed Vegetable	95	410
WHOLE EARTH		
Brown Rice & Vegetables		
298g tin	95	460

Sausages, Sausage Products

There is very little variation in the carbohydrate and calorie content of sausages from one manufacturer to another, and this includes those with added spices, herbs etc. The table below is an accurate guide and the figures given are for the UNCOOKED product. Sausages by their nature are high in fat, therefore, we strongly recommend that they are always GRILLED and NEVER fried.

	Carbohydrate in grams	Calories
Beef Chipolatas		
12 to 1lb (1).....................	4-5	120-150
Beef Sausages		
Thick 8 to 1lb (1)...............	8	180
Thick Economy 8 to 1lb (1)....	8-10	200-240
Thin 16 to 1lb (1)...............	2-4	90-110
Thin Economy 16 to 1lb (1)....	3-4	100-120
Skinless 16 to 1lb (1)..........	2-4	100-120
Pork Chipolatas		
12 to 1lb (1).....................	3-4	120-140
Pork Sausages		
Jumbo 4 to 1lb (1)	15	340
Skinless 16 to 1lb (1)..........	2	90
Thick 8 to 1lb (1)...............	5-8	180-220
Thick Economy 8 to 1lb (1)....	7-9	180-220
Thin 16 to 1lb (1)	2-3	90-110
Thin Economy 16 to 1lb (1)....	3	100
Pork Sausagemeat		
16oz/454g	40	1240
Pork & Beef Chipolatas		
12 to 1lb (1).....................	4-5	100-120
Pork & Beef Sausages		
Jumbo 4 to 1lb (1)	14-16	300-340
Skinless 16 to 1lb (1)..........	3	80
Thick 8 to 1lb (1)...............	7	150-170
Thick Economy 8 to 1lb (1)....	7	150-160
Thin 16 to 1lb (1)	3-4	70-80
Pork & Beef Sausagemeat		
16oz/454g	60	1100
Pork & Tomato Sausages		
Thick 8 to 1lb (1)...............	5	190
Thin 16 to 1lb (1)	3	95
Turkey & Pork Sausages		
Thick 8 to 1lb (1)...............	8	150

There is very little variation in the carbohydrate and calorie content of certain chilled/fresh sausage products. Below is a useful guide for all the popular loose and pre-packed meats.

	Carbohydrate in grams	Calories
Bierwurst 1oz...................................	neg	80
Bratwurst 1oz	1	95

SAUSAGE PRODUCTS - Continued

	Carbohydrate in grams	Calories
Cervelat 1oz	neg	130
Garlic Sausage 1oz	1-2	70-85
Ham Sausage 1oz	1-2	40-50
Luncheon Sausage 1oz	1	85
Polony 1oz	1-2	65-70
Pudding		
Black 1oz	5-7	100
Fruit 1oz	12	100
White 1oz	10	135
Salami 1oz	neg	140-170

BEJAM
Savoury Eggs (1)	9	200

BERNARD MATTHEWS
Turkey & Pork Sausages (uncooked) (1)	7	165

BOWYERS
Savoury Eggs (1)	10	150
Scotch Eggs (1)	23	350
Small Fries (1)	2	35

BUXTED
Chicken Sausages when grilled (1)	9	145

CO-OP
Hot-Dogs in Brine
1 from a 415g tin	1	45

FINDUS
Toad-in-the-Hole
6oz/170g tray	35	355

FRESHBAKE FOODS
Roundas - Sausage
with Beans (1)	18	190
with Cheese (1)	15	210

Sausages - reduced fat
Pork (1)	5	145
Pork & Beef (1)	6	130

ICELAND
Cheese & Onion Savoury Eggs (1)	11	155
Savoury Eggs (1)	12	160

MARKS AND SPENCER
Picnic Eggs
1 from pack of 4	6	185

Scotch Eggs
1 from pack of 2	14	355

	Carbohydrate in grams	Calories
MATTESSON WALLS		
Frankfurters (1)	1	165
MILLERS		
Scotch Egg (1)	26	350
PLUMROSE		
Cocktail/Party Sausages (1)	neg	20
Hot Dog Sausages (2)	1	40
ROBIRCH		
Scotch Egg		
1 from a pack of 2 or 6	10	225
ROSS		
Scotch Fritters with Beans (1)	19	250
Scotch Fritters with Cheese (1)	16	250
SAINSBURY		
Scotch Eggs		
1 from pack of 2	23	345
SAXBY'S		
Scotch Eggs (1)	24	315
TESCO		
Hot Dog Sausages		
226g tin	4	740
Savoury Eggs (1)	10	160

Snacks, Nuts & Sweets

LOW SUGAR

Crisps usually contain 30-40% fat. Therefore they must be an AMBER choice in the diet despite the fact that they contain no sugar and have a reasonable Dietary Fibre content. We have placed the newer ranges of Reduced Fat crisps in the GREEN section if their fat content is 25% and below. However, you are reminded that a packet of crisps still contributes a significant amount of fat to the diet so a maximum use of once a day is recommended, even if the product is in the GREEN section.

	Carbohydrate in grams	Calories
BAHLSEN BISCUITS		
Chipsletten Barbecue		
100g packet	60	520
Chipsletten Paprika		
100g packet	65	510
Salzbrezel		
75g packet	55	315
Salzletten		
75g packet	60	300
Zoo		
150g packet	115	660
BEJAM		
Cheese Shapes		
250g packet	140	1320
Crisps Ready Salted		
200g packet	100	1090
Potato Sticks		
200g packet	115	1010
BN BISCUITS AND FOODS		
Jump Bars –		
Apple (1)	11	80
BOOKER HEALTH		
Barbaras Cookies –		
Fruit & Nut (1)	23	205
Oatmeal & Raisin (1)	23	228
BURTON'S		
Chicken 'n' Chips 1 packet	15	155
Fish 'n' Chips 1 packet	15	155
Piglets 1 packet	11	80
Smax 1 packet	16	130
CALLARD & BOWSER		
Summer Fayre		
Moist Muesli Bar (1)	21	140

	Carbohydrate in grams	Calories

CHESHIRE WHOLEFOODS
Sesame Sticks

	Carbohydrate in grams	Calories
75g packet	20	300

CO-OP
Chip Snacks

50g packet	30	245

Crisps — all flavours

25g packet	10	135
75g packet	30	390

Onion Rings

50g packet	30	260

Streaky Crispies

50g packet	30	230

CRAWFORDS

Cheese Snips 30g packet...................	16	160

FOX'S
Natural Crunch Bars

Fruit and Nut (1)............................	13	95
Honey and Oat (1)	12	90

GOLDEN WONDER
Crackles

1 packet	10	90

Crisps - all flavours

25g packet	10	125
28g packet	12	140
35g packet	15	180
50g packet	20	250
100g packet.................................	40	500

Jacket Crisps - all flavours

1 packet	12	155

Odduns - all flavours

1 packet	15	120

Ringos - all flavours

1 packet	15	100

Stix - all flavours

1 packet	20	120

Wotsits - all flavours

1 packet	15	130

HEDGEHOG FOODS
"Hedgehog Brand" - crisps, all flavours

27g packet	10	100

HOLLAND AND BARRETT

Bombay Mix 1oz	8	140
Dessert Island Delight 1oz...................	9	160
Safari Munch Mix 1oz........................	9	130
Tropical Nut Cocktail 1oz....................	8	145

HOLLY MILL	Carbohydrate in grams	Calories
Apple & Hazelnut Bar (1)	17	150
Apricot & Almond Bar (1)	18	140
Avalanche Citrus Flavour Bar (1)	21	195
Avalanche Fruit & Nut Bar (1)	20	190
Banana Fruit Bar (1)	20	95
Carob Chip Bar (1)	18	150
Castaway – 40g bars		
Apple & Hazelnut (1)	25	200
Banana (1)	27	215
Original (1)	24	200
Crunchy Square Snack (1)	25	190
Muesli Square Snack (1)	32	220
Oat & Sesame Bar (1)	17	135
Oat & Sunflower Bar (1)	17	140
Oat Apple & Raisin Bar (1)	25	170
Oat Apricot & Almond Bar (1)	26	200
Protein Square Snack (1)	17	185
Roasted Peanut Bar (1)	14	160
JORDANS		
Chewy Bar		
with Raisin & Hazelnut (1)	17	120
with Raspberry & Apple (1)	18	120
Original Crunchy Bars		
with Coconut and Honey (1)	17	140
with Honey and Almonds (1)	16	135
with Orange and Carob (1)	17	140
KP		
Cheesy Crunchies		
16g packet	11	80
Crispi – 1 packet		
Beefies	10	80
Meanies	8	60
Crisps – all flavours		
28g packet	11	140
1 from multi-pack (25g)	10	125
Crunchy Waffles – all flavours		
30g packet	15	160
Discos – all flavours		
35g packet	18	170
Dry Roast Peanuts – all flavours		
50g packet	5	280
100g packet	10	555
Hula Hoops – all flavours		
30g packet	18	160
64g packet	40	340
McCoy's – all flavours		
40g packet	17	195
Minichips – all flavours		
30g packet	17	150

KP – Continued

	Carbohydrate in grams	Calories
Mixed Nuts and Raisins		
50g packet	11	245
Peanuts and Raisins		
100g packet	30	445
Skips – all flavours		
18g packet	10	95
Space Raiders – all flavours		
26g packet	15	125
Trebles		
50g packet	20	220
100g packet	40	440
Tropical Blend		
100g packet	35	445
Twirlers – all flavours		
32g packet	18	175
LITTLEWOODS		
Burger Bites		
50g packet	30	275
Crisps		
1 from multipack/variety pack	12	140
Crinkle Cut 75g packet	40	400
Family Pack 150g packet	75	800
Ready Salted 75g packet	40	420
Spring Onion 75g packet	40	410
Crunchy Sticks – 50g packet		
Ready Salted	32	240
Salt & Vinegar	32	240
Onion Rings		
50g packet	30	250
Pizza Bites		
50g packet	30	275
Salt & Pepper Fries		
50g packet	35	220
MARKS AND SPENCER		
Burger Bites		
50g packet	25	270
Corn Chips – Californian		
75g packet	40	420
Crisps — 75g packet		
Bar-B-Q Beef and Onion	35	400
Cheese and Onion	35	410
Crinkle Cut	50	365
Prawn Cocktail	35	405
Ready Salted	40	410
Salt and Vinegar	35	395
Deltas		
100g packet	60	515
Multipack Crisps – 25g packet		
Ready Salted	13	140
Shakers	12	140

	Carbohydrate in grams	Calories
Pistachios Nuts		
60g packet	12	360
Potato Rings		
75g packet	45	390
Potato Sticks		
75g packet	45	380
Potato Thins		
50g packet	30	240
Potato Waffles		
40g packet	20	185
Prawn Cocktail Snacks		
50g packet	25	245
Prawn Crackers		
40g packet	25	175
Salt and Vinegar Chiplets		
50g packet	35	245
Sizzles		
50g packet	25	230
Tortilla Chips		
100g packet	65	475
Wheat Crunchies		
75g packet	50	365
McVITIE'S		
Mini Cheddars		
30g packet	16	160
NABISCO		
Cheese Sticks all flavours (1)	1	22
NUT KERNAL PRODUCTS		
Friendships		
1 packet	9	75
Onion Rings		
Jumbo pack	16	130
Small pack	8	65
Prairie Wheels		
1 packet	8	65
Salt & Vinegar Rings		
Jumbo pack	16	130
Shrimps		
1 packet	9	75
Starfish		
Jumbo pack	21	175
Thinga-Me-Bobs		
Jumbo pack	18	150
Small pack	9	75
Thinga-Me-Jigs		
Jumbo pack	18	150
Small pack	9	75
Yankee Stars		
1 packet	9	75

	Carbohydrate in grams	Calories
PHILEAS FOGG		
Californian Corn Chips		
40g packet	20	225
100g packet	50	575
Mignon Morceaux		
40g packet	25	200
100g packet	55	510
Shanghai Nuts		
100g packet	50	520
Tortilla Chips		
40g packet	25	190
100g packet	65	475
PLANTERS		
Sesame Crunch		
40g packet	10	240
80g packet	20	480
QUAKER		
Harvest Chewy Bars		
Fruit & Nut (1)	15	110
SAFEWAY		
Bacon Streaks		
50g packet	32	230
Crisps – all flavours		
25g packet	10	125
1 from multi-pack......................	10	125
75g packet	30	375
150g packet	60	750
Crispy Squares 50g packet		
Ready Salted	30	240
Salt & Vinegar........................	30	230
Mixes – 100g packet		
Carnival Mix..........................	80	340
Trial Mix.............................	35	495
Tropical Mix	60	450
Onion Rings		
50g packet	30	250
Ready Salted Crunchy Sticks		
75g packet	50	360
Ready Salted Potato Sticks		
75g packet	45	380
Salt and Vinegar Crunchy Sticks		
75g packet	50	360
Salt and Vinegar Twirls		
50g packet	35	220
Savoury Puffs		
50g packet	20	300
Wheat Crunchies		
75g packet	50	365

SAINSBURY

	Carbohydrate in grams	Calories
Bacon Crispies		
50g packet	30	235
Cheese Flavour Puffs		
50g packet	30	260
Cheese Flavour Snacks		
50g packet	35	245
Cheesy Nik Naks		
75g packet	50	115
Crisps		
Cheese and Onion		
75g packet	30	375
Ready Salted		
25g packet	10	130
75g packet	30	390
Salt and Vinegar		
25g packet	10	125
75g packet	30	375
Crunch Bars		
Fruit, Bran & Honey (1)	21	140
Onion Rings		
50g packet	30	260
Potato Squares		
50g packet	30	275
Prawn Cocktail Snacks		
50g packet	25	270
Ready Salted Potato Chips		
75g packet	42	390

SMITHS

	Carbohydrate in grams	Calories
Cheezers		
1 packet	12	150
Chipsticks – all flavours		
1 packet	15	120
Crisps – all flavours		
1 packet	12	150
Frazzles		
1 packet	16	125
Mixed Nuts and Raisins		
30g packet	8	135
Monster Munch – all flavours		
1 packet	17	155
Quavers Cheese		
1 packet	10	100
Savoury Moments		
28g packet	13	145
Scampi/Bacon Fries		
1 packet	15	125
Square Crisps		
1 packet	15	125
Tubes		
1 packet	15	130
Twists		
1 packet	14	85

SOONER FOODS

	Carbohydrate in grams	Calories
Caribbean Cocktail		
40g packet	12	200
Champs		
1 packet	18	60
Crisps		
27g packet	14	145
Mixed Nuts & Raisins		
25g packet	4	125
Nik-Naks		
30g packet	20	150
Rounders		
1 packet	18	105
Wheat Crunchies		
30g packet	20	145

SUN-PAT

Salted Mixed Nuts		
198g tin	24	1200

SUNWHEEL FOODS

Kalibu No Added Sugar Carob - 60g bars		
Fruit & Nut	25	290
Krunchy Bran 'n' Raisin	26	260
Peanut	22	305
Peppermint	25	295
Plain/Orange	25	295
Kalibu No Added Sugar Yogurt		
Coated Snacks - 30g bars		
Banana	15	100
Yogurt Break - 60g bars		
all flavours	27	315

TESCO

Bacon Bites		
50g packet	35	225
Bombay Mix		
150g packet	65	720
Corn Curls		
50g packet	25	85
Crisps - all flavours		
1 from multi-pack (25g)	13	140
75g packet	40	410
100g packet	50	570
150g packet	75	820
Crunch Curls		
50g packet	25	85
Crunchy Sticks — 75g packet		
Ready Salted	55	330
Salt and Vinegar	50	350
Exotic Fruit and Nut Mix		
100g packet	45	455

TESCO - Continued	Carbohydrate in grams	Calories
Nuts Raisins & Choc Chips		
150g packet	45	695
Onion Rings		
50g packet	32	250
Potato Chips – all flavours		
75g packet	40	400
Potato Rings		
75g packet	45	395
Potato Triangles		
100g packet	60	485
Prawn Cocktail Snacks		
50g packet	30	255
Tortilla Chips		
100g packet	65	500
Yoghurt Coated Raisins		
100g packet	65	450
THE WRIGLEY COMPANY		
Orbit Chewing Gum		
Peppermint 1 stick	neg	10
Spearmint 1 stick	neg	10
TREBOR		
Coolmints Sugar Free (1)	1	6
TUCKER FOODS		
Nature's Choice Jacket Potato Crisps		
1 packet	12	150
TUDOR		
Crisps – all flavours		
25g packet	12	150
WAITROSE		
Bacon Snacks		
50g packet	30	235
Cheese Puffs		
50g packet	25	300
Cheese Savouries		
100g packet	55	520
Cheese Twists		
100g packet	50	465
Crinkle Crisps		
75g packet	37	400
Crisps – all flavours		
1 from multi-pack/six pack	12	140
75g packet	32	400
Crispy Thins		
100g packet	60	485
Exotic Fruit & Nuts		
100g packet	60	450

	Carbohydrate in grams	Calories
Fruit Nuts & Seeds		
100g packet	40	470
Onion Rings		
50g packet	30	250
Potato Rings		
113g packet	70	585
Potato Sticks		
113g packet	65	575
Prawn Cocktail Snacks		
50g packet	30	260
Salt & Vinegar Potato Swirls		
50g packet	35	215
Salt & Vinegar Savoury Sticks		
50g packet	32	245
Tropical Fruit & Nuts		
100g packet	50	470
Wheat Crunchies		
75g packet	50	360
Yogurt Coated Fruit & Nuts		
200g packet	75	1140
WALKERS		
Crisps – all flavours		
28g packet	15	160
French Fries		
1 packet	18	100
Say Cheese		
26g packet	15	140
Snaps		
1 packet	9	70

Soups

BATCHELORS

	Carbohydrate in grams	Calories
Cup-a-Soup — 1 sachet		
Beef and Tomato	16	80
Chicken	15	100
Chicken and Leek	15	95
Golden Vegetable	15	80
Mushroom	16	110
Oxtail	15	90
Tomato	17	90
Vegetable and Beef	14	90
Cup-a-Soup Foreign — 1 sachet		
Chinese Sweetcorn with Chicken	12	65
Indian Mild Curry	13	70
Mexican Spicy Tomato	17	85
Oriental Beef & Mushroom	11	60
Cup-a-Soup (Special) — 1 sachet		
Beef & Tomato with Croutons	17	100
Cream of Asparagus with Croutons	19	140
Cream of Chicken & Sweetcorn with Croutons	16	125
Cream of Chicken & Vegetable with Croutons	14	125
Cream of Vegetables with Croutons	18	135
French Onion with Croutons	8	55
Minestrone with Croutons	13	80
Tomato and Vegetable with Croutons	22	135
Vegetable & Beef with Croutons	17	100
1 Pint Soups — 1 sachet		
Beef & Tomato	30	180
Chicken & Vegetable	40	300
Chicken Noodle	25	135
Cream of Chicken	30	335
Cream of Mushroom	40	295
Cream of Tomato	60	360
Cream of Tomato & Vegetable	55	350
Cream of Vegetable	40	310
Farmhouse Vegetable	30	150
Golden Vegetable	35	235
Lincoln Pea	45	265
Minestrone	30	135
Oxtail	25	190
Spring Vegetable	25	105
Vegetable & Beef	25	145
2 Pint Soups — 1 sachet		
Chicken Noodle	50	270
Cream of Chicken	65	670
Cream of Mushroom	75	590
Cream of Tomato	115	725
Farmhouse Vegetable	55	295

	Carbohydrate in grams	Calories
BATCHELORS – Continued		
Minestrone..................................	55	265
Slim-a-Soup — 1 sachet		
Beef & Tomato/Chicken....................	6	40
Chicken & Leek..............................	6	40
Clear Beef with Croutons	4	40
Clear Chicken with Croutons..............	3	40
Golden Vegetable..........................	7	40
Vegetable & Beef...........................	7	40
Slim-a-Soup Special — 1 sachet		
Beef & Vegetable...........................	8	60
Chicken & Vegetable.......................	11	60
Golden Vegetable..........................	11	60
Minestrone.................................	11	60
Snack-A-Soup — 1 sachet		
Beef 'n' Tomato with Croutons	28	160
Chicken 'n' Mushroom with Croutons.....	30	200
Chicken 'n' Sweetcorn with Croutons	28	160
BAXTERS		
Soups — 15oz/425g tins		
Beef & Pepper	30	200
Chicken Broth...............................	25	145
Cock-a-Leekie Soup.........................	20	100
Cream of Asparagus Soup	20	280
Cream of Chicken Soup....................	20	280
Cream of Leek Soup........................	20	220
Cream of Mushroom Soup.................	25	230
Cream of Pheasant Soup	20	260
Cream of Scampi Soup.....................	25	245
Cream of Smoked Trout Soup.............	20	240
Cream of Tomato Soup.....................	40	300
French Onion Soup	20	115
Game Consomme	3	40
Highlander's Broth..........................	30	190
Lentil Soup.................................	45	225
Lobster Bisque..............................	30	270
Minestrone Soup	30	155
Oxtail Soup..................................	20	200
Pea and Ham Soup	45	245
Poachers Broth..............................	20	175
Royal Game Soup	25	180
Scotch Salmon Bisque	25	335
Scotch Broth	35	200
Scotch Vegetable Soup.....................	25	120
CAMPBELLS		
Bumper Harvest Soups — 15oz/425g tins		
Chicken.....................................	20	190
Lentil..	40	200
Minestrone..................................	40	190
Mushroom	20	180

CAMPBELLS - Continued

	Carbohydrate in grams	Calories
Ox Tail	25	190
Pea	50	245
Scotch Broth	30	170
Tomato	45	250
Vegetable	40	170
Condensed Soups — 4.9oz/140g tins		
Cream of Celery	7	115
Cream of Chicken	10	140
Cream of Mushroom	8	120
Cream of Tomato	20	175
Golden Vegetable	15	70
Lentil	20	125
Ox Tail	15	120
Scotch Broth	15	100
Turkey & Vegetable Broth	20	110
Vegetable	20	95
Condensed Soups — 10.4oz/295g tins		
Chicken Rice	25	150
Consommé	neg	25
Cream of Celery	15	245
Cream of Chicken	20	290
Cream of Leek & Potato	25	320
Cream of Mushroom	15	250
Golden Vegetable	30	140
Minestrone	40	235
Oxtail & Vegetable	60	180
Tomato	40	195
Condensed Soups — 10.6oz/300g tins		
Beef Broth	35	205
Chicken Noodle	20	105
Cream of Tomato	40	370
Lentil	40	265
Ox Tail	30	260
Pea & Ham	60	370
Scotch Broth	35	215
Tomato Rice	55	290
Turkey & Vegetable Broth	35	230
Vegetable	45	205
Condensed Soups — 19oz/540g tins		
Cream of Chicken	35	530
Cream of Tomato	75	665
Golden Vegetable	50	255
Lentil	70	475
Scotch Broth	60	385
Vegetable	85	365
Granny's Soups — 15oz/425g tins		
Chicken	30	255
Chicken and Vegetable Broth with Rice	25	160
Lentil	45	235
Pea and Ham	45	255
Potato and Leek	40	185

CAMPBELLS – Continued	Carbohydrate in grams	Calories
Scotch Broth	35	215
Tomato	45	195
Vegetable	35	165
Vegetable Broth with Beef	30	150
Main Course Soups — 15oz/425g tins		
Beef and Vegetable	30	240
Chicken and Vegetable	30	220
Chilli Con Carne	40	265
Steak & Potato	35	225
Steak, Kidney and Vegetable	30	240
Superior Soups — 295g tins		
Asparagus	20	185
Chicken and Sweetcorn	25	265
Crab Bisque	20	225
Cream of Smoked Salmon	20	320
French Onion	15	90
Goulash	35	260
CO-OP		
Soup – 10oz/283g tins		
Cream of Chicken Soup	15	175
Cream of Mushroom Soup	15	160
Cream of Tomato Soup	30	215
Oxtail Soup	15	120
Vegetable Soup	20	95
Soup – 15oz/425g tins		
Cream of Chicken Soup	20	260
Cream of Mushroom Soup	20	235
Cream of Tomato Soup	40	320
Lentil Soup	25	140
Oxtail Soup	25	180
Vegetable Soup	30	145
Cup Soup – 1 sachet		
all flavours	9-15	60-70
Special Cup Soup – 1 sachet		
all flavours	14-22	80-130
CROSSE AND BLACKWELL		
Four Seasons Soup – 400ml pack		
Cream of Mushroom	20	195
Five Vegetable & Beef	25	145
Highland Game	21	130
Lentil & Bacon	22	255
Oriental Chicken & Vegetable	18	170
Oxtail	22	170
Spicy Beef	35	200
Soupe De Poisson	15	145
Tomato	40	285
Ready to Serve Soup – 10oz/283g tins		
Cream of Chicken	13	180
Cream of Mushroom	9	155

CROSSE AND BLACKWELL — Continued

	Carbohydrate in grams	Calories
Harvest Thick Vegetable	30	150
Oxtail........................	15	140
Vegetable........................	30	135
Ready to Serve Soup - 15oz/425g tins		
Cream of Chicken........................	20	270
Cream of Mushroom	15	230
Creamed Tomato	45	300
Harvest Thick Vegetable	45	225
Oxtail........................	20	210
Vegetable........................	40	200
Speciality Soups - 15oz/425g tins		
Consomme........................	2	95
Vichyssoise	15	200

HEINZ

	Carbohydrate in grams	Calories
Big Soups - 15.3oz/435g tins		
Beef and Vegetable	30	150
Beef Broth	25	130
Chicken and Vegetable	30	180
Golden Vegetable........................	30	160
Vegetable........................	35	170
Ready to Serve Soups - 10.2oz/290g tins		
Cream of Chicken........................	15	135
Cream of Mushroom	15	130
Oxtail........................	20	125
Ready to Serve Soups - 10.6oz/300g tins		
Beef Broth	20	120
Beef Soup........................	15	110
Cream of Celery	15	130
Cream of Tomato	30	190
Golden Chicken and Mushroom	15	125
Golden Chicken and Vegetable	20	100
Golden Vegetable Soup	25	125
Homestyle Country Vegetable	25	130
Homestyle Potato & Leek..................	25	110
Homestyle Beef & Vegetable	20	120
Minestrone........................	15	95
Scotch Broth	20	120
Vegetable........................	20	110
Ready to Serve Soups - 15.3oz/435g tins		
Invaders Soup	50	310
Mulligatawny	20	210
Scottish Vegetable with Lentils............	30	190
Spring Vegetable	35	145
Special Recipe Soups - 425g tins		
Cock-a-Leekie	15	85
Cream of Asparagus	20	185
Cream of Chicken with White Wine	20	215
Game	20	130
Weight Watchers Soups - 295g tins		
Asparagus/Celery/Chicken	10	65

	Carbohydrate in grams	Calories
Beef Noodle	8	55
Chicken and Vegetable	11	60
Chicken Noodle	10	55
Mushroom	10	70
Oxtail	9	75
Spring Vegetable/Vegetable	14	65
Tomato	13	75
Vegetable and Beef	12	70

KNORR
1.5 pint packets

Chicken Noodle	30	190
Cornish Seafood	45	280
Crofter's Thick Vegetable	45	250
Farmhouse Chicken and Leek	35	235
Florida Spring Vegetable	20	110
Highland Lentil	50	300
Minestrone	45	250
Oxtail	40	250
Pea Soup with Ham	35	210
Virginia Sweetcorn	55	330
Cream of Quick Soups with Croutons – 1 sachet		
all flavours	16	140
Low Calorie Quick Soups – 1 sachet		
all flavours	7	30-40
Quick Soups – 1 sachet		
all flavours except Tomato	10-12	65-90
Tomato	16	95

Special Recipe Quick Soups with Croutons – 1 sachet

Bacon & Mushroom	13	90
Chicken and Ham	13	100
Chicken & Vegetable	14	105
Country Vegetable	10	90
Lentil & Lamb	13	80
Minestrone	14	90
Tomato Vegetable & Beef	15	80

LITTLEWOODS
Canned Soup – 425g tin

Chicken	20	250
Ox Tail	25	190
Tomato	25	235
Vegetable	25	190

Packet Soup – 1 pint

Chicken	20	380
Minestrone	25	340
Oxtail	25	350
Spring Vegetable	25	320
Thick Vegetable	25	360
Tomato	25	320

MARKS AND SPENCER

Soups - 15oz/425g tins	Carbohydrate in grams	Calories
Beef & Vegetable	35	325
Chicken & Vegetable	35	250
Cream of Asparagus	25	275
Cream of Smoked Trout	25	265
Cream of Tomato	25	235
Lobster Bisque	25	215
Mediterranean Vegetable	25	170
Pea and Ham	40	260

MR CHANG

	Carbohydrate in grams	Calories
Chicken and Sweetcorn 8oz/241g pack	12	110

SAFEWAY

Canned Soup - 15oz/425g tins	Carbohydrate in grams	Calories
Cream of Chicken	20	260
Cream of Mushroom	20	215
Cream of Tomato	30	255
Oxtail	20	155
Scotch Broth	30	160
Vegetable	45	215
Packet Soup - 1 pint packet		
Chicken Noodle	20	110
Cream of Asparagus	25	285
Cream of Mushroom	35	305
Cream of Tomato	55	355
Golden Vegetable	35	170
Minestrone	35	160
Oxtail	30	170
Spring Vegetable	25	135
Special Instant Soup-in-a-Cup - 1 sachet		
Chicken & Mushroom	20	110
Chicken & Vegetables & Croutons	15	100
French Onion & Croutons	10	70
Minestrone & Croutons	15	85
Tomato & Vegetables & Croutons	20	120

SAINSBURY

Gourmet Range - 425g tins	Carbohydrate in grams	Calories
Consomme	4	60
French Onion	10	110
Lobster Bisque	25	250
Vichysoisse	20	195
Soup - 15oz/425g tins		
Extra Thick Vegetable	40	215
Minestrone	30	195
Oxtail	20	215
Scotch Broth	25	235
Tomato	40	290
Vegetable	40	180

	Carbohydrate in grams	Calories
Packet Soup - 1 pint sachet		
Asparagus	25	265
Chicken	25	220
Chicken Noodle	30	170
French Onion	20	85
Minestrone	30	130
Onion	30	165
Spring Vegetable	20	90
Tomato	40	190

TESCO

	Carbohydrate in grams	Calories
Canned Soup - 425g tins		
Cream of Celery	17	185
Cream of Chicken	25	300
Cream of Mushroom	17	235
Cream of Tomato	35	250
Lentil	45	235
Minestrone/Thick Vegetable	40	220
Oxtail	20	195
Scotch Broth	30	260
Vegetable	30	160
Packet Soup - 1.5 pint sachet		
Asparagus	35	220
Chicken Noodle	45	220
French Style Onion	30	140
Minestrone	40	220
Mushroom	35	220
Oxtail	35	200
Scotch Broth	35	210
Spring Vegetable	35	140
Tomato	40	210

WAITROSE

	Carbohydrate in grams	Calories
Low Calorie Soup - 295g tins		
Asparagus/Mushroom	8	50
Celery/Tomato & Beef	10	60
Chicken & Vegetable	7	45
Tomato	8	55
Vegetable	15	65
Soups - 425g tins		
Beef Broth	25	170
Beef Consommé	5	60
Chicken	25	250
Chicken & Sweetcorn	25	225
Clam Chowder	20	185
Cock-a-Leekie	22	105
Crab Bisque	30	330
Cream of Asparagus	20	235
Cream of Celery	22	230
French Onion	15	65
Goulash	25	285

	Carbohydrate in grams	Calories
Lentil & Bacon	35	210
Lobster Bisque	25	215
Minestrone	45	200
Mushroom	20	225
Oxtail	25	160
Pea & Ham	40	240
Scotch Broth	30	160
Tomato	30	270
Vegetable	40	190
Vichyssoise	25	230

New Additions

New Additions

New Additions

New Additions

New Additions

New Additions

New Additions

New Additions

New Additions

New Additions

New Additions

RED SECTION

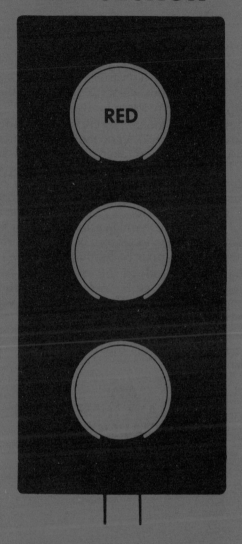

GO SLOW
Stop and think.
Try to save these foods
for special occasions.

Red - Watch Out!

Low in fibre . . . can be high in added sugar and fat . . . may also be high in calories, so even if you are not trying to lose weight, it is still advisable to limit your intake of these foods.

This does not mean they can never be eaten. Most dietitians would agree that a small amount of a Red Section Food taken as part of a prudent diet is quite acceptable. If you occasionally eat sweet foods, try to have them at the end of a meal rather than as an in-between meal snack. This is because the foods you have eaten in the meal (particularly the high fibre foods) can help to slow down the sharp rise in blood sugar which normally occurs after eating sugary foods.

Red Section Foods can be useful during illness (when appetite may be reduced), for treating hypoglycaemia (low blood sugar) or when exercising.

Seek the advice of your dietitian for further guidance on careful use of foods from this section.

RED
TRY TO SAVE THESE FOODS
FOR SPECIAL OCCASIONS

Biscuits

SWEET

	Carbohydrate in grams	Calories
ALLINSON		
Carob Bites all flavours (1)	3	24
Carob Fruit and Nut (1)	9	85
Carob Ginger and Bran (1)	10	75
Carob Oatmeal (1)	9	80
Carob Raisin & Bran Biscuits (1)	8	86
Wholemeal Tea Biscuits		
Ginger Biscuits (1)	8	54
Honey Biscuits (1)	8	50
Oatmeal Biscuits (1)	8	54
APPLEFORD'S		
Cluster Bars - 1 bar		
Apple & Hazelnut	18	115
Apricot & Chocolate Chip	19	115
Hazelnut & Raisin	19	125
Peanut & Almond	15	140
BAHLSEN BISCUITS		
Choco-Leibniz Milk (1)	9	72
Choco-Leibniz Plain (1)	9	72
Choco-Star M (1)	5	60
Waffeletten (1)	5	38
BEJAM		
Bourbon Cream Biscuits (1)	11	68
Custard Creams (1)	9	60
Ginger Nuts (1)	8	43
Half Coated Chocolate Biscuits (1)	9	65
Mini-Choc-Chip Cookies (1)	3	16
BN BISCUITS AND FOODS		
Jump Bars		
with Chocolate Chips (1)	10	85
with Raisin (1)	12	80
BOOTS		
Digestive Cream Biscuits (1)	9	62
Ginger Fingers (1)	6	33
Nice Biscuits (1)	5	30
BURTON'S		
Chocolate Chip Cookies (1)	6	51
Coconut Delights (1)	16	105
Coconut Macaroons (1)	6	50
Custard Creams (1)	9	62
Gingernuts (1)	8	44
Jaffa Cakes (1)	8	40

BURTON'S Continued	Carbohydrate in grams	Calories
Jammie Dodgers (1)	13	84
Milk Chocolate Homeblest (1)	9	70
Mint/Orange Viscount (1)	10	89
Mr. Men and Little Miss (1)	3	19
Teacakes (1)	7	43
Toffypops (1)	10	73
Wagon Wheels (1)	23	172

CADBURY

Animal Biscuits (1)	4	30
Bournville Assorted		
Oval (1)	7	50
Ring (1)	8	60
Sandwich (1)	10	80
Shamrock (1)	6	45
Wafer (1)	7	65
Bournville Digestive (1)	7	45
Butter Shorties (1)	7	45
Chocolate Cabarets (1)	7	45
Chocolate Fingers (1)	3	25
Coconut Coasters (1)	6	45
Cookies original (1)	7	45
Milk Assorted		
Oval (1)	7	55
Ring (1)	8	60
Sandwich (1)	10	75
Shamrock (1)	6	45
Wafer (1)	7	65
Milk Digestive (1)	6	50
Orange Cremes (1)	10	80

CHILTONIAN

Gingerella (1)	5	28

CO-OP

Ginger Nut (1)	8	42
Milk Cookie (1)	6	44

CRAWFORD

Bargain Bags		
Chocolate Chip and Hazelnut (1)	5	39
Chocolate Chip and Orange (1)	5	39
Ginger Snaps (1)	5	27
Iced Shorties (1)	7	41
Pennywise		
Bourbon Creams (1)	10	63
Custard Creams (1)	10	66
Frosted Creams (1)	9	43
Jam Rings (1)	10	63
Orange Creams (1)	5	58
Raspberry Creams (1)	10	66
Wafers (1)	5	46

	Carbohydrate in grams	Calories
DOVES FARM		
Wholemeal Bourbon (1)	8	60
FORTTS		
Chocolate Oliver (1)	12	69
FOX'S		
All Butter Sultana Cookie (1)	12	74
Bran Crunch (1)	5	36
Butter Crinkle (1)	6	37
Choc Chip and Almond Natural Crunch Bar (1)	13	100
Choc Chip Nut Shortie (1)	5	34
Ginger Finger (1)	6	32
Ginger Snaps (1)	7	35
Golden Crunch (1)	5	32
Nice (1)	5	38
Oaten Crunch (1)	5	36
Shortbread Finger (1)	7	60
Traditional Brandy Snap (1)	10	55
Triple Biscuits (1)	13	98
HOLLY MILL		
Ginger Cookies (1)	7	55
HUNTLEY AND PALMERS		
Butter Biscuits (1)	7	48
Coconut Biscuits (1)	5	51
Dutch Shortcake (1)	9	40
Lemon Puff (1)	9	80
Milk Chocolate Digestive (1)	9	66
Plain Chocolate Digestive (1)	9	65
Sponge Fingers (1)	5	21
ICELAND		
Bourbon Creams (1)	9	62
Coconut Rings (1)	7	49
Custard Creams (1)	9	63
Ginger Nuts (1)	9	44
Milk Chocolate Malted Milk (1)	7	53
Orange Creams (1)	9	63
Shorties (1)	7	49
ITONA		
Granny Ann Biscuits -		
Hi-Fi Biscuits (1)	15	110
Hi-Protein Biscuits (1)	6	65
JACOBS		
Club		
Coffee (1)	14	113
Fruit (1)	15	113

JACOBS - Continued

	Carbohydrate in grams	Calories
Milk (1)	15	117
Mint (1)	15	113
Orange (1)	15	113
Plain (1)	15	113
Wafer (1)	12	100
Coated Mallows (1)	9	46
Trio (1)	17	127

KP
Choc Dips - Mini Pots		
1 pot	19	175

LITTLEWOODS
Choc and Nut Cookies (1)	7	52
Jaffa Cakes (1)	7	40
Mallow Tea Cakes (1)	7	47
Milk Chocolate Sandwich		
all flavours (1)	13	100
Party Rings (1)	5	27
Toffee Biscuits (1)	11	76

LYONS
Maryland Cookie		
Choc Chip and Coconut (1)	6	51
Choc Chip and Hazelnut (1)	6	50

MACDONALDS
Taxi (1)	10	80
Yo Yo		
Mint (1)	13	100
Toffee (1)	15	98

MARKS AND SPENCER
All Butter Sultana Cookie (1)	12	75
Break In (1)	14	119
Butter Crunch Creams (1)	9	65
Chocolate Chip Cookie (1)	7	52
Crunchy Sandwich Bars (1)	13	100
Fruit & Nut Creams (1)	8	58
Ginger Snaps (1)	6	33
Half Coated Digestive		
Milk (1)	9	65
Plain (1)	9	65
Jaffa Cakes (1)	9	44
Milk Chocolate Caramel Wafers (1)	11	96
Milk Chocolate Crunch (1)	5	34
Muesli Cookies (1)	10	79
Plain Chocolate Biscuit Thins (1)	3	27
Plain Chocolate Ginger Biscuits (1)	10	64
Rich Tea Finger Creams (1)	7	51

MARKS & SPENCER – Continued

	Carbohydrate in grams	Calories
Tea Cakes		
Milk Chocolate Topped (1)	10	72
Viennese Chocolate Sandwich (1)	8	77
McVITIE		
54321	14	100
Abbey Crunch Creams (1)	10	67
Abbey Crunch (1)	7	47
Bandit (1)	12	105
Chocolate Biscuit Finger (1)	4	25
Chocolate Digestive (1)	13	98
Chocolate Sports Milk (1)	14	108
Crumblecake Creams (1)	10	92
Digestive Creams (1)	10	69
Ginger Nuts (1)	8	46
Gipsy Creams (1)	10	82
Jaffa Cakes (1)	10	47
Milk Chocolate Homewheat (1)	12	85
Munchmallow (1)	11	82
Penguin (1)	18	125
Plain Chocolate Homewheat (1)	12	85
TUC Savoury Creams (1)	6	70
United (1)	16	110
United Extra Time (1)	29	223
MORRISONS		
Choc 'n' Nut Cookies (1)	6	50
Coconut Cookies (1)	7	50
NABISCO		
Dutch Shortcake (1)	9	40
Happy Faces (1)	11	77
Jam Creams (1)	10	76
THRIFTIES		
Bourbon (1)	9	54
Coffee (1)	8	53
Custard (1)	8	54
PATERSON-BRONTE		
Golden Crunch (1)	8	60
Oatflake (1)	11	80
Shortcake (1)	11	81
PEEK FREANS		
Bourbon (1)	9	60
Citrus Creams (1)	8	58
Coated Mallows (1)	8	52
Coffee Creams (1)	17	56
Country Crunch (1)	5	36
Crunch Creams (1)	8	58
Custard Creams (1)	16	53
Devon Creams (1)	8	59

PEEK FREANS – Continued	Carbohydrate in grams	Calories
Iced Gem 4 Biscuits	6	24
Jamboree Mallows (1)	14	77
Jersey Creams (1)	8	58
Megabar (1)	20	97
Neapolitan Wafers (1)	5	36
Nice (1)	7	44
Nice Creams (1)	8	57
Shortcake (1)	7	49
Snow Balls (1)	13	131

QUAKER
	Carbohydrate in grams	Calories
Harvest Chewy Bars with		
Apple & Raisin (1)	17	110
Chocolate Chip (1)	17	115
Mint Chocolate Chip (1)	17	115
Harvest Crunch Bars with		
Chocolate & Hazelnut (1)	10	80
Peanut (1)	10	85
Raisin (1)	11	80
Tropical Fruit & Nut (1)	10	75

RENSHAW
	Carbohydrate in grams	Calories
Ratafias (4)	6	36

SAFEWAY
	Carbohydrate in grams	Calories
Assorted Creams – 400g pack		
Bourbon Creams (1)	9	56
Butter Crunch Creams (1)	9	66
Chocolate Creams (1)	9	63
Coconut Nice Creams (1)	9	80
Custard Creams (1)	8	65
Finger Creams (1)	7	50
H/C Milk Choc Coronet Creams (1)	11	90
Jam Sandwich Creams (1)	10	70
Lemon Creams (1)	9	64
Oaten Crunch (1)	6	35
Almond Biscuits (1)	5	44
Bourbon Creams (1)	10	62
Butter Biscuits (1)	6	42
Butter Crinkle (1)	6	38
Choc Nut Cookies (1)	7	54
Coconut Rings (1)	6	41
Cornish Creams (1)	9	73
Currant Crunch (1)	6	40
Ginger Creams (1)	9	66
Ginger Nuts (1)	9	45
Golden Crunch Creams (1)	10	68
H/C Milk Choc Sunota (1)	8	60
Milk Chocolate Fives –		
Caramel Shortcake Biscuits (1)	14	100
Digestive Bar (1)	12	100

	Carbohydrate in grams	Calories
Fruit & Nut Bar (1)	12	95
Orange Sandwich Biscuits (1)	17	130
Sandwich Biscuit (1)	17	130
Shortcake Biscuit (1)	12	100
Milk Caramel Wafers (1)	11	95
Milk Orange Fingers (1)	5	40
Milk/Plain Chocolate Digestive (1)	9	66
Party Rings (1)	6	34
Plain Chocolate Finger (1)	5	47
Shorties (1)	7	48

SAINSBURY

	Carbohydrate in grams	Calories
Bourbon (1)	9	60
Butter Sandwich Creams (1)	8	63
Caramel Wafers (1)	12	85
Chocolate & Nut Cookies (1)	7	50
Chocolate Chip Nibble Cookies (1)	2	15
Chocolate Digestive		
Milk (1)	8	60
Plain (1)	8	60
Chocolate Milk Fingers (1)	3	25
Chocolate Wafers Milk (1)	5	45
Crunch Creams (1)	8	60
Digestive Sweetmeal (1)	6	45
Fig Roll (1)	11	60
Fruit & Nut Creams (1)	8	55
Ginger Snaps (1)	8	40
Honey & Bran Crunch (1)	7	45
Iced Bears (1)	6	40
Jaffa Cakes (1)	9	44
Lemon Puffs (1)	8	76
Lincoln (1)	5	35
Malted Milk (1)	6	40
Marie (1)	5	30
Morning Coffee (1)	4	25
Nice (1)	7	45
Oatmeal Crunch (1)	5	35
Peanut Crunch (1)	6	45
Rich Tea (1)	7	45
Sandwich Creams (1)	10	73
Shortbread Fingers (1)	12	105
Spicy Fruit Crunch (1)	7	45
Sponge Fingers (1)	5	21
Thistle Shortbread (1)	12	105
Wholemeal Honey Sandwich (1)	11	75

TESCO

	Carbohydrate in grams	Calories
All Butter Thins (1)	4	23
Almond Shorties (1)	6	46
Bakewell Creams (1)	10	61
Bourbon Creams (1)	10	67

	Carbohydrate in grams	Calories
Caramel Cookie Rings (1)	6	39
Choc Chip Shortbread Cookies (1)	13	102
Chocolate Chip Cookies (1)	7	48
Coconut Crumble Creams (1)	8	67
Coconut Macaroons (1)	6	51
Coconut Rings (1)	5	46
Coffee Creams (1)	9	61
Currant Crunch Creams (1)	8	66
Custard Creams (1)	9	61
Economy Bourbon Creams (1)	10	61
Economy Chocolate Chip Cookies (1)	6	49
Economy Custard Creams (1)	10	62
Economy Fruit Shortcake (1)	5	32
Flapjack (1)	20	135
Ginger Crunch Creams (1)	10	61
Ginger Nuts (1)	7	33
Golden Crunch Creams (1)	8	65
Honey & Oatmeal Cookies (1)	12	81
Jaffa Cakes (1)	7	38
Jam and Cream Sandwich (1)	11	115
Lemon Crisp Biscuits (1)	6	42
Lincoln Biscuits (1)	5	39
Malted Milk Creams (1)	9	63
Milk Chocolate Biscuits – 1 from pack of 5		
Caramel Coated Wafers	16	107
Digestive	12	96
Fruit & Nut Biscuits	12	95
Muesli	12	94
Orange Sandwich	16	121
Sandwich	16	123
Shortcake	12	96
Wafers	12	99
Milk Chocolate Mint Wafer Fingers (1)	5	41
Milk Chocolate Sweetmeal (1)	9	65
Milk Chocolate Tea Cakes (1)	9	61
Milk Chocolate Wafer Fingers (1)	5	41
Mini Chocolate Chip & Fruit Cookies (1)	3	18
Mini Chocolate Chip & Nut Cookies (1)	3	19
Muesli Cookies (1)	7	46
Nice Biscuits (1)	6	36
Orange Creams (1)	9	61
Peanut Crunch (1)	7	49
Petticoat Tails (1)	7	55
Plain Chocolate Digestive (1)	9	65
Spicy Fruit Crunch (1)	7	45
Stem Ginger Cookies (1)	12	81
Strawberry Crumble Creams (1)	9	64
Sultana Cookies (1)	12	81
Treacle Crunch Creams (1)	9	64

	Carbohydrate in grams	Calories
WAITROSE		
Coconut Cookies (1)	6	55
Coconut Creams (1)	8	65
Iced Ring Biscuits (1)	5	30
Wafer Sandwich Biscuits		
Chocolate Filling (1)	13	85
WALKERS SHORTBREAD		
Hazelnut Biscuits (1)	10	84
Hazelnut & Choc Chip (1)	11	85
Honey & Oatmeal (1)	12	81
Muesli (1)	11	74
Orange & Chocolate Chip (1)	11	80
Stem Ginger (1)	11	80
Sultana (1)	12	80
Treacle (1)	11	66
Walkers Pure Butter –		
Chocolate Chip Shortbread (1)	12	103
Chocolate Chip Shortbread		
Rings (1)	8	66
Highland Shortbread (1)	15	118
Walnut Biscuits (1)	10	84

Cakes, Ingredients, Mixes

CAKES

	Carbohydrate in grams	Calories
BAHLSEN CAKES		
Large Cakes — 250g		
Lemon Cake	135	1215
Madeira Cake	135	1200
BIRDS EYE		
Cheesecake Fruit	185	1560
CADBURY		
Chocolate Cake	160	1065
Chocolate Whirls (1)	18	130
Flake Cakes (1)	16	125
Mini Rolls (1)	16	115
Swiss Gateau	150	1020
Swiss Roll	140	945
CHAMBOURCY		
Cheesecakes - 90g pack		
Black Cherry	30	225
Blackcurrant	27	260
Strawberry	25	245
EDEN VALE		
Cheesecake - 100g packs		
Blackcurrant	27	205
Raspberry	24	195
Strawberry	25	200
LITTLEWOODS		
Battenberg	200	1170
Cherry Bakewells (1)	31	200
Coconut Decorated Sandwich	150	1200
Decorated Genoa 1oz	16	95
Fondant Fancies (1)	18	105
Walnut Layer Cake	165	1250
LYONS		
Apple/Almond Slices (1)	17	120
Bakewell Tarts (1)	27	175
Battenberg	180	980
Cup Cake		
Chocolate (1)	30	130
Orange and Lemon (1)	29	135
Date & Apple Slices (1)	14	100
Iced Tarts (1)	22	125
Jam Tarts		
3 flavours (1)	25	140

	Carbohydrate in grams	Calories
Junior Choc Roll		
Caramel (1)	15	110
Jam & Vanilla (1)	18	115
Lemon Meringues (1)	24	145
Madeleines (1)	19	110
Paradise Slices (1)	23	155
Sponge Sandwich		
Chocolate	120	870
French	145	935
Raspberry Jam	150	755
Swiss Roll		
Chocolate & Vanilla	95	660
Raspberry	125	560
Raspberry and Vanilla	115	635
Viennese Whirls (1)	15	135

MARKS AND SPENCER

	Carbohydrate in grams	Calories
All Butter Eccles Cakes (1)	25	170
All Butter Viennese Fancies (1)	33	285
Angel Sandwich Cut Cake approx.	190	1955
Apple Sponge Sandwich approx.	85	755
Apricot Sponge Roll	180	1000
Assorted Jam Tarts (1)	20	110
Battenberg approx	195	965
Blackcurrant Sundaes (1)	33	205
Caramel Cake	125	1085
Cheesecake (frozen)		
Apricot	100	1000
Blackcurrant	195	1400
Cherry & Chocolate	200	1145
Raspberry & Redcurrant	165	1520
Cherry Madeira Cut Cake	170	1200
Chocolate Sponge Curls (1)	21	200
Chocolate Sponge Roll approx.	155	1070
Chocolate with Choc Buttercream		
Junior Rolls (1)	17	135
Chorley Cakes (1)	40	290
Coconut Sandwich Cake	140	1210
Corn Crisp Whole Round	115	815
Country Cake	205	1660
Creme Doughnuts (frozen) 1 from pack of 4.	16	185
Custard Slices (1)	30	240
Doughnuts (1)	22	175
Egg Custard Tarts (1)	27	230
Fondant Fancies (1)	22	110
Fresh Cream Meringues (1)	25	125
Iced Ring Doughnuts (1)	25	200
Meringue Nests (1)	16	60
Milk Chocolate Covered Mini Rolls (1)	21	165
Mini Rum Babas (1)	47	250
Rice Crisp with Raisins Whole Round	105	500
Snowballs (1)	18	105

13

	Carbohydrate in grams	Calories
Sponge Gateau		
Chocolate Butter Cream	130	935
Sultana & Cherry Cake	185	890
Swiss Roll		
Chocolate	125	875
Jam	180	870

McVITIE'S CAKES

Banana Cake	175	1115
Cherry Fruit Pieces	185	1095
Cherry Genoa	185	1155
Chocolate Cake	180	1135
Dark Orange	175	1095
Dundee	360	2115
Fruit Cake Slices		
Individual (1)	23	105
Golden Syrup 291g	185	1140
Jamaica Ginger 291g	180	1075
Kensington Pieces	185	1200
McVitie Iced Top Xmas Cake	635	2950
McVitie Marzipan Top Xmas Cake	690	3205
Tunis	580	4520

McVITIE'S FROZEN FOODS

Black Forest Cake	130	990
Black Forest M.R. Gateau	150	1320
Strawberry Pavlova	140	1345

MR KIPLING

Almond Slices (1)	21	125
Angel Layer Cake	155	1080
Apple Bakewell Tart	200	1280
Assorted Crumbles (1)	32	200
Bakewell Slices (1)	27	185
Bakewell Tart	195	1235
Battenberg	200	965
Battenberg Treats (1)	30	175
Blackcurrant/Apple Crumbles (1)	32	195
Celebration Slices (1)	30	170
Cherry Bakewell Tarts (1)	31	200
Cherry Fruit Cake	195	1140
Cherry Slices (1)	19	150
Cherry Walnut Slices (1)	22	145
Chocolate Fudge Cake	145	1020
Chocolate Slices (1)	21	145
Chocolate Swiss Roll	110	620
Coffee Gateau	225	1310
Coconut Macaroons (1)	16	115
Country Slices (1)	19	120
French Fancies (1)	18	105
French Jam Sponge	170	900
Jaffa Fingers (1)	20	140

MR KIPLING — Continued	Carbohydrate in grams	Calories
Jam Swiss Roll	120	535
Jam Tarts (1)	22	130
Manor House Cake	190	1710
Raspberry Bakewell	195	1280
Treacle Tart	245	1250

ROSS

Black Forest Gateau	195	1350
Cheesecake		
Blackcurrant	290	2480
Raspberry	280	2480
Strawberry	270	2380
Lemon Torte	175	1450
Pineapple Pavola	140	1295
Rum Babas (1)	60	350

SAFEWAY

All Butter Coconut Cake 11oz	175	1190
All Butter Madiera Cake 10oz	160	1035
Chocolate Chip Cake 385g	200	1420
Chocolate Log & Buttercream 412g	230	1765
Chocolate Mini Rolls		
(1 from pack of 6)	15	120
Gateau -		
Blackforest (frozen)	230	2170
Chocolate and Blackcurrant 260g	165	975
Coconut Buttercream 260g	150	975
Praline and Apricot 260g	155	950
Giant Yule Log	230	1765
Meringue Nests (1)	13	55
Rich Fruit Christmas Cake 1oz	18	110
Snowballs (1)	14	60
Sponge Sandwich with Buttercream-		
Blackcurrant/Raspberry Jam	130	820
Coconut	125	990
Trifle Sponge (1)	18	80

SAINSBURY

Almond Slices (1)	25	150
Angel Sandwich and Lemon Icing	190	1320
Chocolate Cup Cakes (1)	30	130
Chocolate Delights (1)	20	130
Junior Chocolate and Buttercream		
Swiss Roll (1)	19	120
Junior Jam Swiss Roll (1)	17	70
Junior Milk Chocolate Swiss Roll (1)	15	120
Swiss Roll -		
Jam large	155	680
small	115	515
Jam/Vanilla large	155	800
Milk Chocolate	125	880

	Carbohydrate in grams	Calories
ST IVEL		
Devonshire Cheesecake - 90g		
Blackcurrant/Strawberry..................	24	225
Gateau - 80g		
Black Forest.................................	17	160
Strawberry	20	190
SUNBLEST		
Jam Doughnuts (1)	34	260
TESCO		
Angel Layer Cake 1oz	16	115
Cherry Madeira 1oz..........................	17	100
Corn Crisp..................................	105	685
Meringue Flan	75	295
Meringue Nests (1)	13	55
Rice Crisp..................................	85	585
Sponge Fingers (1)...........................	5	20
Sponge Flan Case -		
large	130	600
medium	50	225
TIFFANY		
Sponge Sandwich Cakes — 200g		
Chocolate..................................	120	940
Lemon.....................................	105	845
Orange	105	845
Walnut	105	1070
VITBE		
Raisin Brans (1).............................	23	155
WAITROSE		
All Butter Coconut Cake 1oz	15	110
All Butter Madeira 1oz......................	16	105
Angel Sandwich 1oz	20	115
Cherry Genoa 1oz	17	105
Lemon Iced Madeira Sandwich 1oz	17	120
WALKERS SHORTBREAD		
Meringues -		
Fingers/Shells (1)	9	35
Nests (1)...................................	13	52
Stars (1)...................................	5	18
Traditional Scotch Bun 1oz	20	95
YOUNGS		
Individual Cheesecakes		
Blackcurrant	30	260
Raspberry.................................	28	260
Strawberry	30	270

CAKE INGREDIENTS

The following carbohydrate and calorie guide to cake-making ingredients is sufficiently accurate for all brand names.

	Carbohydrate in grams	Calories
Cooking Chocolate		
Milk 1oz	15	155
Plain 1oz	15	145
Glace Cherries 1oz	15	55
Marzipan		
250g pack	175	1030
Mixed Peel 1oz	18	70

HOMEPRIDE
Top 'n' Fill all varieties

1 sachet	150	925

PEARCE DUFF

Assorted Dragees 1oz	28	110
100's/1000's 1oz	28	105
Choc Sugar Strands 1oz	22	120
Hazelnut Crunch 1oz approx	20	105
Jelly Diamonds 1oz	27	100
Orange/Lemon Slices 1oz	24	95
Sugar Strands 1oz	27	105
Sunnyfruit Jelly Crystals 1oz	24	100

RENSHAW
Crunchnut Topping

100g pack	40	530

CAKE MIXES

GRANNY SMITH

	Carbohydrate in grams	Calories
Butterfly Tops Cake Mix*		
215g packet	210	1570
Cheesecake Mix*		
210g packet	160	1070
Chocolate Sandwich Cake Mix*		
300g packet	300	2100
Doughnut Mix*		
225g packet	175	1665
Lemon Madeira Cake Mix*		
225g packet	140	930
Lemon Meringue Crunch Mix*		
260g packet	300	1970
Lemon Tops Cake Mix*		
225g packet	210	1105

GREENS CAKE MIXES

	Carbohydrate in grams	Calories
Almond Slices†		
233g packet	185	1110
American Style Chocolate Fudge Brownie*		
264g packet	200	1265
Apple Crunch*		
317g packet	270	1790
Apple & Blackcurrant Crunch*		
317g packet	265	1770
Austrian Flavourmoist Cake*		
325g packet	275	1755
Bakewell Slice Mix†		
301g packet	150	1045
Bakewell Tart Mix†		
240g packet	185	1095
Bavarian Flavourmoist Sandwich*		
385g packet	330	2070
Cartoons Cake – 1 packet		
Disneys†	120	595
Mr Men/My Little Pony†	120	600
Snow Whites†	125	600
Cheesecake		
Luxury Recipe†		
198g packet	155	900
Luxury Recipe Blackberry†		
318g packet	180	970
Luxury Recipe Black Cherry†		
334g packet	190	1000
Luxury Recipe Blackcurrant†		
318g packet	170	925
Luxury Recipe Red Cherry†		
334g packet	175	940

†before additions
*when made up according to instructions

18

GREENS CAKE MIXES — Continued

	Carbohydrate in grams	Calories
Original†		
210g packet	160	890
Tangy Lemon†		
203g packet	160	925
Classic Madeira Cake Mix*		
225g packet	180	1080
Classic Victoria Cake Mix†		
225g packet	175	1000
Flavourmoist Chocolate Drop Tea Cakes*		
205g packet	170	980
Flavourmoist Devon Sponge Cake†		
244g packet	270	1290
Fruit Loaf*		
300g packet	230	1320
Lemon Meringue Pie Mix*		
288g packet	205	1150
Iced Mocha Luxury Flavourmoist Cake Mix*		
385g packet	340	2065
Strawberry Flavour Cake Mix*		
325g packet	280	1785
Swiss Style Chocolate Cake Mix*		
325g packet	270	1800
Traditional Recipe Chocolate Sponge†		
184g packet	150	655
Traditional Recipe Plain Sponge†		
184g packet	165	675
Walnut Flavour Cake†		
385g packet	340	2075

LYONS TETLEY

Home Classics - 340g packets		
Blackcurrant*	170	1365
Cherry*	180	1395
Strawberry*	180	1385
King Size (untopped) Cheesecake Mix*		
252g packet	175	1590

ROYAL

Cheesecake Mix*		
210g packet	170	1690
Chocolate Mint Crunch Mix*		
240g packet	180	1675
Rum & Raisin Crunch Mix*		
225g packet	145	1270

TESCO

Cheesecake†		
210g packet	155	900

†before additions
*when made up according to instructions

19

VIOTA

Chocolate Cup Cakes Water Icing*
  215g packet.................................. 170 935
Chocolate Fudge Cake*
  241g packet.................................. 165 1400
Coconut Macaroons*
  155g packet.................................. 100 755
Golden Shred Orange Marmalade Cake*
  255g packet.................................. 195 1120
Iced Fairy Cakes*
  198g packet.................................. 150 1040

WHITWORTHS

Cheesecake Mixes*
  Black Cherry
    11oz packet............................... 175 1340
  Blackcurrant
    11oz packet............................... 175 1340
  Cherry
    11oz packet............................... 175 1340
  Plain
    7oz packet................................ 145 1005

*when made up according to instructions

Cereals-Sugar Coated

	Carbohydrate in grams	Calories
KELLOGG		
Coco Pops 1oz	25	105
Crunchie Nut Cornflakes 1oz	23	110
Frosties 1oz	25	100
Honey Smacks 1oz	24	100
Ricicles 1oz	25	100
Smacks 1oz	25	105
Special K 1oz	22	100
Start 1oz	23	95
QUAKER		
Sugar Puffs 1oz	25	105
SAINSBURY		
Honey Nut Cornflakes 1oz	22	100
WEETABIX		
Farmhouse Bran with Honey & Nut 1oz	17	95
Chocolate Flavour Wheat Hoops 1oz	21	95

Dairy Products

SWEETENED

	Carbohydrate in grams	Calories
CARNATION		
Build-Up†		
all flavours 1 envelope......................	25	130
Slender†		
all flavours 1 envelope......................	21	100
FARLEY HEALTH PRODUCTS		
Complan all flavours		
per 2oz/57g serving approx	30	250
FUSSELL'S		
Blue Butterfly		
Skimmed Sweetened Condensed Milk		
383g can...................................	210	1075
KELLOGG		
Two Shakes all flavours		
1 sachet approx.............................	33	145
NESQUIK		
Milk Shakes all flavours		
2 heaped teaspoons approx	15	60
NESTLE		
Condensed Milk sweetened		
14oz/397g can.............................	225	1290
RAYNER AND CO		
Milk Shakes Syrup		
all flavours except Chocolate		
1 level tablespoon approx...............	5	20
Chocolate flavour		
1 level tablespoon approx...............	7	25

†before making up

Desserts & Pancakes

SWEETENED

JELLIES, most 1 pint jellies provide between 80-100g Carbohydrate and 340-380 Calories.

AMBROSIA

	Carbohydrate in grams	Calories
Chocolate Desserts — 1 pot		
all flavours	21	140
Creamed Macaroni		
439g tin	70	405
Creamed Rice		
170g tin	30	155
439g tin	70	400
Creamed Sago		
439g tin	65	355
Creamed Semolina		
439g tin	60	365
Creamed Tapioca		
439g tin	65	365
Devon Custard		
532g carton	90	540
425g tin	70	430
Topsy Turvy Dessert - 150g pot		
4 flavours	28	155
Traditional Rice Pudding		
439g tin	75	450

BATCHELORS

Quick Custard		
90g sachet	80	385

BEJAM

Knickerbocker Glory (1)	45	275
Mousse - 1 tub		
all flavours	11	80

BIRD'S

Angel Delight* all flavours except Chocolate/Mint Chocolate,		
69g sachet	55	320
Chocolate and Mint Chocolate flavours		
69g sachet	50	305
Blancmange* all flavours		
35g sachet	35	125
Dream Topping* all flavours		
40g sachet	15	250
Ice Magic (1 serving) approx	5	75
Instant Whip* all flavours		
64g sachet	65	240

*when made up according to instructions

BIRD'S — Continued

	Carbohydrate in grams	Calories
Trifle Mix* all flavours		
1 packet	125	620
Whisk and Serve Custard* all flavours		
79g sachet	65	335
Whisk and Serve Semolina*		
90g sachet	65	400
Yogurt Whirl* all flavours		
73g sachet	45	325

BIRDS EYE

	Carbohydrate in grams	Calories
Lovely		
Chocolate 1 tub	22	235
Mousse – 1 tub		
Chocolate	16	100
Strawberry	14	90
Sherry Trifle 1 tub	27	180
Supermousse – 1 tub		
Choc 'n' Nut	16	150
Mint Choc Chip	17	140
Raspberry/Strawberry	18	120
Superwhip 1 tub	60	885

BROWN AND POLSON

	Carbohydrate in grams	Calories
Instant Mix Custard*		
90g sachet	80	420

CHAMBOURCY

	Carbohydrate in grams	Calories
Creme Desserts – 1 pot		
Chocolate/Vanilla	23	140
Creme Vienna – 1 pot		
Chocolate	22	135
Strawberry	18	125
Dalky (a la Crème) – 1 pot		
Chocolate	22	135
Strawberry	18	120
Flanby – 1 pot		
Caramel	20	95
Kremly – 1 pot		
Exotic Fruit/Strawberry	20	110
Lemon	18	95
Le Grand Desserts – 200g pot		
Chocolate & Vanilla	40	265
Strawberry & Vanilla	40	255
Petit Chambourcy - Aromatises 1 pot		
Apricot	9	70
Exotic Fruits	10	75
Strawberry	10	75

†before additions
*when made up according to instructions

CHIVERS

	Carbohydrate in grams	Calories
Jelly Creams† all flavours		
74g packet approx	60	260

CO-OP

Instant Delight† all flavours		
69g packet	60	295
Instant Whip† all flavours without milk		
64g packet	65	240
Macaroni Pudding		
15oz/425g tin	70	380
Rice Milk Pudding		
15oz/425g tin	70	385
Sago Pudding		
15oz/425g tin	65	350
Semolina Pudding		
15oz/425g tin	65	360
Tapioca Pudding		
15oz/425g tin	70	360

EDEN VALE

Cheesecake - 100g pack		
Blackcurrant	25	220
Raspberry	23	215
Strawberry	25	200
Supreme Desserts - 1 pot		
Caramel	21	130
Chocolate	21	135
Strawberry	20	120
Trifle - 100g pot		
all flavours	25	160

FINDUS

Ripple Mousse — 1 tub		
all flavours	15	100

GREENS

Carmelle†		
70g packet	65	240
Chocolate Sponge Pudding*		
264g packet	230	1295
Egg Custard Dessert†		
54g packet	50	220
Fruit Sponge & Custard Pudding*		
256g packet	220	1170
Strawberry Fruit Whisk†		
260g packet	80	315
Treacle Sponge Pudding*		
297g packet	275	1340

†before additions
*when made up according to instructions

GOLDEN WONDER

	Carbohydrate in grams	Calories
Pot Sweet - 1 pot		
Apple & Blackberry Crumble..............	45	230
Peach with Apple & Almond Topping....	45	220
Pear with Apple & Caramel Crunch	45	205
Spicy Apple Crunch.....................	50	220

HEINZ

Sponge Puddings — 10.6oz/300g tins		
Apple & Blackberry........................	135	800
Chocolate................................	135	890
Mixed Fruit..............................	140	900
Raspberry/Strawberry	150	860
Treacle	160	870

HP FOODS

Sauces - 1 level tablespoon approx.		
Chocolate Dessert	11	45
Raspberry Dessert	5	20
Strawberry Dessert	7	25

ITONA

Beanmilk Custard		
400g pack...............................	60	360

LIBBY

Creamed Rice		
439g tin.................................	70	380
624g tin.................................	100	545

LITTLEWOODS

Fruit Cocktail Trifle 397g	70	540
Trifle - 113g pack		
Raspberry/Strawberry	20	155

LYONS MAID

Dessert Sauces, all flavours		
1 level tablespoon approx	11	50

MARKS AND SPENCER

Baked Jam Roll................................	240	1660
Caramel Delight Dessert (1)	28	180
Chocolate Delight Dessert (1)	26	180
Chocolate Dessert		
1 from pack of 3	24	145
Chocolate Souffle (1 from pack of 2).........	14	95
Chocolate Sponge Pudding	100	730
Creme Caramel 1 pot.......................	27	190
Fresh Cream Fruit Trifle		
16oz	95	830
30oz	190	1460
Individual Cream Fruit Trifle (1)	27	220
Raspberry Ring Dessert	110	695

MARKS AND SPENCER — Continued	Carbohydrate in grams	Calories
Raspberry Royal Dessert (1)	24	145
Rice Dessert and Apricot Puree (1)	23	155
Spotted Dick	105	725
Strawberry Delight Dessert 1 pot	22	150
Syrup Sponge Pudding		
7oz/199g pack..........................	140	745
Tropical Royale Dessert 1 pot	18	160

McDOUGALLS
Saucy Sponges* — 1 packet

	Carbohydrate in grams	Calories
Apple.........................	135	810
Apricot/Blackcurrant/Lemon/		
Raspberry	145	855
Treacle	145	815

McVITIE'S FROZEN FOODS

	Carbohydrate in grams	Calories
Apple Crumble 430g........................	150	810
Apple/Blackcurrant Crumble 430g	165	875

NESTLE

	Carbohydrate in grams	Calories
Double Top Dessert Topping Mix†		
1 sachet	7	80
Tip Top Dessert Topping		
14.1oz/400g can........................	34	440

PEARCE DUFF

	Carbohydrate in grams	Calories
Instant Custard†		
85g packet	70	320
Sorbet†		
69g packet	65	240

ROBERTSONS

	Carbohydrate in grams	Calories
Christmas Pudding		
8oz/227g................................	120	675
1lb/454g................................	240	1345

ROSS

	Carbohydrate in grams	Calories
Apple/Apple & Blackberry Dumplings (1) ..	50	335
Creme Caramel (1)	25	155
Devonshire Individual Trifles (1)	28	180
Jam Roly Poly..............................	205	1360
Mousse all flavours, 1 tub	12	90
Spotted Dick	175	1250
Treacle Roly Poly	205	1435

ROWNTREE MACKINTOSH

	Carbohydrate in grams	Calories
Creamola Rice		
9oz/255g packet........................	220	910
Creamola Steamed or Baked Pudding Mix		
8oz/227g packet........................	195	650

†before additions
*when made up according to instructions

	Carbohydrate in grams	Calories
Instant Custard Mix†		
98g packet	78	415

ROYAL
Simply Topping*		
44g packet	25	330

SAFEWAY
Christmas Pudding		
8oz pudding.................................	145	725
1lb pudding	285	1450
2lb pudding	565	2900
Creamed Rice Pudding		
439g tin..........................	70	390
Creme Caramel 1 pot.........................	27	140
Fresh Cream Fruit Cocktail 14oz	70	530
Fresh Cream Trifle - 14oz		
Pear	75	540
Raspberry	65	505
Strawberry	70	525
Fruit Cocktail 1 pot	23	170
Instant Custard†		
83g packet	70	355
Luxury Christmas Pudding		
1lb pudding	300	1480
Mousse (frozen) — 1 tub		
all flavours............................	13	90
Sponge Puddings — 200g		
Jam...................................	120	720
Syrup	125	745
Supreme Delight - 1 packet		
all flavours.............................	60	310
Traditional Creamed Rice		
440g tin.......................................	80	470

SAINSBURY
Blancmange 1 sachet		
all flavours..............................	33	135
Caramel Dessert 1 tub	21	105
Chocolate Cream Surprise 1 tub	19	155
Creamed Rice Pudding		
439g tin.................................	70	440
Fresh Cream Fruit Trifle 1 tub................	40	230
Instant Custard		
69g packet	40	290
J S Supreme* - 1 sachet		
all flavours..................................	70-75	480
Mousse		
Chocolate 1 tub	24	185

†before additions
*when made up according to instructions

SAINSBURY — Continued

	Carbohydrate in grams	Calories
Yogurt Sundeas – 1 pot		
Black Cherry & Banana	25	200
Strawberry	20	190

ST IVEL

	Carbohydrate in grams	Calories
Creme Caramel 1 pot	27	135
Souffle — 1 pot		
Chocolate	30	245
Lemon/Orange	28	210
Trifles – 1 tub		
all flavours	27	165
Wizard Mousse – 1 tub		
Chocolate	28	240
Raspberry/Strawberry	33	235

TESCO

	Carbohydrate in grams	Calories
Delight Dessert Mix* – 69g packet		
all flavours	70	500
Dessert Topping†		
42g sachet	12	135
Mousse — 1 tub		
Chocolate	14	105
Chocolate and Mint	12	100
Raspberry Ripple/Strawberry	14	100

TIFFANY

	Carbohydrate in grams	Calories
Apple and Blackberry Crumble 454g	175	1090
Apple Roly Poly 385g	185	1025
Apricot Butter Sponge 290g	125	570
Chunky Apple Crumble 454g	240	1410
Gooseberry Crumble 454g	155	1045
Jam Roly Poly 340g	190	1070
Red Cherry Butter Sponge 330g	105	505
Spotted Dick 350g	190	1090
Upper Crust Vienna Desserts		
Red Morello Cherry	195	1560
Spicy Apple & Sultana	170	1380

WAITROSE

	Carbohydrate in grams	Calories
Creamed Rice Pudding		
440g tin	75	390
Original Plum Pudding		
4oz	75	370
1lb	295	1490

WALLS

	Carbohydrate in grams	Calories
Dessert Sauces all flavours		
1 level tablespoon approx	11	45

†before additions
*when made up according to instructions

WHITWORTHS

	Carbohydrate in grams	Calories
Crumble Mix		
8oz/227g packet...........................	150	1100

YOUNGS

Individual Desserts - 1 pot

	Carbohydrate in grams	Calories
Creme Caramel............................	24	140
Mixed Fruit Trifles	27	170
Real Raspberry Trifles......................	27	170
Real Strawberry Trifles.....................	28	170

PANCAKES

	Carbohydrate in grams	Calories
MOTHERS PRIDE		
Scotch Pancakes (1).............................	16	85
SAINSBURY		
Scotch Pancakes (1).............................	16	85
SUNBLEST TEATIME		
Raisin & Lemon Pancakes (1).................	15	80
Sultana & Syrup Pancakes (1).................	19	80

Drinks

SWEETENED

CORDIALS, SPARKLING DRINKS & SQUASHES

With such a variety of sugar-free cordials and squashes available it is not necessary to use sweetened drinks EXCEPT to treat hypo-glycaemia or when more concentrated carbohydrate sources are required, i.e. during illness. Ask your dietition for advice before using any of the drinks in this section. This table is a reasonably accurate guide to the carbohydrate and calorie values per fluid ounce of a variety of sweetened UNDILUTED drinks.

	Carbohydrate in grams	Calories
Apple & Blackberry	7	25
Blackcurrant Cordial	7	30
Blackcurrant Concentrate, i.e. Syrup	20	80
Grapefruit	8	30
Grapefruit Barley Water	8	30
Grapefruit and Pineapple	8	30
Lemon	7	25
Lemon Barley	7	35
Lemon and Lime Barley Water	8	30
Lemon/Lime	7	25
Lime Cordial	7	25
Orange	8	30
Orange and Apricot	8	30
Orange and Grapefruit	8	30
Orange and Lemon	8	30
Orange and Passionfruit	7	25
Orange and Pineapple	8	30
Orange Barley	8	30
Peppermint Cordial	9	35
Strawberry Cordial	9	35
Tropical Orange	9	35

There is very little variation in the carbohydrate and calorie values for all SWEETENED Still Fruit Drinks. These are all between 9-13% carbohydrate and 35-50 calories per 100ml.

		Carbohydrate	Calories
i.e.	200ml carton	18-26	70-100
	250ml carton	22-32	90-125
	1 litre pack	90-130	350-500

BEECHAMS
Baby Ribena Ready to Drink
all flavours, 125ml pack 6   25

BEECHAMS — Continued

	Carbohydrate in grams	Calories
**Diet Sparkling Ribena Reduced Calorie		
Blackcurrant Juice Drink		
330ml can...............................	17	65
Ferguzade Glucose Syrup Beverage		
1fl.oz/25ml................................	6	25
Hycal all flavours		
171ml bottle	110	415
Lucozade all flavours		
1fl.oz/25ml................................	5	20
250ml bottle	50	180
Lucozade Light +		
250ml bottle	23	90
**Low Sugar Ribena		
Light Blackcurrant Juice Drink		
1fl.oz/25ml................................	7	25
250ml tetra bik..........................	13	50
Ribena ready to drink		
250ml carton	39	150
Ribena Dry		
250ml bottle	30	120
700ml bottle	90	330
Sparkling Ribena		
Blackcurrant Juice Drink		
330ml can................................	47	175

BOOTS

Glucose Drink 1fl. oz/25ml	5	20
Tropical Fruit Squash 1fl. oz/25ml	12	45

BRITVIC

High Juice Squash/Cordial		
Lemon Squash 1fl. oz/25ml..................	10	40
Lime Juice Cordial 1fl. oz/25ml.............	8	35
Orange Squash 1fl. oz/25ml	9	35

CORONA

C Vit Blackcurrant Health Drink		
1fl.oz/25ml................................	14	55
C Vit Blackcurrant & Lemon Barley		
1fl. oz/25ml................................	13	50

MASONLINE

Class Energy Drinks		
Lemon/Orange flavours		
15g powder	15	60

+ We would not recommend this for treating hypoglycaemia

** Although this product is in the Red Section it is a much better choice than the ordinary Ribena. Must still be used with care.

	Carbohydrate in grams	Calories
QUOSH		
Real Orange Squash 1 fl. oz/25ml............	10	35
SCHWEPPES		
Kia-Ora Double Strength –		
Lemon/Orange 1 fl. oz/25ml...............	13	50
SOMPORTEX		
Slush Puppie		
7oz/200ml serving	19	75

FIZZY DRINKS

With such a variety of sugar-free fizzy drinks available it is not necessary to use sweetened drinks. This table is a reasonably accurate guide to the carbohydrate and calorie values per half pint of most flavours of sweetened fizzy drinks.

	Carbohydrate in grams	Calories
American Ginger Ale	21	80
Bitter Lemon	25	100
Blackcurrantade	18	70
Cherryade	19	70
Cola	25	100
Cream Soda	20	75
Cydeela	15	55
Dandelion and Burdock	15	55
Dry Ginger Ale	12	45
Ginger Beer	22	85
Indian Tonic Water	18	65
Lemonade	19	70
Lemonade Shandy	15	70
Lemon and Lime	15	60
Limeade	17	65
Orangeade	20	75
Shandy	15	75
Strawberryade	18	70
Traditional Lemonade	30	110
Tropical Flavour	19	75

BRITVIC
Orange Drink

330ml can	39	145

CARIBA
Sparkling Pineapple and Grapefruit Crush

330ml can	30	115

COCA COLA
Coca Cola

330ml can	35	135

Lilt

330ml can	38	155

CORONA
Coola

200ml can	23	85
330ml can	38	140

Lager Shandy

330ml can	17	80

Limeade & Lager

330ml can	25	105

	Carbohydrate in grams	Calories

IDRIS
Old English Ginger Beer
330ml can	29	115

Old English Ginger Beer with Lemonade
330ml can	33	125

KENWOOD CASCADE
Bitter Lemon Squash* 22ml	14	60
Blackcurrant* 22ml	16	60
Cola* 22ml	17	65
Ginger Ale American* 22ml	12	50
Ginger Beer* 22ml	14	55
Indian Tonic Water* 22ml	11	45
Iron Brew* 22ml	15	60
Lemon and Lime* 22ml	13	55
Lemonade* 22ml	13	50
Orange Squash* 22ml	14	65
Shandy* 22ml	12	50
Strawberry* 22ml	15	60

LITTLEWOODS
Drinks – 330ml cans
Irn Bru	34	130
Tizer	34	130
Vimto	22	80

MARKS AND SPENCER
Citro – 320ml can
Lemon Drink	35	135
Orange & Apricot Drink	29	115
Sparkling Orange Drink	48	190

Crush – 250ml can
Mandarin	30	120
Sun Fruit	23	80

PEPSI
Pepsi Cola
250ml bottle	28	110
330ml can	37	145

ROWNTREE MACKINTOSH
Creamola Foam Drink Crystals
5oz/142g pack	122	455

SCHWEPPES
American Ginger Ale
113ml bottle	7	25
180ml bottle	10	40

Dry Ginger Ale
113ml bottle	5	20
180ml bottle	7	30

* Amount of Concentrate recommended to make 1 bottle when following manufacturers instructions.

SCHWEPPES - Continued

	Carbohydrate in grams	Calories
Ginger Beer		
170ml bottle	15	60
Lemonade		
113ml bottle	8	30
180ml bottle	12	45
Lemonade Shandy		
330ml can	18	85
Russchian		
113ml bottle	7	30
Sparkling Bitter Lemon		
113ml bottle	10	40
180ml bottle	16	60
Sparkling Limon Crush		
330ml can	37	140
Sparkling Orange Crush		
330ml can	39	150
Sparkling Orange & Passionfruit Drink		
330ml can	30	115
Tonic Water		
113ml bottle	6	25
180ml bottle	10	40

SODA STREAM

	Carbohydrate in grams	Calories
American Ginger† 1fl.oz/25ml	17	70
Blackcurrant† 1fl.oz/25ml	20	80
Cherry† 1fl.oz/25ml	19	80
Cola† 1fl.oz/25ml	16	65
Ginger Beer† 1fl.oz/25ml	20	80
Grapefruit and Pineapple† 1fl.oz/25ml	17	70
Iron Brew† 1fl.oz/25ml	14	55
Lemonade† 1fl.oz/25ml	18	70
Lime and Lemonade† 1fl.oz/25ml	15	60
Orange† 1fl.oz/25ml	20	80
Raspberry† 1fl.oz/25ml	19	75
Shandy† 1fl.oz/25ml	16	65
Strawberry† 1fl.oz/25ml	19	75
Tizer† 1fl.oz/25ml	24	95
Tonic† 1fl.oz/25ml	14	55
Vimto† 1fl.oz/25ml	12	45

TANGO

Sparkling Drinks — 330 ml cans

	Carbohydrate in grams	Calories
Apple	31	120
Grapefruit	38	140
Lemon Drink with Lime Juice	30	115
Orange	40	155
Orange & Passion Fruit	38	145
Orange and Pineapple	38	145

† before making up

37

TOP DECK

	Carbohydrate in grams	Calories
Lemonade & Cider		
330ml can	28	125
Limeade & Lager		
330ml can	25	105

FRUIT JUICES

	Carbohydrate in grams	Calories
BIRD'S		
Apeel all flavours		
1 litre when made up	90	340
BRITVIC		
Britvic 55 – 180ml bottle		
Apple Juice Drink	21	80
Grapefruit Juice Drink	24	90
Orange Juice Drink	25	95
Pineapple Juice Drink	25	95
Britvic 55 – 250ml can		
Apple Juice Drink	29	110
Orange Juice Drink	29	110
Pineapple Juice Drink	35	130
COCA COLA		
Five Alive – Citrus		
200ml carton	24	100
1 litre carton	125	480
Five Alive – Tropical		
200ml carton	20	80
1 litre carton	100	390
HEINZ		
Grapefruit Juice sweetened		
120ml can	20	80
H P BULMER		
Orangina		
200ml carton	21	80
HUNTS		
Sweetened Fruit Juices — 107ml bottles		
Grapefruit	17	70
Orange	14	55
Pineapple	15	60
KELLOGG		
Rise and Shine all flavours		
60g sachet approx	53	200
LIBBY		
Grapefruit 'C' sweetened		
930ml bottle	145	540
Grapefruit Juice sweetened		
525ml can	51	200
Orange 'C' sweetened		
930ml bottle	125	475
Orange Juice sweetened		
525ml can	68	270

LIBBY — Continued

	Carbohydrate in grams	Calories
Ready to Drink -		
Moonshine Drink		
200ml pack	22	85
500ml pack	54	200
Umbongo Fruit Drink		
200ml pack	22	85
500ml pack	55	200
SCHWEPPES		
Grapefruit Juice		
113ml bottle	14	55
180ml bottle	23	85
Hi-Juice 66		
170ml bottle	23	90
Orange Juice (Sweetened)		
113ml bottle	17	65
180ml bottle	27	100
Tomato Juice Cocktail		
113ml bottle	5	20
180ml bottle	8	30

HOT BEVERAGES

There is very little variation in the carbohydrate and calorie values for Bedtime Drinks. We give below a guide to cover all the popular brands:

	Carbohydrate in grams	Calories
Drinking Chocolate,		
1 level teaspoon approx.....................	4-5	15-20
Malted Milk Drink,		
1 level teaspoon approx.....................	3-4	15-20
CADBURY		
Chocolate Break		
1 sachet	18	115
CARNATION		
Hot Chocolate		
1 sachet	19	110
CARO		
Caro Instant		
2 heaped teaspoons.........................	3	15
Caro Extra		
2 heaped teaspoons.........................	3	15
GEORGE PAYNE		
Lift Lemon Tea Sweet and Less Sweet		
2 teaspoons serving approx.................	10	35
HORLICKS		
Low Fat Instant Horlicks — 1 sachet		
Chocolate Malted Food Drink	24	125
Hot Chocolate Drink........................	21	130
Malted Food Drink...........................	23	120

Fruit-in Syrup, Pie Fillings

FRUIT-IN SYRUP

With the wide range of fruits in natural juice or low calorie syrup (see green section), you should not need to use fruits in syrup at all. However, during illness or in an emergency, fruits in syrup may be used. The table below is an approximate guide to the carbohydrate and calorie content of an average 15oz/425g can of most brand names.

	Carbohydrate in grams	Calories
Apple	70	300
Apricots	105	360
Blackberries	80	310
Cherries	90	390
Fruit Cocktail Salad	90	340
Gooseberries	70	380
Grapefruit Segments	60	210
Loganberries	105	420
Mandarin Oranges	60	260
Peaches	85	340
Pears	85	340
Pineapple	80	300
Plums	75	290
Prunes	130	500
Raspberries	85	360
Rhubarb	60	240
Strawberies	130	440

Fruit Pie Fillings

SWEETENED

	Carbohydrate in grams	Calories
ARMOUR		
Fruit Fillings — 28oz/795g tins		
Blackcurrant	210	795
Cherry	240	915
Gooseberry	185	710
Raspberry	250	950
Strawberry	270	1035
BATCHELORS		
Pack-a-Pie — 1 jar		
Apple	80	295
Apple & Blackberry	95	355
Apple & Raspberry	80	350
Blackcurrant	95	385
Cherry	95	360
Strawberry	105	395
BIRD'S		
Lemon Pie Filling Mix†		
71g pack	70	255
CHIVERS		
Fruit For All — 1 pouch		
Apricot/Blackcurrant	95	345
Morello Cherry	90	330
CO-OP		
Fruit Pie Fillings — 1 tin		
Apple	65	250
Apple and Blackberry	70	260
Apple and Raspberry	70	255
Blackcurrant	75	285
Red Cherry	80	315
Strawberry	80	300
GREENS		
Lemon Pie Filling*		
twin pack, 1 sachet	70	335
MORTON		
Fruit Filling — 1 tin		
Apple	80	305
Apple and Blackberry	65	250
Apple and Raspberry	70	255
Black Cherry	75	280
Blackcurrant	80	315

†before making up

	Carbohydrate in grams	Calories
Pineapple	70	260
Red Cherry	90	330
Redcurrant & Raspberry	55	225
Strawberry	80	305

PICKERINGS
Pie Fillings — 385g tins

Apple	65	250
Apple and Raspberry	65	255
Strawberry	85	325

ROYAL
Lemon Fie Filling Mix*

70g pack	90	485

SAINSBURY
Pie Fillings — 14oz/400g tins

Apricot	90	350
Blackcurrant	95	375

TESCO
Pie Fillings — 1 tin

Apple	60	240
Apple and Blackberry	65	260
Apple and Raspberry	60	240
Cherry	95	370
Gooseberry	70	280
Strawberry	70	235

*when made according to instructions

Ice Cream and Lollies

ICE CREAM

Ice cream is a very popular product and one the many individuals with diabetes are reluctant to give up. Therefore most dietitians advise that ice cream may be selected as a dessert after a well balanced high fibre, low sugar main meal, though not usually more than a MAXIMUM of TWICE in any one week.

The figures quoted below are a sufficiently accurate guide to the Carbohydrate (CHO) and Calorie contribution of most ice creams if measured out using an ice cream scoop. It assumes that a rounded scoop will weigh a maximum of 50 grams (just less than 2 ounces). It is important that you check this weight (whether you use a scoop or a serving spoon) particularly in the early days after diagnoses to ensure that this weight is not exceeded.

Plain Ice Cream (Dairy/Non Dairy), Soft Scoop
i.e. Chocolate, Coffee, Mint, Strawberry, Vanilla etc.

	Carbohydrate in grams	Calories
1 scoop minimum	10	80
1 scoop maximum	15	120

Sweeter Ice Cream
i.e. those with added Chocolate Chips/Sauce, Dried Fruit, Liqueurs, Toffee etc.

1 scoop minimum	15	100
1 scoop maximum	20	150

BEJAM

Choc Ice all flavours (1)	10	115
Dairy Choc 'n' Nut Cornets (1)	35	260
Ice Cream Roll	95	495

BIRDS EYE

Arctic Circles (1)	21	155
Arctic Gateau		
Choc 'n' Cherry	95	630
Strawberry	90	660
Arctic Log	115	720
Arctic Roll	95	525

CO-OP

Ice Cream Roll	75	480

LYONS MAID

Cutting Brick – 1 brick

Chocolate Ripple	150	930
Cornish Dairy	130	905

LYONS MAID — Continued	Carbohydrate in grams	Calories
Neapolitan	120	835
Peach Melba	140	900
Raspberry Ripple	140	880
Vanilla	120	850
Weight Watchers	115	515
Dairy Milk Ices		
1 from multi-pack	9	50
Dark Satin Choc Ice (1)	13	130
Family Brick - 1 brick		
Chocolate/Banana	60	400
Cornish Dairy	65	510
Fruit Harvest -		
Pineapple	75	380
Raspberry	75	450
Neapolitan	55	400
Vanilla	60	405
Weight Watchers	55	245
Gold Seal - 1 pot		
Caramel Toffee	150	1140
Chocolate Coconut Flake	160	1100
Chocolate Swirl	185	1170
Mint Choc Chip	150	1055
Rum & Raisin	150	1010
Vanilla Choc Flake	155	1200
Handy Pack Vanilla 1 pack	40	265
Hostess	90	705
King Cóne		
Chocolate (1)	26	220
Cornish Dairy (1)	26	230
Mint Choc (1)	27	205
Royale (1)	29	205
Strawberry (1)	29	195
Vanilla (1)	24	205
Silky Smooth Choc Ice (1)	12	135
Sundae Cups		
Chocolate (1)	16	160
Raspberry (1)	18	90
Vanilla Bar (1)	10	75
Vanilla Cup (1)	12	85
PEARCE DUFF		
Ice Cream Mix† — all flavours		
69g pack	50	320
PENDLETONS		
Big Top Cones (1)	20	260
Choc Ice Vanilla (1)	10	125
Dark Choc Ice		
Mint (1)	10	125
Vanilla (1)	10	125
Vanilla Flavour Bar (1)	6	55
Vanilla Flavour Cup (1)	13	115

†before additions

	Carbohydrate in grams	Calories
ROSS		
Choc Ice (1)	11	130
SAFEWAY		
Choc Ices all flavours (1)	11	135
Cutting Brick – 1 marked portion		
Cornish	9	70
Raspberry Ripple	10	60
Vanilla	8	60
Family Brick – 1 brick		
Cornish	65	490
Raspberry Ripple	75	440
Vanilla	55	390
Ice Cream Roll	60	340
SAINSBURY		
Choc Ice		
Dark (1)	14	130
Light (1)	14	130
TESCO		
Choc Ices (1)	13	130
WAITROSE		
Sorbet – 1 scoop		
Blackcurrant	16	70
Lemon	15	60
WALLS		
Choc and Nut Slice		
1 family sweet	70	530
Choc Bar		
Dark and Golden (1)	13	130
Golden Vanilla (1)	14	130
Nutty Choc Bar (1)	16	190
Complete Desserts		
Sonata	90	775
Viennetta	85	815
Cornetto		
Choc and Nut (1)	24	220
Mint Choc Chip (1)	24	225
Strawberry (1)	30	200
Cup Italiano		
Choc and Nut (1)	16	175
Strawberry (1)	19	110
Ice Cream Bar Golden Vanilla (1)	12	85
Individual Slices Vanilla (1)	8	65
Neapolitan		
1 family sweet	60	430
Raspberry Ripple		
1 family sweet	80	480

	Carbohydrate in grams	Calories
Sliceable		
Bananarama	125	840
Blue Ribbond Vanilla	125	920
Cream of Cornish	130	985
Neapolitan	130	935
Pinacoolada	140	830
Raspberry Ripple	170	1040
Rum & Raisin	155	990
St Clements Orange & Lemon	150	880
Snofrute 'n' Cream		
Strawberry (1)	14	85
Snofrute 'n' Juice		
Orange/Pineapple (1)	17	65
St Clements Orange & Lemon		
1 family sweet	70	415
Strawberry Ripple Slice		
1 family sweet	75	500

ICE LOLLIES

	Carbohydrate in grams	Calories
BEJAM		
Raspberry Split	10	60
Rio-Choc	14	120
LYONS MAID		
Big Squeeze	23	110
Chocolate Supreme (1)	12	75
Coconut Flake	20	185
Cola Quench	8	30
Fab	12	70
1 from multi-pack	14	85
Hungry Hound	12	85
Juice Bar		
Grapefruit	10	40
Orange/Pineapple	11	45
Merlins Brew	8	65
Mint Crisp	21	160
Mr Men	5	20
Orange Maid	12	45
Panda (1)	12	80
Raspberry Mivvi Fun Size	10	60
Real Milk Ice all flavours	9	50
Strawberry Mivvi	14	80
Super Juice Bar	13	50
Toffee Crumble	18	170
Triple Choc	18	220
Twango	15	120
Zoom	9	40
PEARCE DUFF		
Ice Pops	2	6
PENDLETONS		
Black Knight Lolly	5	40
Blackcurrant Ace Lolly	5	25
Cider Lolly	12	50
Cornish Twicer	11	65
Double Flavour Lolly	5	25
Hat Trick Lolly	9	75
Iced Orange Lolly	12	50
King Size Twicer Lolly	11	65
Lager and Lime Lolly	12	50
Lemon Ace Lolly	5	25
Mexi Choc Lolly	10	75
Pen Cola Lolly	5	25
Raspberry Ace Lolly	5	25
Twicer Rocket Lolly	5	40
SAFEWAY		
Orange Ice Lollies	5	25

WALLS

	Carbohydrate in grams	Calories
Big Dipper – Buttermint/Toffee (1)	19	150
Fat Frog	13	50
Feast	21	260
Funny Feet	10	85
Mini Milk – Strawberry/Vanilla	6	40
Orange Frutie	16	60
Romero	16	170
Sparkles Lemonade/Orangeade/Strawberry	8	40
Starship 4	10	35
Strawberry Split	15	85
Tongue Twister	11	90
Woppa	11	40

Pastry Goods

SWEETENED

	Carbohydrate in grams	Calories
DORSET FOODS		
Apple Strudel (1)	25	195
Apple Turnover (1)	24	215
FINDUS		
Lemon Cream Pie	100	1220
FRESHBAKE FOODS		
Apple Turnover (1)	27	270
Mince Pies (1)	32	220
JUS-ROL		
Frozen Apple Strudel	115	800
Frozen Apple Turnover (1)	18	140
LITTLEWOODS		
Apple Pies small (1)	30	185
Apple & Blackcurrant Pies small (1)	28	180
Mince Pies small (1)	35	215
LYONS		
Blackcurrant Puffs (1)	14	120
Dessert Pie Apple	180	1110
Fruit Pies – 1 from pack of 2 4 or 6		
Apple	30	190
Apple and Blackcurrant	30	190
Harvest	30	190
Lattice Pie		
Apple and Blackcurrant	170	1000
Cherry and Apple	170	1015
Popular Pie		
Apple	65	385
Apple and Blackcurrant	65	390
Apricot	65	400
Sundaes – all flavours (1)	30	195
MARKS AND SPENCER		
Apple Pies (1)	34	185
Apple Puffs (1)	16	115
Blackcurrant & Apple Pie frozen	210	1665
Choux Ring Dessert frozen 241g	65	1020
Deep Filled Apple Pie frozen 737g	260	1620
Gooseberry Slice	210	1560
Lemon Cream Flan frozen	145	1475
Trellis Bramley Apple Tart	150	985

	Carbohydrate in grams	Calories
McVITIE'S FROZEN FOODS		
Apple Pie 438g	160	1240
Apple/Blackcurrant Pie	175	1100
Mr KIPLING		
Apple Pies		
individual (1)	65	405
1 from pack of 6	32	195
Apple and Blackcurrant Pies (1)	28	180
Assorted Fruit Pies (1)	28	200
Mince Pies (1)	35	215
ROSS		
Apple Pie Baked	460	3145
Apple and Blackberry Pie	460	3145
SAFEWAY		
Bramley Apple Pies (1)	24	155
Deep Mince Pies (1)	36	210
SAINSBURY		
Bramley Apple Pies (1)	42	260
Mince Pies (1)	33	190
TESCO		
Fruit of the Forest Pies (1)	36	200

Preserves and Spreads

All preserves contain a lot of added sugar. For this reason sugar-free or low sugar versions are recommended for everyday use. The approximate carbohydrate and calorie values per level teaspoon of most types of preserve are 5g carbohydrate and 15 calories. The table below gives the values for some other popular spreads.

	Carbohydrate in grams	Calories
Honey 1oz	21-22	75-80
Lemon/Orange Curd 1oz	18	80
Mincemeat 1oz	18-19	65-70
Syrup 1oz	22	85
Treacle 1oz	19-20	70-75

CADBURY

Chocolate Spread 1oz	21	90
Hazelnut Spread 1oz	16	160

LEDBURY PRESERVES

Del'ora Exotic Mincemeat 1oz	18	65

Sweets

There is very little variation from one manufacturer to another in respect of the following sweets. Below is a sufficently accurate guide per ounce:

	Carbohydrate in grams	Calories
Dolly Mixtures 1oz	25	110
Jelly Babies 1oz	25	95
Jelly Beans 1oz	25	105
Jelly Bears 1oz	24	95
Mini Jellies 1oz	22	90

ALLINSON
Carob-Coated Sesame Crunch Bar (1)	17	120
Carob-Crunch Bar (1)	22	150
Sesame Crunch Bar 40g pack	29	170

BARKER & DOBSON
Victory V (1)	2	10

BASSETT
Bassetti Sticks (1)	12	52
Candy Foams 1oz	25	105
Jelly Buttons 1oz	22	90
Jelly Eggs 1oz	26	100
Lico-Jet (1)	7	20
Liquorice Allsorts		
113g carton	90	390
120g film bag	95	410
Liquorice Comfits 1oz	25	100
Liquorice Cuttings 1oz	20	85
Liquorice Torpedos 1oz	25	100
Mini Allsorts 1oz	22	105
Mint Imperials 1oz	28	105
Pontefract Cakes		
4oz/113g film bag	85	335
Toasted Tea Cakes 1oz	15	125
Wine Gums		
4oz/113g carton	90	370

BEECHAMS
Lucozade glucose tablets (1)	3	12

BOOTS
Barley Sugar Drops (1)	5	20
Bran & Apple Crunch Bar (1)	16	115
Coconut Crunch Bar (1)	16	150
Glucose Drops (1)	6	22
Glucose Tablets all flavours (1)	3	12
Honey Crunch Bar (1)	21	140

BOOTS — Continued

	Carbohydrate in grams	Calories
Milk Chocolate Bar with Fruit Muesli (1)	34	170
Milky Coating Swiss Style Muesli Bar (1)	30	160
Natural Poppy Seed Bar (1)	19	135
Natural Sesame Seed Bar (1)	18	140
Natural Sunflower Seed Bar (1)	18	140
Plain Chocolate Coated		
Date & Muesli Bar (1)	29	145
Ginger & Pear Bar (1)	29	155

CADBURY

	Carbohydrate in grams	Calories
Bar 6	24	220
Boost	28	255
Bournville Dark		
50g bar	31	255
100g bar	62	510
Bournville Selection		
8oz/227g box	140	1065
Cadbury's Dairy Milk		
20g bar	12	105
60g bar	36	320
100g bar	60	530
vending machine bar	29	255
Caramel		
50g bar	32	245
Chocolate Buttons		
large bag	31	270
standard bag	20	175
Contrast Assortment		
8oz/227g box	160	1020
Creme Eggs (1)	30	170
Crunchie standard	26	165
Curly Wurly	21	135
Double Decker		
Standard bar	34	235
Mini Bar (1)	12	85
Eclairs 1 sweet	3	20
Flake	21	180
'99' Flake	7	65
Fry's Chocolate/Peppermint Cream	39	210
Fry's Five Centres	38	215
Fry's Turkish Delight (1 bar)	38	185
Fudge (1 roll)	22	130
Gambit	25	210
Milk Brazil Nut		
100g bar	50	550
Milk Fruit and Nut		
standard bar	33	270
100g bar	57	470
vending machine bar	28	225
Milk Sultana		
100g bar	62	450

CADBURY — Continued	Carbohydrate in grams	Calories
Milk Tray Assortment		
8oz/227g box	160	1110
Milk Wholenut		
standard bar	28	305
100g bar	51	550
vending machine bar	24	265
Mini Eggs (1)	2	15
Picnic	25	230
Roses Assortment		
97g packet	65	470
220g box	145	1065
Shortcake Snack		
1 packet	29	210
Skippy	25	190
vending machine bar	30	215
Star Bar	29	260
Wispa Bar	19	200

CALLARD AND BOWSER
Barley Sugar (1)	6	25
Brazil Nut Toffees (1)	5	40
Butterscotch (1)	6	25
Chocolate Toffees (1)	5	40
Chocolate Toffee Rolls (1)	6	40
Coffee Chocolates (1)	5	30
Coffee Toffees (1)	6	40
Cream-line Toffees (1)	6	40
Creamy Fudge Bar	49	275
Dessert Nougat (1)	10	60
Juicy Jellies (1)	8	35
Licorice Toffees (1)	6	40
Milk Chocolate Toffee Rolls (1)	6	40
Mint Chocolates (1)	5	30
Mint Toffees (1)	6	40
Mintoes		
1 from bag or box	6	25
1 from stick pack	4	15
Plain Jane Almond Toffees (1)	5	40
Rock Drops all flavours (1)	2	10
Soft Mints (1)	4	15
Treacle Brittle (1)	6	25
Treacle Toffees (1)	6	40

CLARNICO
Mint Creams (1)	10	30
Real Fruit Jellies (1)	10	30

DEXTROSOL
Dextrosol all flavours (1)	3	12

	Carbohydrate in grams	Calories
FERRERO		
Tic Tac (3) approx	1	5
per packet	15	65
FOX'S		
Glacier Fruits		
1 from 113g bag	5	20
1 from stick pack	3	12
Glacier Mints		
1 from 113g pack	5	20
1 from stick pack	3	12
GRANOSE		
Carob Fruit Bar 35g (1)	26	145
Carob Muesli Pineapple Bar 35g (1)	25	145
HALLS		
Bubblicious 1 tablet	4	14
Dentyne 1 tablet	1	4
Freshen-Up 1 tablet	2	10
HORLICKS		
Horlicks Tablets		
1 packet	15	75
ITONA		
Chunky Bar 36g bar (1)	33	390
Granny Ann Granymel Caramels		
all flavours, 100g pack	65	400
Noot Bar (1)	36	430
Roasted Noots		
4oz/113g pack	28	475
KALIBU		
Carob Bars with Raw Sugar –		
60g bars, all flavours	33	300
LITTLEWOODS		
Barley Sugars 1oz	28	105
Butterscotch 1oz	26	110
Filled Bars –		
Caramel 100g	55	495
Mint/Orange 50g	25	240
Pineapple/Raspberry 50g	26	255
Fudge 35g bar	25	140
Milk Chocolate Honeycomb Gemini 30g	22	130
Mint Humbugs		
35g bag	30	125
Liquorice Allsorts		
8oz/227g bag	180	840
Sugar Letters		
92g pack	85	345

LOFTHOUSE OF FLEETWOOD

	Carbohydrate in grams	Calories
Fisherman's Friend Lozenge		
Aniseed & Original (1)....................	1	5

MARKS AND SPENCER

	Carbohydrate in grams	Calories
Assorted Fruit Pastilles		
200g pack................................	125	505
Buttermints		
200g pack................................	170	880
Chews stick pack (1)...........................	9	40
Cream Filled Chocolate — 50g bars		
Lemon/Orange/Strawberry...............	32	210
Hazelnut Toffee Nougat Bar...............	30	220
Honeycomb Crunch Bar	80	695
Jaffa Assortment		
8oz/227g bag.............................	215	795
Liqueur Truffles		
200g pack................................	85	1040
Liquorice Allsorts		
8oz/227g pack	180	835
Milk Chocolate Buttons		
75g bag..................................	45	385
Mini Sticks — 1 pack		
Hazelnut	36	400
Mint......................................	36	345
Mocca....................................	48	400
Mintoes		
8oz/227g bag.............................	195	930
Pastilles		
8oz/227g bag.............................	185	780
Plain Chocolate		
100g bar	65	530
Popcorn		
35g bag..................................	30	120
Real Fruit Gum Teddy Bears		
125g bag.................................	100	425
Swiss Chocolate — 50g bars		
Milk......................................	28	270
Plain	30	265
Walnut Whips (1)	15	130
Wine Gums		
200g pack................................	160	685

MARS

	Carbohydrate in grams	Calories
Bounty Milk		
funsize	17	140
twin pack	35	280
Bounty Plain		
funsize	18	140
twin pack	36	280
Galaxy		
50g bar..................................	28	275
85g bar..................................	48	465

MARS — Continued	Carbohydrate in grams	Calories
100g bar	56	550
Lockets		
1 packet	40	150
M+M's Peanut		
50g pack	27	250
100g pack	54	500
M+M's Plain		
50g pack	34	240
100g pack	67	485
Maltesers		
funsize bag	14	110
large bag, 150g	94	750
medium bag, 85g	53	425
small bag, 55g	35	275
small bag, 41g	25	200
Marathon		
fun size	11	100
standard	32	295
Mars		
extra large	70	455
fun size	13	90
standard	48	310
Milky Way		
fun size	13	75
twin bar	40	240
Minstrels		
family bag	70	525
standard bag	33	245
Opals stick pack	44	200
Peanut Treets		
family bag	59	515
standard bag	27	235
Revels Total Mix		
family bag	75	550
standard bag	24	175
Ripple	17	160
Topic	32	265
Tracker -		
Choc Chip		
29g bar	17	145
40g bar	26	210
Roasted Nut		
29g bar	16	145
40g bar	24	215
Tunes all varieties		
1 packet	36	135
Twix		
teabreak pack	20	150
twin pack (2 bars)	39	300
NESTLE		
Milky Bar 1oz	16	155

	Carbohydrate in grams	Calories
PASCALL		
Butter Mints (1)	6	30
Fresh Mints (1)	7	25
Fruit Bonbons (1)	7	25
Murray Fruits (1)	7	25
Murray Mints (1)	7	25
RENSHAW		
Amandines (1)	4	35
Assorted Chocolate Pralines (1) approx	7	70
Luxuries		
185g pack	115	830
Marzipan Fruits (1) approx	8	45
Marzipan Ovals (1)	3	25
Petits Fours (1 piece)	6	40
Pralines (1)	6	65
ROWNTREE MACKINTOSH		
Aero		
Countline	19	175
Milk Chocolate	23	210
Orange/Peppermint	23	210
After Eight Mints (1)	6	35
Assorted Toffees (1)	5	30
Blue Riband	12	100
Breakaway		
Milk and Plain (1 bar)	12	105
Milk and Plain (2 bar)	25	210
Cabana	34	235
Caramac		
Countline	20	185
Medium	15	145
Caramel Wafer	11	75
Drifter (2 biscuit pack)	40	260
Fruit Gums (1)	1	5
Fruit Pastilles (1)	2	11
Golden Cup small	14	100
Golden Toffee (1)	5	30
Kit Kat		
4 finger pack	31	250
2 finger pack	15	110
Lion Bar	29	210
Matchmakers		
Long Coffee (1)	3	20
Long Mint (1)	3	20
Long Orange (1)	3	20
Mintola (1)	4	25
Munchies (1)	3	25
Nutty	22	255
Polo Fruits (1)	2	8
Polo Peppermints (1)	1	6
Rolo (1)	4	25

ROWNTREE MACKINTOSH — Cont	Carbohydrate in grams	Calories
Smarties small tube	26	160
Toffee Crisp	27	225
Toffo		
Assorted (1)	3	25
Mint/Plain (1)	3	20
Tooty Frooties (1)	2	8
Tooty Minties (1)	2	9
Tots — 1 packet		
Bunnytots	45	180
Candytots	42	175
Jellytots	42	160
Tigertots	37	165
Walnut Whip		
Milk Chocolate Coffee flavour	22	170
Milk Chocolate Vanilla flavour	22	170
Plain Chocolate Vanilla flavour	22	165
Yorkie — standard bar		
Milk Chocolate	35	320
Almond	31	350
Raisin and Biscuit	33	260

SAFEWAY

	Carbohydrate in grams	Calories
Chocolate Buttons		
50g pack	31	245
Chocolate Coated Fudge		
funtime size	14	95
Honeycomb Crunch		
1 from pack of 5	15	85
funtime size	12	70
Milk Chocolate Brazils (1)	4	55
Plain Chocolate Brazils (1)	5	55

SAINSBURY

	Carbohydrate in grams	Calories
Butterscotch		
6oz/170g pack	150	660
Chocolate Milk Buttons		
44g packet	28	220
Clear Fruits/Mints		
8oz/227g pack	200	805
Devon Toffees		
8oz/227g pack	160	1040
Fruit Jellies		
8oz/227g pack	200	805
Liquorice Allsorts		
8oz/227g pack	180	840
Marshmallows		
6oz/170g pack	135	540
Mint Humbugs		
8oz/227g pack	225	840

	Carbohydrate in grams	Calories
Mint Imperials		
6oz/170g pack	150	570
Wine Gums		
8oz/227g pack	140	585

SHARPS

Bon Bons (1)	6	25
Dairy Fudge (1)	7	45
Extra Strong Mints (1)	3	10
Super Toffee (1)	5	30
Top Cream Toffee (1)	6	35

TERRY

All Gold		
1lb/454g box	285	n/a
Chocolate Coffee Creams		
200g pack	150	755
Chocolate Orange (Milk)	100	965
Chocolate Orange (Plain)	110	945
Chocolate Orange Bar	27	255
Devon Milk		
1lb/454g box	240	n/a
Hazelnut Whirls		
7oz/200g box	95	n/a
Marzipan Bar (1)	22	190
Moonlight		
1lb/454g box	275	n/a
Neapolitans (Solid)		
192g box	116	1025
Pastilles		
1 sweet	2	<10
Peppermint Creams		
46g pack	40	150
Plain Chocolate Bar		
50g bar	32	265
100g bar	63	535
Waifa		
Milk	22	190
Plain	23	185

THE WRIGLEY COMPANY

Doublemint 1 stick	2	10
Freedent Peppermint/Spearmint 1 stick	2	10
Juicy Fruit 1 stick	2	10
P.K. Arrowmint/Peppermint 1 pellet	2	6
Wrigley's Spearmint 1 stick	2	10

TREBOR

Acid Drops (1)	6	22
Assorted Tools (1)	5	48

	Carbohydrate in grams	Calories
Barley Sugar (1)	6	23
Beatall Lollies (1)	8	32
Bitter Lemon/Orange (1)	4	14
Blackcurrant and Aniseed Twist (1)	7	26
Black Jack (1)	3	15
Black 'n' White Chews (1)	8	36
Brazil Nut Toffee (1)	3	28
Cherry Drops (1)	3	16
Chocolate Dairy Toffee (1)	6	45
Chocolate Eclairs (1)	5	39
Chocolate Fruits/Limes (1)	4	16
Chocolate Fudge (1)	6	43
Chocolate Mint Creams (1)	7	40
Chocolate Mints (1)	5	24
Chuckles (1)	3	11
Cola Sherbets (1)	6	23
Cough Candy Twist (1)	7	26
Crystals (1)	1	5
Dairy Fudge (1)	6	43
Dairy Toffee (1)	4	31
Everton Mints (1)	6	23
Extra Strong Mints (1)	2	10
Fish 'n' Chips (1)	6	54
Frosties (1)	6	23
Fruit Creams (1)	8	31
Fruit Salad (1)	3	15
Glitter Fruits/Mints (1)	6	22
Imperial Mints		
1 sweet from Giant Roll	5	18
1 small sweet	2	10
Kola Kubes (1)	4	17
Kopp Kops (1)	4	16
Lemon Bon Bons (1)	6	27
Little Big Feet (1)	3	13
Liquorice Toffee (1)	4	31
Lolly Bag small (1)	8	32
Lolly Bag large (1)	8	37
Lollyade (1)	29	109
Mint Creams (1)	8	32
Mint Toffee (1)	4	51
Pancho Peanuts/Raisins (1)	neg	6
Pear Drops (1)	4	15
Penny Coins (1)	1	16
Pineapple Chunks (1)	4	17
Polar Mints (1)	5	19
Raisin Fudge (1)	6	40
Real Fruit Jellies (1)	8	36
Refreshers (1)	1	6
Sherbet Lemons (1)	6	23
Soft Centre Drops (1)	6	24
Softmints (1)	3	16

	Carbohydrate in grams	Calories
Splits (1)	3	15
Strawberry Bon Bons (1)	6	27
Strawberry Sherbets (1)	6	23
Supa 5 (1)	4	16
Sweet Peanuts (1)	5	26
Toffee Bon Bons (1)	6	27
Toffee Crunch (1)	5	27
Toffee Lollies (1)	8	30
Top Cream Toffee (1)	5	36
Trebor Mints (1)	1	6

New Additions

New Additions

New Additions

New Additions

New Additions

New Additions

New Additions

New Additions

Alcohol

Having diabetes does not mean that you cannot drink alcohol, but it does mean that you must think more carefully about what you drink and when.

Too much alcohol is not good for anyones health so try not to drink more than your doctor or dietitian advises. If you have had no advice and are not overweight, we would recommend a **daily maximum of 3 standard drinks for men and 2 standard drinks for women.**

By 1 standard drink we mean:
$\frac{1}{2}$ pint beer/lager/cider OR
1 pub measure of spirit (e.g. Barcardi, Whisky, Gin, Vodka) OR
1 small glass of sherry/port OR
1 standard glass of wine OR
1 pub measure of vermouth/aperitif/liqueur.

Alcohol can make you more likely to experience hypoglycaemia (a 'hypo'), partly because it impairs the mechanism by which the liver automatically releases some of its store of glucose into the blood when the blood sugar drops too low. If you have drunk too much, then your liver does not work properly and this protective mechanism does not come into play. This may put you at risk of hypoglycaemia (a 'hypo') up to several hours after drinking alcohol. Therefore, **always** have something to eat with your drink OR shortly afterwards. If possible, choose high fibre foods such as a wholemeal sandwich, or wholemeal biscuits or crackers (preferably varieties from the Green Section of Countdown).

Do not substitute alcoholic drinks for your usual meals and do not count the carbohydrate of the alcoholic drink into your diet.

If the recommended alcohol intake is not exceeded, the carbohydrate content of the drinks will not be enough to disturb control.

Always wear or carry some form of diabetic identification. A developing hypo could easily be mistaken for drunkenness if alcohol is smelt on the breath.

Never drink and drive or undertake other tasks which may be dangerous if hypoglycaemia occurred, i.e. the operation of potentially dangerous machinery.

How to use the Section

Each section contains a brief introduction and general advice. As we recommend that the carbohydrate content of alcoholic beverages should not be counted into the diet, we have removed the carbohydrate values from this section. Please note, however, that low alcohol drinks should be treated as a sugared drink and therefore their carbohydrate content is shown.

The calories are shown for all drinks and where appropriate the alcohol content.

APERITIFS

Always try to use the low calorie mixers. Diluting a drink will not make the alcohol less potent but it will make the drink last longer. Watch home measures!

Calories

Advocaat (Sainsbury)
fluid ounce	65
pub measure 24ml	55

Advocaat (Warnicks)
fluid ounce	85
pub measure 24ml	75

Babycham Dry
100ml bottle	60
25cl can	150

Babycham Sweet
100ml bottle	80
25cl can	200

Campari
fluid ounce	65
pub measure 24ml	55

Cherry B
95ml bottle	130

Cherry B White
95ml bottle	80

Cinzano Bianco
fluid ounce	45
pub measure 50ml	75

Cinzano Extra Dry
fluid once	30
pub measure 50ml	50

Cinzano Rosé
fluid ounce	40
pub measure 50ml	70

Cinzano Rosso
fluid ounce	45
pub measure 50ml	75

Crabbie's Green Ginger Wine
fluid ounce	50

Dubonnet Red
fluid ounce	50
pub measure 50ml	80

Goldwell Snowball
113ml bottle	120

Martini Bianco
fluid ounce	45
pub measure 50ml	80

Martini Extra Dry
fluid ounce	35
pub measure 50ml	60

	Calories
Martini Rosé	
fluid ounce	45
pub measure 50ml	80
Martini Rosso	
fluid ounce	45
pub measure 50ml	80
Noilly Prat Dry French	
fluid ounce	40
pub measure 50ml	70
Pimms Vodka Base	
fluid ounce	55
pub measure 50ml	100
Pimms No 1 Cup	
fluid ounce	55
pub measure 50ml	100
Primavera	
fluid ounce	30
pub measure 50ml	50
Pony	
95ml bottle	120
Riccadonna Bianco Vermouth	
fluid ounce	45
pub measure 50ml	75
Riccadonna Extra Dry Vermouth	
fluid ounce	30
pub measure 50ml	50
Riccadonna Rosé Vermouth	
fluid ounce	45
pub measure 50ml	75
Riccadonna Rosso Vermouth	
fluid ounce	50
pub measure 50ml	80
Safeway British Rich Ruby Wine	
fluid ounce	40
pub measure 50ml	65
Safeway Vermouth Dry	
fluid ounce	30
pub measure 50ml	50
Safeway Vermouth Bianco/Rosso	
fluid ounce	45
pub measure 50ml	80
Safeway Vermouth Light Dry	
fluid ounce	25
pub measure 50ml	45
Scotsmac Medium Dry	
fluid ounce	35
pub measure 50ml	55
Scotsmac Medium Sweet	
fluid ounce	40
pub measure 50ml	65
Stone's Ginger Wine	
fluid ounce	n/a
pub measure 24ml	n/a

LOW ALCOHOL BEERS AND LAGERS

As the drinks below are not a significant source of alcohol and are often high in sugar, they should be treated as a sugared drink and therefore their carbohydrate content **SHOULD** be counted into your dietary allowance.

	Carbohydrate in grams	Calories	Alcohol Content
Barbican Alcohol-Free Lager			
275ml bottle/can	8	35	0.02%
440ml can	13	55	0.02%
Bass L.A.			
275ml bottle	12	65	1%
440ml can	20	105	1%
Birell			
275ml bottle	15	65	0.6%
Carlton L.A.			
330ml can	11	60	0.9%
Clausthaler			
330ml can	19	95	0.6%
Danish Light			
275ml bottle	8	45	0.9%
440ml can	13	70	0.9%
Dansk L.A.			
330ml bottle	12	70	0.9%
Gerstel Low Alcohol Lager			
330ml bottle	17	95	0.5%
Kaliber			
275ml bottle	12	50	<0.05%
330ml bottle	14	60	<0.05%
McEwans L.A. Lager			
330ml can	12	65	0.9%
Panther			
25cl bottle	10	55	0.9%
330ml bottle	13	75	0.9%
Prostel			
330ml bottle	22	85	0.5%
Sainsbury Low Alcohol Lager			
330ml can	19	95	0.6%
St. Christopher			
half pint bottle.....................	10½	40	0.05%
Swan Special Light			
375ml can	14	75	0.9%
Talisman Low Alcohol Larger			
275ml bottle	9	50	<0.9%
330ml can	11	60	<0.9%
Tennent's L.A.			
330ml can	10	60	1%
Whitbread White Label Low Alcohol Bitter			
half pint/275ml bottle	19	85	1%
440ml can..........................	30	135	1%

BEERS, LAGERS AND STOUTS

We would recommend a variety which has an alcohol content of less than 5%. The percentage (%) figures refer to the alcohol content expressed as % by volume. We would **not** recommend the low sugar "diat" lagers/beers as these tend to have a higher alcohol content.

	Calories	Alcohol Content
Artic Lite (Draught)		
half pint..	80	3.66%
Artic Lite		
275ml bottle	75	3.66%
Bass Blue Triangle		
275ml bottle	100	4.4%
Bass (Cask Draught)		
half pint..	105	4.3%
Bentley Yorkshire Bitter		
half pint..	80	3.0%
Breaker Malt Liquor		
440ml can	180	5.4%
Budweiser		
275ml bottle	110	4.5%
330ml can	130	4.5%
Budweiser (Draught)		
half pint..	110	4.5%
Bulldog Pale Ale		
275ml bottle	175	5.9%
Carling Black Label (Draught)		
half pint..	100	4.1%
Carling Black Label		
275ml can	90	4.0%
440ml can	140	4.0%
Carlsberg Export		
275ml bottle	110	5%
275ml can	110	5%
440ml can	180	5%
Carlsberg Hof		
half pint..	110	4.5%
Carlsberg Pilsner		
275ml bottle	75	3.2%
275ml can	75	3.2%
440ml can	120	3.2%
Carlsberg Pilsner (Draught)		
half pint..	80	3.4%
Carlsberg Special Brew		
275ml bottle	210	8.7%
275ml can	210	8.7%
440ml can	335	8.7%
Charger		
440ml can	125	3.3%
Colt 45 Strong Malt Lager		
440ml can	180	5.1%

	Calories	Alcohol Content
Courage Best Bitter		
half pint...........................	100	3.9%
Courage Bitter		
440ml can	140	3.8%
Courage Brown Ale		
275ml can	80	2.4%
Courage Directors Bitter		
half pint...........................	115	4.6%
Courage Light Ale		
275ml can	80	3.0%
440ml can	130	3.0%
Double Diamond (Draught)		
half pint...........................	100	3.47%
Double Diamond		
440ml can	190	3.98%
Falcon		
440ml can	120	3.27%
Faust Pils Lager		
440ml can	135	4.5%
Fosters Lager		
375ml can	150	4.9%
Fosters Lager (Draught)		
half pint...........................	90	3.5%
Fourex (Draught)		
half pint...........................	90	3.66%
Gold Cross (Draught)		
half pint...........................	100	4.17%
Gold Label		
nip bottle	170	10.4%
275ml can	255	10.4%
Guinness Draught Stout		
half pint...........................	90	4.0%
pint.................................	180	4.0%
Guinness Extra Stout		
half pint bottle.................	100	4.3%
pint.................................	195	4.3%
275ml can	100	4.3%
440ml can	155	4.3%
485ml can	170	4.3%
Harp Lager		
275ml bottle	80	3.3%
440ml can	130	3.3%
485ml can	170	3.3%
Harp Extra (Draught)		
half pint...........................	100	4.3%
Harp Master Lager		
440ml can	65	7.0%
Harp Premier Lager		
330ml bottle	45	5.0%

	Calories	Alcohol Content
Heineken Lager		
pint bottle....................................	170	3.4%
275ml bottle	85	3.4%
275ml can	85	3.4%
440ml can	135	3.4%
Heldenbrau		
275ml can	70	3.9%
440ml can	115	3.9%
Heldenbrau Draught		
half pint..	70	3.8%
Heldenbrau Special		
440ml can	265	8.6%
Hemeling Lager (Draught)		
half pint.......................................	80	4.1%
Hemeling		
275ml bottle	75	4.1%
440ml can	125	4.1%
Henninger Pils		
275ml bottle	110	5.6%
High Life		
half pint..	80	3.27%
Hofmeister Lager		
440ml can	130	3.4%
Holsten Larger Pils		
275ml bottle	105	5.8%
440ml can	170	5.8%
Holsten Export		
275ml bottle	110	5.0%
440ml can	180	5.0%
Holsten Export (Draught)		
half pint..	120	5.0%
John Courage Strong Pale Ale		
275ml bottle	105	4.2%
440ml can	170	4.2%
John Courage Strong Pale Ale (Draught)		
half pint..	110	4.2%
John Smith's Bitter		
440ml can	160	3.8%
Kaltenberg Diat Pils		
275ml bottle	115	6.1%
440ml can	185	6.1%
Kronenburg 1664 Strong Lager		
440ml can	185	4.7%
Kronenburg 1664 Strong Lager (Draught)		
half pint..	120	4.7%
Lamot Pilsor Strong Lager		
275ml bottle	105	6.0%
440ml can	165	6.0%
Long Life (Draught)		
half pint..	100	4.17%

	Calories	Alcohol Content
Long Life		
275ml can	100	4.17%
440ml can	155	4.17%
500ml can	175	4.17%
Lowenbrau (Draught)		
half pint.......................................	105	4.36%
Lowenbrau Pils		
275ml bottle	115	6.03%
440ml can	180	6.03%
Lowenbrau Special Export		
330ml bottle	150	5.49%
Mackeson Stout		
275ml bottle	115	3.0%
275ml can	115	3.0%
1 pint bottle	230	3.0%
Marston's Low 'C'		
275ml bottle	75	4.2%
McEwan's Export		
440ml can	165	4.2%
McEwan's Lager		
440ml can	140	3.3%
McEwan's Pale Ale		
440ml can	125	3.0%
Miller Lite		
440ml can	120	4.2%
Miller Lite (Draught)		
half pint.......................................	80	4.2%
Moravia Strong Lager		
half pint bottle..............................	115	4.85%
Newcastle Amber Ale		
275ml bottle	80	3.2%
550ml bottle	140	3.2%
Newcastle Best Scotch		
440ml can	140	3.4%
Newcastle Brown Ale		
275ml bottle	110	4.5%
550ml bottle	220	4.5%
440ml can	175	4.5%
Northern Clubs Federation Ace Lager		
440ml can	145	3.4%
Northern Clubs Federation Ace Lager (Draught)		
half pint.......................................	95	3.4%
Northern Clubs Federation Best Bitter (Draught)		
half pint.......................................	105	3.7%
Northern Clubs Federation Best Scotch Ale		
440ml can	135	3.6%
Northern Clubs Federation Best Scotch Ale (Draught)		
half pint.......................................	90	3.6%

	Calories	Alcohol Content
Northern Clubs Federation Dark Mild Ale (Draught)		
half pint	90	3.2%
Northern Clubs Federation Export Ale		
275ml bottle	125	4.6%
440ml can	200	4.6%
Northern Clubs Federation Export Ale (Draught)		
half pint	130	4.6%
Northern Clubs Federation High Level Brown Ale		
550ml bottle	245	4.6%
Northern Clubs Federation Low Carbohydrate Lager		
275ml bottle	110	4.7%
440ml can	180	4.7%
Northern Clubs Federation Low Carbohydrate Lager (Draught)		
half pint	115	4.7%
Northern Clubs Federation Medallion Lager		
440ml can	150	4.0%
Northern Clubs Federation Medallion Lager (Draught)		
half pint	100	4.0%
Northern Clubs Federation Pale Ale		
440ml can	135	3.2%
Northern Clubs Federation Pale Ale (Draught)		
half pint	90	3.2%
Northern Clubs Federation Special Ale		
275ml bottle	115	4.2%
550ml bottle	230	4.2%
440ml can	185	4.2%
Northern Clubs Federation Special Ale (Draught)		
half pint	120	4.2%
Northern Clubs Federation Sweet Stout		
275ml bottle	175	4.2%
Orangeboom (Draught)		
half pint	85	3.63%
Orangeboom de Luxe		
275ml bottle	115	5.0%
Red Stripe Lager		
275ml can	110	4.6%
440ml can	180	4.6%

	Calories	Alcohol Content
Rowells Farrier Bitter		
440ml can	120	3%
Safeway Bedford Bitter		
440ml can	125	2.5%
Safeway Dutch Lager		
440ml can	115	2.4%
Safeway Lager		
440ml can	140	2.7%
Safeway Light Ale		
440ml can	125	2.5%
Safeway Ruddles Bitter		
275ml bottle	75	2.5%
Sainsbury Extra Strength Lager		
440ml can	180	4.8%
Sainsbury Midland Mild		
440ml can	130	2.3%
Sainsbury Rutland Bitter		
275ml can	90	3.0%
Sainsbury Stout		
275ml can	90	2.3%
Sainsbury Yorkshire Bitter		
440ml can	155	3.6%
Satzenbrau		
275ml bottle	110	6.1%
440ml can	180	6.1%
Scottish Pride Lager		
440ml can	120	3.6%
Skol (Draught)		
half pint	95	3.79%
Skol		
275ml bottle	85	3.53%
275ml can	85	3.53%
440ml can	140	3.66%
Skol Special Strength (Draught)		
330ml bottle	135	4.82%
440ml can	180	4.82%
Skol Special Strength (Wrexham Brewed)		
half pint	115	4.82%
Stella Artois Lager		
330ml bottle	145	5.0%
440ml can	195	5.0%
Stones Bitter		
half pint	90	4.1%
440ml can	140	4.1%
Tennent's Extra		
440ml can	175	5.0%
Tennent's Extra (Draught)		
half pint	110	5.0%

	Calories	Alcohol Content
Tennent's Lager		
275ml bottle	90	4.0%
440ml can	140	4.0%
Tennent's Lager (Draught)		
half pint......................................	95	4.1%
Tennent's Pilsner		
440ml can	125	3.5%
Tennent's Pilsner (Draught)		
half pint......................................	85	3.8%
Toby Brown Ale		
275ml bottle	75	3.0%
Toby Light Ale		
275ml bottle	75	3.4%
Top Brass Lager		
440ml can	125	3.3%
Trent Bitter		
275ml bottle	75	2.95%
440ml can	120	2.95%
Trent Mild		
440ml can	130	2.31%
Tuborg Gold		
275ml bottle	105	5%
440ml can	170	5%
Tuborg Pilsner		
275ml bottle	75	3.2%
440ml can	120	3.2%
Watneys Brown Ale		
275ml bottle	70	2.7%
275ml can	70	2.7%
440ml can	110	2.7%
Watneys Pale Ale		
275ml bottle/can	80	3.0%
440ml can	130	3.0%
Whitbread Best Bitter		
440ml can	145	3.7%
Whitbread Best Mild		
half pint......................................	85	2.7%
Whitbread Brewmaster		
half pint bottle.............................	110	3.8%
pint bottle...................................	220	3.8%
Whitbread English Ale		
275ml bottle	105	5.4%
Whitbread Export Ale		
440ml can	160	3.9%
Whitbread Forest Brown		
275ml bottle	85	2.8%
275ml can	85	2.8%
pint bottle...................................	170	2.8%

	Calories	Alcohol Content
Whitbread Light Ale		
275ml bottle	75	3.1%
550ml bottle	150	3.1%
275ml can	75	3.1%
440ml can	120	3.1%
Whitbread Pale Ale		
275ml bottle/can	90	3.5%
550ml bottle	180	3.5%
440ml can	145	3.5%
Whitbread Tankard		
half pint	100	3.8%
Whitbread Trophy		
half pint	90	3.6%
440ml can	145	3.6%
Worthington 'E'		
half pint	100	4.4%
Worthington's Export Ale		
275ml bottle	100	4.4%
440ml can	160	4.4%
Worthington's Light Ale		
440ml can	120	3.0%
Worthington's Special Bitter		
440ml can	120	3.0%
Worthington's White Shield		
275ml bottle	125	5.6%
Wrexham Draught Lager		
half pint	85	3.36%
Younger's Brown Ale		
275ml bottle	80	2.9%
Younger's Kestrel Lager		
440ml can	125	3.3%
Younger's Light Ale		
440ml can	125	3%
Younger's Sweet Stout		
275ml bottle	80	2.4%
Younger's Tartan Special or Bitter		
440ml can	145	3.5%

CHAMPAGNES POMAGNES AND SPARKLING WINES

COLMANS OF NORWICH

Calories

Moussec Sparkling Medium Dry White
- 4 fluid ounce/113ml glass 65
- 75cl bottle 465

Moussec Sparkling Sweet White
- 4 fluid ounce/113ml glass 100
- 75cl bottle 645

Veuve du Vernay Demi-Sec
- 4 fluid ounce/113ml glass 90
- 700ml bottle 540

Veuve du Vernay Rosé
- 4 fluid ounce/113ml glass 130
- 700ml bottle 805

Veuve du Vernay Brut
- 4 fluid ounce/113ml glass 75
- 700ml bottle 465

HARVEYS

Pirrot Champagne
- 70cl bottle 585

HP BULMER

Perry
- 4 fluid ounce/113ml glass 50

Pomagne –
  Medium Dry
  - 4 fluid ounce/113ml glass........................ 60
  - 750ml bottle 400

  Medium Sweet
  - 4 fluid ounce/113ml glass........................ 75
  - 750ml bottle 495

INTERNATIONAL DISTILLERS AND VINTNERS

Chanterelle Brut
- 4 fluid ounce/113ml glass 75

Chanterelle Demi Sec
- 4 fluid ounce/113ml glass 90

Le Piat Crystal Brut
- 4 fluid ounce/113ml glass 80

Le Piat Cyrstal Demi Sec
- 4 fluid ounce/113ml glass 90

Volari Medium Red Wine
- 4 fluid ounce/113ml glass 75

Volari Medium White Wine
- 4 fluid ounce/113ml glass 70

MARTINI AND ROSSI
Asti Spumante
- 4 fluid ounce/113ml glass **90**
- 75cl bottle **585**

PERCY FOX
Piper Brut Extra Champagne
- 4 fluid ounce/113ml glass **85**
- 75cl bottle **570**

Piper Brut Sauvage Champagne
- 4 fluid ounce/113ml glass **80**
- 75cl bottle **530**

SAFEWAY
Asti Spumante
- 4 fluid ounce/113ml glass **85**
- 75cl bottle **570**

SAINSBURY
Champagne
- 4 fluid ounce/113ml glass **80**
- 37.5cl bottle **265**
- 75cl bottle **525**

Deutscher Sekt
- 4 fluid ounce/113ml glass **70**
- 75cl bottle **470**

Vino Spumante
- 4 fluid ounce/113ml glass **80**
- 75cl bottle **525**

SHOWERINGS
Calviere Sparkling Pear Drink
- 4 fluid ounce/113ml glass **70**
- 25cl bottle **150**

LOW ALCOHOL CIDERS

As the drinks below are not a significant source of alcohol and are often high in sugar, they should be treated as a sugared drink and therefore their carbohydrate content **SHOULD** be counted into your dietary allowance.

HP BULMER Strongbow L.A.	Carbohydrate in grams	Calories	Alcohol Content
275ml bottle	8	50	0.9%

CIDERS

We would recommend a variety which has an alcohol content of less than 5%. The percentage (%) figures refer to the alcohol content expressed as % by volume.

HP BULMER	Calories	Alcohol Content
Bulmer Original		
half pint...............................	105	5.25%
Bulmer Conditioned Draught		
Dry half pint............................	80	4.25%
Medium half pint	85	4.25%
Sweet half pint.........................	95	4.25%
GL -		
Dry half pint............................	100	5%
Medium Sweet half pint	80	3.5%
SL Keg Draught		
half pint...............................	100	4.0%
Number 7		
half pint bottle........................	100	6%
Special Reserve		
Dry half pint............................	150	8%
Strongbow Draught		
half pint...............................	100	4.5%
Strongbow		
half pint bottle........................	100	5.25%
440ml can	160	5.25%
Strongbow 1080		
half pint	140	7.5%
Strongbow Keg (Draught)		
half pint...............................	100	4.75%
West Country Still Draught		
Dry half pint............................	100	5.5%
Extra Dry half pint.....................	90	5.5%
Medium half pint	110	5.4%
Woodpecker		
half pint bottle........................	80	3.5%
440ml can	125	3.5%
Woodpecker Draught		
half pint...............................	100	4%
Woodpecker Dry		
half pint...............................	85	4%
Woodpecker Still		
half pint...............................	100	4.75%

MERRYDOWN		
Country Cider		
half pint...............................	140	6%
Traditional Cider		
half pint...............................	125	5%
Vintage Cider		
half pint...............................	170	8%

	Calories	Alcohol Content

MERRYDOWN - Continued
Vintage Dry Cider
half pint... 145   8%

SAFEWAY
Medium Sweet Cider
half pint... 80   2.8%
Special Dry Cider
half pint... 125   4.9%
Strong Old Vat Cider
half pint... 105   4.2%

SAINSBURY
Medium Sweet Sparkling Cider
75cl bottle 505   8.2%
Medium Sweet Cider
half pint... 80   3.4%
Normandy Cider
75cl bottle 240   3.5%
Strong Medium Dry Cider
half pint... 115   6.0%

SHOWERINGS
Addlestones Draught Cider
half pint... 100   5.8%
Coates Special Farmhouse
half pint... 140   6%
Coates Triple Vintage
half pint... 155   7%
Copperhead
half pint... 100   5%
Festival Vat Medium Sweet
half pint... 90   4%
Festival Vat Strong Medium Dry
half pint... 120   5%
Gaymers Lite
275ml bottle 80   5%
Gaymers Norfolk Dry
half pint... 110   5.9%
Gaymers Olde English
275ml bottle 115   6%
Gaymers Olde English Draught
440ml can 145   5%
Gaymers Olde English Keg
half pint... 95   5%
Somerset
275ml bottle 90   4%

THE TAUNTON CIDER COMPANY
Autumn Gold Cider
half pint bottle................................. 85   3.3%
440ml can 135   3.3%

THE TAUNTON CIDER CO. - Continued

	Calories	Alcohol Content
Autumn Gold Cider (Draught)		
half pint	**115**	**5%**
Diamond White Cider		
half pint	**145**	**8.2%**
Dry Blackthorn Cider		
half pint	**100**	**5%**
440ml can	**150**	**5%**
Dry Blackthorn Cider (Draught)		
half pint	**100**	**5%**
Special Vat Cider		
half pint bottle	**125**	**5.9%**
440ml can	**195**	**5.9%**
Taunton Cool Cider		
half pint	**100**	**3%**
Traditional Draught Dry Cider		
half pint	**85**	**5.2%**

HOME BREWING WINEMAKING

When brewing beers and lagers, choose the ones which have an alcohol content of less than 5%. The percentage (%) figures refer to the alcohol content expressed as % by volume. Home brews can be notoriously high in alcohol so follow the manufacturers instructions as closely as possible.

BOOTS

	Calories	Alcohol Content
Budget Beer Kit—		
Bitter		
half pint	90	4.4%
Lager		
half pint	95	4.4%
Seasonal Beer Kit—		
Old Winter Ale		
half pint	155	7.9%
Special Beer Kit—		
Barley Wine		
half pint	155	8%
Best Bitter		
half pint	95	4.6%
Continental Lager		
half pint	95	4.6%
Dry Irish Stout		
half pint	115	5.8%
Extra Strong Bitter		
half pint	120	6.2%
London Bitter		
half pint	90	4.5%
Tyneside Brown Ale		
half pint	105	5.2%
Yorkshire Strong Ale		
half pint	135	6.7%
Standard Beer Kit—		
Bitter		
half pint	95	4.6%
Brown Ale		
half pint	95	4.6%
Cider Kit-		
half pint	90	4.4%
Lager		
half pint	100	4.6%
Light Ale		
half pint	95	4.6%
Stout		
half pint	95	4.6%
Strong Export		
half pint	105	5.3%

GEORDIE HOME BREW

Bitter		
half pint......................................	105	n/a

JOHN BULL HOMEBREWS
(Diabetic Version)

	Calories	Alcohol Content

Best Bitter
half pint.. **90   4-5%**
Lager
half pint.. **90   4-5%**

TOM CAXTON HOMEBREW
Bitter
half pint.. 115
Brown Ale
half pint.. 115
Gravity 45
half pint.. 135
Indian Pale Ale
half pint.. 140
Lager
half pint.. 115
Mild Ale
half pint.. 115
Pale Ale
half pint.. 115
Special Lager
half pint.. 140

UNICAN HOME BREW KITS
Country Reserves (1kg size)
Fruit Wines —
  Elderberry/Blackberry
    4 fluid ounce/113ml glass................. 100
    70cl bottle.............................. 610
  Elderflower/Peach
    4 fluid ounce/113ml glass................. 100
    70cl bottle.............................. 610
Home Brew Beer —
  Barley Wine
    half pint 150
  Bitter/Lager/Light Ale/
  Northern Mild
    half pint 110
  Extra Stout/Extra Strong Bitter/
  Extra Strong Lager
    half pint 170
House Reserve (1 and 5 Gallon) —
  Dry Red
    4 fluid ounce/113ml glass................. 70
    70cl bottle.............................. 440
  Medium White/Rosé
    4 fluid ounce/113ml glass................. 75
    70cl bottle.............................. 445
  Sweet White
    4 fluid ounce/113ml glass................. 80
    70cl bottle.............................. 495

UNICAN HOME BREW KITS – Continued
Special Blend (1kg size) —

Calories

Dry Red/White
4 fluid ounce/113ml glass................. 90
70cl bottle..................................... 550

Light Dry White/Medium White
4 fluid ounce/113ml glass................. 95
70cl bottle..................................... 565

Sweet Red/White
4 fluid ounce/113ml glass................. 100
70cl bottle..................................... 610

Special Reserves (1.45kg size) —
Vermouth

Rosé
4 fluid ounce/113ml glass................. 125
70cl bottle..................................... 765

White
4 fluid ounce/113ml glass................. 135
70cl bottle..................................... 830

Wine —
Dry Red/White
4 fluid ounce/113ml glass................. 95
70cl bottle..................................... 575

Light Dry White/Rosé/
Medium White
4 fluid ounce/113ml glass................. 95
70cl bottle..................................... 590

Sweet White
4 fluid ounce/113ml glass................. 105
70cl bottle..................................... 635

Standard Wines (1kg size) —
Dry Red/Dry White/
Full Bodied Dry Red
4 fluid ounce/113ml glass................. 85
70cl bottle..................................... 535

Light Dry Red/White
4 fluid ounce/113ml glass................. 90
70cl bottle..................................... 540

Medium White/Rosé
4 fluid ounce/113ml glass................. 90
70cl bottle..................................... 545

Sherry/Port
4 fluid ounce/113ml glass................. 95
70cl bottle..................................... 585

Sweet White
4 fluid ounce/113ml glass................. 95
70cl bottle..................................... 585

Three Week Wines (1.45kg size) —
Medium White/Red/Rosé
4 fluid ounce/113ml glass................. 75
70cl bottle..................................... 470

Sweet White
4 fluid ounce/113ml glass................. 80
70cl bottle..................................... 495

LIQUEURS

Liqueurs are drunk in small quantities and their sugar content is therefore quite concentrated. Take care! Also, watch home measures!

Calories

Bailey's Irish Cream Liqueur
- fluid ounce 90
- pub measure 24ml 75

Benedictine
- fluid ounce 85
- pub measure 24ml 70

Cherry B Cream Liqueur
- fluid ounce 90
- pub measure 24ml 80

Cherry Brandy (De Kuyper)
- fluid ounce 55
- pub measure 24ml 50

Chocolate Orange Cream Liqueur (Sainsbury)
- fluid ounce 90
- pub measure 24ml 80

Coffee Cream Liqueur (Sainsbury)
- fluid ounce 90
- pub measure 24ml 80

Cointreau
- fluid ounce 90
- pub measure 24ml 80

Creme de Cassis (Sainsbury)
- fluid ounce 80
- pub measure 24ml 70

Drambuie
- fluid ounce 105
- pub measure 24ml 90

Grand Marnier
- fluid ounce 85
- pub measure 24ml 70

Irish Velvet
- fluid ounce 120
- pub measure 24ml 100

Kirsch (De Kuyper)
- fluid ounce 70
- pub measure 24ml 60

Tia Maria
- fluid ounce 85
- pub measure 24ml 70

Waterford Cream
- fluid ounce 170
- pub measure 24ml 140

SHERRIES PORTS

JOHN HARVEY   Calories
Cockburns Dry Tang Port
   fluid ounce 35
   pub measure 50ml 60
Cockburns Fine Old Ruby Port
   fluid ounce 45
   pub measure 50ml 80
Cockburns Special Reserve Port
   fluid ounce 45
   pub measure 50ml 80
Harveys Bristol Cream Sherry
   fluid ounce 50
   pub measure 50ml 85
Harveys Bristol Dry Sherry
   fluid ounce 35
   pub measure 50ml 60
Harveys Bristol Milk Sherry
   fluid ounce 50
   pub measure 50ml 90
Harveys Club Amontillado
   fluid ounce 35
   pub measure 50ml 65
Harveys Finesse
   fluid ounce 40
   pub measure 50ml 75
Harveys Luncheon Dry Sherry
   fluid ounce 30
   pub measure 50ml 55
Harveys Malmsey Maderia
   fluid ounce 50
   pub measure 50ml 85
Harveys Manzanilla Sherry
   fluid ounce 30
   pub measure 50ml 55
Harveys Sercial Maderia
   fluid ounce 35
   pub measure 50ml 60
Harveys Tico
   fluid ounce 45
   pub measure 50ml 75

**INTERNATIONAL DISTILLERS
AND VINTNERS**
Croft Delicado Sherry
   fluid ounce 30
   pub measure 50ml 50
Croft Distinction Port
   fluid ounce 40
   pub measure 50ml 70

Croft Original Sherry

fluid ounce	40
pub measure 50ml	70

Croft Particular Sherry

fluid ounce	35
pub measure 50ml	55

Croft Triple Crown Port

fluid ounce	40
pub measure 50ml	70

PEDRO DOMECQ
Celebration Cream

fluid ounce	45
pub measure 50ml	75

Double Century Amontillado

fluid ounce	35
pub measure 50ml	60

Double Century Cream

fluid ounce	40
pub measure 50ml	70

Double Century Fino

fluid ounce	30
pub measure50ml	55

Double Century Original

fluid ounce	35
pub measure 50ml	60

Double Century Pale Cream

fluid ounce	45
pub measure 50ml	75

La Ina

fluid ounce	25
pub measure 50ml	45

Primero

fluid ounce	30
pub measure 50ml	55

Rio Viejo

fluid ounce	35
pub measure 50ml	55

SAFEWAY
Aperitif White Port

fluid ounce	40
pub measure 50ml	70

British Sherry Cream

fluid ounce	40
pub measure 50ml	65

British Sherry Medium

fluid ounce	35
pub measure 50ml	60

British Sherry Pale Cream

fluid ounce	40
pub measure 50ml	65

	Calories
British Sherry Pale Dry	
fluid ounce	30
pub measure 50ml	50
Manzanilla	
fluid ounce	30
pub measure 50ml	50
Montilla Dry	
fluid ounce	25
pub measure 50ml	45
Montilla Medium	
fluid ounce	30
pub measure 50ml	50
Montilla Pale Cream	
fluid ounce	40
pub measure 50ml	70
Ruby Port	
fluid ounce	45
pub measure 50ml	80
Spanish Sherry Amontillado	
fluid ounce	30
pub measure 50ml	55
Spanish Sherry Cream	
fluid ounce	45
pub measure 50ml	75
Spanish Sherry Fino	
fluid ounce	30
pub measure 50ml	50
Spanish Sherry Oloroso	
fluid ounce	35
pub measure 50ml	65
Spanish Sherry Pale Cream	
fluid ounce	40
pub measure 50ml	70
Tawny Port	
fluid ounce	45
pub measure 50ml	75

SAINSBURY

British Sherry Cream	
fluid ounce	40
pub measure 50ml	65
British Sherry Medium Dry	
fluid ounce	35
pub measure 50ml	60
British Sherry Pale Cream	
fluid ounce	40
pub measure 50ml	65
British Sherry Pale Dry	
fluid ounce	30
pub measure 50ml	50

Calories

Montillla Medium Dry
fluid ounce 25
pub measure 50ml 45

Montilla Pale Cream
fluid ounce 35
pub measure 50ml 65

Montilla Pale Dry
fluid ounce 25
pub measure 50ml 40

Ruby Port
fluid ounce 45
pub measure 50ml 80

Spanish Sherry Amontillado
fluid ounce 35
pub measure 50ml 60

Spanish Sherry Rich Cream
fluid ounce 40
pub measure 50ml 70

Spanish Sherry Fino
fluid ounce 30
pub measure 50ml 50

Spanish Sherry Manzanilla
fluid ounce 25
pub measure 50ml 45

Spanish Sherry Pale Cream
fluid ounce 40
pub measure 50ml 70

Vintage Character Port
fluid ounce 40
pub measure50ml 70

LOW ALCOHOL "MIXED" DRINKS

As the drinks below are not a significant source of alcohol, they should be treated as a sugared drink and therefore the carbohydrate content SHOULD be counted into your dietary allowance.

BRITVIC Drivers – 180ml bottles	Carbohydrate in grams	Calories	Alcohol Content
Gin & Tonic Flavour	15	55	<0.5%
Whisky & American Ginger Ale Flavour.....................	15	60	<0.5%
White Rum & Cola Flavour	18	70	<0.5%

SPIRITS

Spirits tend to be high in alcohol so take care. Always try and use the low calorie mixers. Diluting a drink will not make the alcohol less potent, but it will make the drink last longer. Be careful with home measures!

Calories

Brandy
fluid ounce **65**
pub measure 24ml **55**
Gin
fluid ounce **65**
pub measure 24ml **55**
Malibu
fluid ounce **60**
pub measure 24ml **50**
Pernod
fluid ounce **75**
pub measure 24ml **65**
Rum Dark
fluid ounce **65**
pub measure 24ml **55**
Rum White
fluid ounce **65**
pub measure 24ml **55**
Southern Comfort
fluid ounce **80**
pub measure 24ml **70**
Tequila
fluid ounce **60**
pub measure 24ml **50**
Vodka
fluid ounce **60**
pub measure 24ml **50**
Whisky
fluid ounce **65**
pub measure 24ml **55**

LOW ALCOHOL WINES

As the drinks below are not a significant source of alchol, they should be treated as a sugared drink and their carbohydrate content SHOULD therefore be counted into your daily allowance.

	Carbohydrate in grams	Calories	Alcohol Content
Elsberg — 75cl bottle			
French	40	235	0.05%
German	38	210	0.05%
Jung's Extra Dry White			
70cl bottle	14	65	0.05%
Jung's Red			
70cl bottle	35	175	0.05%
Jung's Rose			
70cl bottle	35	175	0.05%
Jung's Schloss Bossenburg Sparkling White			
75cl bottle	35	175	0.05%
Jung's White			
70cl bottle	35	175	0.05%
Masson Light White			
75cl bottle	60	240	0.49%
Shloer Nouveau – 70cl bottle			
Red	70	300	0.9%
White	75	315	0.9%
Wunderbar Red			
70cl bottle	35	185	0.3%
Wunderbar Silver			
70cl bottle	28	140	0.3%
Wunderbar Gold			
70cl bottle	35	190	0.3%
Wunderbar Sparkling			
70cl bottle	35	185	0.03%

WINES

Try and choose the dry or medium rather than the sweet varieties.

COLMAN'S OF NORWICH
Red and Rosé Wine

	Calories
Charbonnier	
Red	
4 fluid ounce/113ml glass	80
70cl bottle	485
Rose	
4 fluid ounce/113 ml glass	80
70cl bottle	485
Cotes du Roussillon	
4 fluid ounce/113ml glass	80
500ml carafe	340
French Red Wine	
4 fluid ounce/113ml glass	80
25cl bottle	175
Moussec	
Red	
4 fluid ounce/113ml glass	70
70cl bottle	430
Soproni Kekfrankos	
4 fluid ounce/113ml glass	75
70cl bottle	465

White Wines

	Calories
Balatonfuredi Olasz Riesling	
4 fluid ounce/113ml glass	90
70cl bottle	560
Bereich Bernkastel	
4 fluid ounce/113ml glass	85
70cl bottle	510
Bergerac Blanc	
4 fluid ounce/113ml glass	80
500ml carafe	355
Bereich Nierstein	
4 fluid ounce/113ml glass	85
70cl bottle	510
Charbonnier Dry	
4 fluid ounce/113ml glass	70
70cl bottle	435
Charbonnier Medium	
4 fluid ounce/113ml glass	80
70cl bottle	500
Charbonnier Sweet	
4 fluid ounce/113ml glass	95
70cl bottle	590
French Medium White	
4 fluid ounce/113ml glass	80
70cl bottle	500

Calories

Kecskemeti Welsch Riesling
4 fluid ounce/113ml glass 70
70cl bottle 435

Kiskunhalasi Muscat
4 fluid ounce/113ml glass 90
70cl bottle 540

Liebfraumilch
4 fluid ounce/113ml glass 85
25cl bottle 185
70cl bottle 510

Mosel Blumchen
4 fluid ounce/113ml glass 70
70cl bottle 420

Moussec Medium Dry White
4 fluid ounce/113ml glass 70
700ml bottle 415

Niersteiner Gutes Domtal
4 fluid ounce/113ml glass 85
70cl bottle 510

Pecsi Olasz Riesling
4 fluid ounce/113ml glass 85
70cl bottle 520

Piesporter Michelsberg
4 fluid ounce/113ml glass 85
70cl bottle 510

COUNTRY MANOR WINES
White Wines
Country Manor Medium Dry
fluid ounce 20
4 fluid ounce/113ml glass 65
Country Manor Medium Sweet
fluid ounce 20
4 fluid ounce/113ml glass 75

INTERNATIONAL DISTILLERS AND VINTNERS
Red and Rosé Wines
Beau Soleil Vin du Table Red
4 fluid ounce/113ml glass 70
Beau Soleil Vin du Table Rose
4 fluid ounce/113ml glass 75
Carafino Red
4 fluid ounce/113ml glass 80
Cotes du Rhone
4 fluid ounce/113ml glass 80
Cotes du Rousillon
4 fluid ounce/113ml glass 80
Dao Ribalonga
4 fluid ounce/113ml glass 75

I.D.V - Continued

	Calories
La Cour Pavillon Red	
4 fluid ounce/113ml glass	**80**
La Vista Spanish Red	
4 fluid ounce/113ml glass	**75**
Le Piat de Beaujolais	
4 fluid ounce/113ml glass	**75**
Le Piat D'or Red	
4 fluid ounce/113ml glass	**75**
Pedrotti Rosato	
4 fluid ounce/113ml glass	**65**
Pedrotti Rosso	
4 fluid ounce/113ml glass	**65**
Peter Dominic Vin du Table Red	
4 fluid ounce/113ml glass	**70**
Peter Dominic Vin du Table Rose	
4 fluid ounce/113ml glass	**75**
Pierre Ricard Red	
4 fluid ounce/113ml glass	**65**
Real Sangria Red	
4 fluid ounce/113ml glass	**105**
Rose d'Anjou	
4 fluid ounce/113ml glass	**75**
Sonnelle Cotes du Rhone	
4 fluid ounce/113ml glass	**80**
Sonnelle Red Table Wine	
4 fluid ounce/113ml glass	**75**

White Wines

	Calories
Beau Soleil Vin du Table Blanc-	
Dry	
4 fluid ounce/113ml glass........................	**70**
Medium	
4 fluid ounce/113ml glass........................	**85**
Sweet	
4 fluid ounce/113ml glass........................	**95**
Bourgogne Aligote	
4 fluid ounce/113ml glass	**75**
Carafino White	
4 fluid ounce/113ml glass	**75**
La Cour Pavillon White	
4 fluid ounce/113ml glass	**80**
La Vista Dry White	
4 fluid ounce/113ml glass	**75**
La Vista Medium Dry White	
4 fluid ounce/113ml glass	**85**
La Vista Sweet White	
4 fluid ounce/113ml glass	**90**
Leibfraulmilch St. Dominic	
4 fluid ounce/113ml glass	**70**
Leibfraulmilch Three Kings	
4 fluid ounce/113ml glass	**70**

Calories

Mosel Spezial
4 fluid ounce/113ml glass 70
Pedrotti Bianco
4 fluid ounce/113ml glass 65
Peter Dominic Vin du Table Blanc–
Dry
4 fluid ounce/113ml glass........................ 70
Medium
4 fluid ounce/113ml glass........................ 75
Sweet
4 fluid ounce/113ml glass........................ 95
Piat D'or White
4 fluid ounce/113ml glass 80
Pierre Ricard White
4 fluid ounce/113ml glass 80
Premieres Cotes de Bordeaux
4 fluid ounce/113ml glass 100
Real Sangria White
4 fluid ounce/113ml glass 65
Sonnelle Lutomer Laski Riesling
4 fluid ounce/113ml glass 80
Sonnelle Muscadet Sevre et Maine
4 fluid ounce/113ml glass 75
Sonnelle White Table Wine
4 fluid ounce/113ml glass 75
St Leger "Cooler"
25cl bottle 105
Vinho Verde
4 fluid ounce/113ml glass 70

JOHN HARVEY
Red Wines
Harveys No 1 Claret
4 fluid ounce/113ml glass 85
70cl bottle 520
Inglenook Cabernet Sauvignon
4 fluid ounce/113ml glass 85
70cl bottle 535
Lan Harveys Red Rioja
4 fluid ounce/113ml glass 90
70cl bottle 550

White Wines
Harveys Selected Moselle
4 fluid ounce/113ml glass 75
70cl bottle 465
Sauvignon Sec White Bordeaux
4 fluid ounce/113ml glass 85
70cl bottle 250

MERRYDOWN

Calories

Apple Wine Medium Dry
4 fluid ounce/113 ml glass 70

Elderberry Wine Sweet
4 fluid ounce/113ml glass 165

Gooseberry Wine Dry
4 fluid ounce/113ml glass 70

Mead Sweet
4 fluid ounce/113ml glass 155

Red Currant Wine Medium Sweet
4 fluid ounce/113ml glass 145

Wheat and Raisin
4 fluid ounce/113ml glass 90

PEDRO DOMECQ
Red Wines
Rioja Wines
Domecq Domain Red
4 fluid ounce/113ml glass 80

Vina Eguia
4 fluid ounce/113ml glass 80

White Wines
Domecq Domain White
4 fluid ounce/113ml glass 80

SAFEWAY
Red and Rosé Wines
Beaujolais
4 fluid ounce/113ml glass 80

Blauer Portugieser Red
4 fluid ounce/113ml glass 90

Bourgogne Rouge
4 fluid ounce/113ml glass 80
70cl bottle 480

Cabernet D'Anjou
4 fluid ounce/113ml glass 80

CH Barrail AC Medoc
4 fluid ounce/113ml glass 105

CH Du Calvaire
4 fluid ounce/113ml glass 110
75cl bottle 740

CH Haut St Lambert (1979)
4 fluid ounce/113ml glass 85

CH la Croix St Emlion
4 fluid ounce/113ml glass 110

CH La Tour Robert Pomerol
4 fluid ounce/113ml glass 110
75cl bottle 730

CH La Tutlerie
4 fluid ounce/113ml glass 75
70cl bottle 450

CH Mondesir Gazin Montaigu
4 fluid ounce/113ml glass 105

35

	Calories
CH Pontet Clauzure (1976)	
4 fluid ounce/113ml glass	85
Clos Yon Figeac (1979)	
4 fluid ounce/113ml glass	90
Cote de Ventoux	
4 fluid ounce/113ml glass	75
Cote du Rhone	
4 fluid ounce/113ml glass	85
Coteaux du Tricastin	
4 fluid ounce/113ml glass	85
Cotes De Beaune Villages	
4 fluid ounce/113ml glass	80
Gevrey Chambertin	
4 fluid ounce/113ml glass	80
Hautes Cotes De Nuits	
4 fluid ounce/113ml glass	80
Lambrusco Red	
4 fluid ounce/113ml glass	75
70cl bottle	455
Luberon Red	
4 fluid ounce/113ml glass	80
70cl bottle	485
Mercurey	
4 fluid ounce/113ml glass	80
Pommard	
4 fluid ounce/113ml glass	80
Prem Cote de Bourdeaux	
4 fluid ounce/113ml glass	115
Rioja Rose	
4 fluid ounce/113ml glass	80
Sangria	
4 fluid ounce/113ml glass	100
Vosnes Romanee	
4 fluid ounce/113ml glass	80

White Wines

	Calories
Bechth Pilger Spatlese	
4 fluid ounce/113ml glass	90
75cl bottle	580
Bereich Bernkastel	
4 fluid ounce/113ml glass	85
Bereich Nierstein	
4 fluid ounce/113ml glass	85
Bernkastel K/Lay	
4 fluid ounce/113ml glass	80
Bordeaux Blanc AOC	
4 fluid ounce/113ml glass	95
Bordeau Sauvignon	
4 fluid ounce/113ml glass	100
Bourgogne Aligote	
4 fluid ounce/113ml glass	80

	Calories
Bourgogne Blanc	
4 fluid ounce/113ml glass	**75**
Dom de Pouvray Vouvray	
4 fluid ounce/113ml glass	**80**
Dom Des Rochettes	
4 fluid ounce/113ml glass	**90**
Dom Garennes Sancerre	
4 fluid ounce/113ml glass	**80**
Dom Terral Blanc	
4 fluid ounce/113ml glass	**90**
70cl bottle	**540**
Grac Himm Kabinet	
4 fluid ounce/113ml glass	**75**
Gruner Veltliner White	
4 fluid ounce/113ml glass	**90**
Kerner Kabinett	
4 fluid ounce/113ml glass	**80**
Lamberhurst Muller Thurgau	
4 fluid ounce/113ml glass	**95**
Liebraumilch	
4 fluid ounce/113ml glass	**85**
Luberon White	
4 fluid ounce/113ml glass	**70**
70cl bottle	**435**
Macon Village	
4 fluid ounce/113ml glass	**80**
Maikammerer Kabinett	
4 fluid ounce/113ml glass	**80**
Mosel	
4 fluid ounce/113ml glass	**80**
Muscadet de Sevre Maine	
4 fluid ounce/113ml glass	**75**
Muskat Ottonel	
4 fluid ounce/113ml glass	**95**
Nir Spieglber Kabinet	
4 fluid ounce/113ml glass	**80**
Oppenheimer Krott	
4 fluid ounce/113ml glass	**80**
Perlwein	
4 fluid ounce/113ml glass	**85**
Piesport Mich Auslese	
4 fluid ounce/113ml glass	**90**
Piesporter M/Berg	
4 fluid ounce/113ml glass	**80**
Rudesheimer Rosegart	
4 fluid ounce/113ml glass	**80**
Scheurebe Kabinett	
4 fluid ounce/113ml glass	**80**
Spat Rotipfler	
4 fluid ounce/113ml glass	**100**
Tafelwein Medium Dry	
4 fluid ounce/113ml glass	**75**

SAFEWAY - Continued

	Calories
Tafelwein Medium Sweet	
4 fluid ounce/113ml glass	80
Verdicchio Classico	
4 fluid ounce/113ml glass	75
Vin Blanc Cassis	
4 fluid ounce/113ml glass	100
Vino da Mesa Dry White	
4 fluid ounce/113ml glass	70
Vino da Mesa Medium/White	
4 fluid ounce/113ml glass	80
Vino da Mesa Sweet	
4 fluid ounce/113ml glass	85
Vin de Table Blanc	
4 fluid ounce/113ml glass	70
W/Heimer DOM Crock	
4 fluid ounce/113ml glass	80
Wilt Scharzberg Kab Crock	
4 fluid ounce/113ml glass	70
Yugoslavian Gewurztraimin	
4 fluid ounce/113ml glass	85
Yugoslavian Laski Riesling	
4 fluid ounce/113ml glass	80

SAINSBURY
Red and Rosé Wines

	Calories
Beaujolais	
4 fluid ounce/113ml glass	80
75cl bottle	500
Beaumes De Venise	
4 fluid ounce/113ml glass	85
75cl bottle	550
Bergerac Rouge	
4 fluid ounce/113ml glass	75
75cl bottle	490
Claret	
4 fluid ounce/113ml glass	70
75cl bottle	470
Dao Portuguese	
4 fluid ounce/113ml glass	80
75cl bottle	500
Portuguese Rosé	
4 fluid ounce/113ml glass	80
75cl bottle	540
Rioja (Red)	
4 fluid ounce/113ml glass	75
75cl bottle	490
Rose Cotes De Provence	
4 fluid ounce/113ml glass	75
75cl bottle	490
Rose D'Anjou	
4 fluid ounce/113ml glass	80
75cl bottle	525

SAINSBURY - Continued

Valpolicella
Calories

4 fluid ounce/113ml glass	75
75cl bottle	490

Vin Rouge De France

4 fluid ounce/113ml glass	80
25cl bottle	180

White Wines

Bergerac Blanc

4 fluid ounce/113ml glass	80
75cl bottle	500

Blanc Anjou

4 fluid ounce/113ml glass	80
75cl bottle	515

Gewurztraminer

4 fluid ounce/113ml glass	85
70cl bottle	555

Klusserather St Michael Riesling Splatlese

4 fluid ounce/113ml glass	65
75cl bottle	440

Libefraumilch

4 fluid ounce/113ml glass	70
75cl bottle	445

Mosel

4 fluid ounce/113ml glass	65
75cl bottle	415

Muscadet Serve et Maine

4 fluid ounce/113ml glass	75
75cl bottle	490

Oppenheimer Krotenbrunnen

4 fluid ounce/113ml glass	65
75cl bottle	440

Piesporter Michelsberg

4 fluid ounce/113ml glass	65
75cl bottle	415

Premieres Cotes De Bordeaux

4 fluid ounce/113ml glass	110
75cl bottle	715

Soave

4 fluid ounce/113ml glass	75
75cl bottle	490

Vin Blance De France Medium

4 fluid ounce/113ml glass	80

Vinho Verde

4 fluid ounce/113ml glass	70
75cl bottle	445

Vino De Espana Dulce

4 fluid ounce/113ml glass	95
75cl bottle	630

Yugoslav Laski Riesling

4 fluid ounce/113ml glass	80
75cl bottle	515

New Additions

New Additions

New Additions

New Additions

New Additions

New Additions

New Additions